# CRISIS OF SUBJECTIVITY
# BOTHO STRAUSS'S CHALLENGE TO
# WEST GERMAN PROSE OF THE 1970'S

# AMSTERDAMER PUBLIKATIONEN ZUR SPRACHE UND LITERATUR

in Verbindung mit

Peter Boerner — Bloomington (Neuere deutsche Literatur)
Hugy Dyserinck — Aachen (Komparatistik)
Friedrich Maurer — Freiburg (Ältere deutsche Literatur)
Oskar Reichmann — Heidelberg (Sprachwissenschaft)

herausgegeben von

COLA MINIS
und AREND QUAK

56. BAND

# CRISIS OF SUBJECTIVITY
# BOTHO STRAUSS'S CHALLENGE TO WEST GERMAN PROSE OF THE 1970'S

by

## Leslie A. Adelson

Amsterdam 1984

CIP-GEGEVENS KONINKLIJKE BIBLIOTHEEK, DEN HAAG

Adelson, Leslie A.

Crisis of subjectivity : Botho Strauss's challenge to West German prose of the 1970's / by Leslie A. Adelson. — Amsterdam : Rodopi. — (Amsterdamer Publikationen zur Sprache und Literatur ; Bd. 56)
ISBN 90-6203-906-5
SISO du 856.6 UDC 830
Trefw.: Duitse letterkunde ; 20e eeuw.

©Editions Rodopi B.V., Amsterdam 1984
Printed in The Netherlands

## ACKNOWLEDGMENTS

To all those whose aid and encouragement contributed to the completion of this study I wish to express my sincere gratitude. Special thanks go to Dörte Nicolaisen and Tineke Ritmeester for their gifts of translation, as well as to Ken Nabors, Sylvia Toombs, and the Interlibrary Loan Staff at Washington University for their expert assistance. To Hanser Verlag, the Theater der Stadt Heidelberg, and their representatives -- Ursula Ruppel and Anne Sorg-Schumacher -- I extend particular thanks. Without their kind cooperation my research would have been less than complete.

I owe thanks to Washington University for the financial assistance that made this study possible and to the College of Humanities at The Ohio State University for the assistance needed to bring the manuscript to publication. For their careful readings and guidance I would like to thank Paul Michael Lützeler, Patricia Herminghouse, and Egon Schwarz; for their collegial generosity I am grateful to Peter Uwe Hohendahl, Helmut Kreuzer, and David Roberts. Jörg Drews merits special mention for his critical insights, keen wit, and invaluable friendship.

To my family and the good friends who have weathered my stormy seas I am, simply, indebted.

# TABLE OF CONTENTS

| CHAPTER | | PAGE |
|---|---|---|
| I. | SUBJECTIVITY AND THE CONCEPT: THE WEST GERMAN STUDENT MOVEMENT, THEODOR W. ADORNO, AND BOTHO STRAUSS | 1 |
| | Introduction | 1 |
| | Tendenzwende and Botho Strauss | 2 |
| | The Student Movement: Politics | 4 |
| |     The student movement and subjectivity | 4 |
| |     The student movement and theory | 11 |
| |     The student movement and history | 14 |
| | The Student Movement: Literature | 17 |
| |     Theory of literature: Uwe Timm and Peter Schneider | 19 |
| |     Novels of the student movement | 22 |
| |         Uwe Timm: Heisser Sommer and Kerbels Flucht | 24 |
| |         Peter Schneider: Lenz | 32 |
| |         Jochen Schimmang: Der schöne Vogel Phönix | 35 |
| |         Nicolas Born: Die erdabgewandte Seite der Geschichte | 40 |
| | Adorno: Subjectivity and the Concept | 45 |
| | The Realism Debate: Uwe Timm and Jörg Drews | 54 |
| | Botho Strauss and the Principle of Diachronic Longing: | |
| |     Between Adorno and the Student Movement | 60 |
| | Botho Strauss and His Critics | 66 |

| CHAPTER | PAGE |
|---|---|

II. "MARLENES SCHWESTER" AND "THEORIE DER DROHUNG":

    AMBIVALENCE     88

    "Marlenes Schwester"     88

    "Theorie der Drohung"     107

III. DIE WIDMUNG: CRISIS OF EXPERIENCE AND ARTICULATION     138

IV. RUMOR: POLARIZATION     181

    Rumor     181

    Excursion on Paare, Passanten     222

V. CONCLUSIONS AND BEGINNINGS     228

    Botho Strauss and Max Frisch     228

    Botho Strauss and the Reception of His Works     236

    Botho Strauss and History: The Challenge to Literature in the 1980's     240

BIBLIOGRAPHY     249

Chapter 1

SUBJECTIVITY AND THE CONCEPT:
THE WEST GERMAN STUDENT MOVEMENT, THEODOR W. ADORNO, AND BOTHO STRAUSS

I. INTRODUCTION

Alternately acclaimed as the great literary hope of his generation and denounced as regression personified, Botho Strauss is nothing if not controversial.[1] This study attempts to delineate the development of his prose oeuvre in the 1970's, both in terms of a progressive inner monologue, composed of a multiplicity of voices, and a dialogue in which the author engages with the socio-historical forces of his age. The four texts to be discussed here--"Marlenes Schwester" (1974), "Theorie der Drohung" (1975), <u>Die Widmung: Eine Erzählung</u> (1977), and <u>Rumor</u> (1980)[2]--have not been chosen on the basis of their publication dates alone. Rather they comprise a single literary endeavor, in which Strauss' deliberate ambivalences express and respond to the postulates of the epoch. Moreover, they are tied to one another and significantly linked to their matrix, West German society, by a factor common to them all: the crisis of subjective agency. The apparent stalemate between subjectivity and the concept in the 1970's compels Strauss to challenge this crisis. In so doing, he addresses the particular disappointments of the West German student movement of the late 1960's and early 1970's and, furthermore, reflects elements of Theodor W. Adorno's critique of advanced capitalist society. Although the actual course of the protest movement and the theoretical insights of Adorno are disparate phenomena, they both evidence a critical stance toward Western society informed by some notion of an emancipatory project and, in addition, have import for the potential function of literature in that project. In this capacity, these phenomena influence Strauss' understanding of the crisis of subjective agency as well as his particular aesthetic challenge to it. These are certainly not the author's only sources of inspiration, but his reactions to them are fundamental to his literary treatment of the dilemma of subjectivity in contemporary West German society.

## II. TENDENZWENDE AND BOTHO STRAUSS

Strauss is in fact often indirectly associated with the student movement, albeit for the wrong reasons. The texts which are the subject of this study first appeared in a decade which bore the marks of the tumultuous West German student protest movement, repressive government policies, and personal insecurities for those who feared reprisals for their political activities or leftist sentiments.[3] In the aftermath of the student movement it became popular to speak of a Tendenzwende, a turning away from a highly politicized, organized strategy for social change towards a retreat from the public political sphere.[4] Generally speaking, Tendenzwende usually refers to a growing disinterest in politics and an increasing focus on what has traditionally been considered private: personal relationships, emotions, the search for personal identity. With regard to literature, Tendenzwende has provided a ready label for a development which seems to favor personal concerns and aesthetic expression over collective interests and political content. While it can be convincingly argued that the use of the term Tendenzwende more often than not glibly obscures the complex reality of both socio-political and literary history,[5] one must nevertheless acknowledge the fact that it is usually applied to Botho Strauss.[6] On the surface, the intensely introspective, reflective nature of his prose does indeed lend itself to such categorization. Botho Strauss' work has been praised by some for its sensitive depiction of subjective anguish and isolation, while condemned by others for its nihilistic, self-indulgent emphasis on the private torment of the individual. Neither position does justice to the complexity of Strauss' prose, which is certainly not intended as a narcissistic retreat into or masochistic celebration of subjective decay.

There is, however, good reason to consider Strauss' prose oeuvre in the broader context of the West German student movement and its impact upon West German literature of the 1970's. Strauss is not, strictly speaking, a product of the student upheaval, a fact of biography that has led some scholars to regard his literary endeavors as independent of that movement.[7] Others, such as Hans Wolfschütz, ascertain a general connection between the tenor of Strauss' literary work and the cultural mood of the times. "Wirklichkeitsverständnis und Ästhetik von Botho Strauss sind entscheidend geprägt von der Erfahrung der gescheiterten Studentenrevolte von 1967/68. Seine Literatur trägt alle Zeichen von Melancholie und Resignation einer als nachrevolutionär erfahrenen Zeit."[8] Yet, even this assertion of

Botho Strauss' indebtedness to the student movement is too vague to be particularly useful. It neither differentiates among Strauss' prose pieces, nor does it provide an analysis as to how the failure of the student movement is manifested in his prose. A discussion of Strauss and the West German student movement is fruitful, not because of a presumedly common cultural nihilism, but rather because of a far more fundamental, even structural legacy of aesthetic epistemology. Strauss' prose is an heir to the student revolt in that it addresses a dilemma which that movement was unable to resolve and which ultimately contributed to its demise. At the heart of this dilemma is the capacity of language to oppress as well as to liberate.[9] Strauss' unique response to this aspect of the crisis of subjective agency can best be understood when compared with other literary texts attempting to deal with the same issue: those novels which make explicit reference to the protest and its failure. First, however, a fairly detailed discussion of the politics of the student movement as they relate to subjectivity, theory, and history must clarify the conflict between subjectivity and abstract language that gave rise to these novels.

### III. THE STUDENT MOVEMENT: POLITICS

<u>The student movement and subjectivity</u>. Although the protest movement underwent many changes in the late 1960's and early 1970's, one could, at the risk of oversimplifying, describe its course as falling into three main phases.[10] The early, anti-authoritarian phase was followed by a dogmatic, Marxist-Leninist phase which, in turn,

preceded the breakdown of the organized movement.[11] The Marxist-Leninist cadres, founded in 1969, established first and foremost the politically "correct" line, which was then applied dogmatically to analyses of social reality and, consequently, to political strategies for changing it.[12] Political praxis did not evolve from lived experience but was instead dictated <u>a priori</u> by a rigid theory, which perceived society as determined solely by class structures. Since social reality was reduced dogmatically to essential and peripheral contradictions, political praxis was logically directed towards eliminating what was considered the essential contradiction, i.e., that between labor and capital. This fundamental assumption designated the factory as the locus of political identity. Students who wanted to contribute to the socialist revolution were thus expected to fulfill their role as the political vanguard by doing political work at the base.[13] The much debated question as to whether one considers the conflict between labor and capital to be the linchpin on which advanced Western societies turn or whether students and intellectuals constitute the revolutionary vanguard is not at issue here. In the context of this study it is, however, important to note that in seeing themselves as the intellectual vanguard, the forces of the student movement had in effect instrumentalized their own lives. The dogma to which they adhered forced them to ignore the specifics of their bourgeois personalities, socialization, and social status. The division of social life into essential and peripheral contradictions did not leave room to address or even to acknowledge as politically significant the personal problems and needs of the alienated students. By the early 1970's, the question of the intellectuals' true identity--as opposed to their assumed identity as the revolutionary vanguard--demanded to be heard. This may be seen in part as a response to a failure of the student movement to succeed in its political undertaking.

> Dass politische Gruppen dezimiert oder lahmgelegt werden, weil ihre Mitglieder erst einmal 'zu sich selber finden müssen'; dass politische Diskussionen erstarren, weil plötzlich von einer Seite die Frage aufkommt, 'was hat das eigentlich mit uns zu tun', diese Wiederkehr der verdrängten Bedürfnisfrage, die ihre Verdrängung wiederum herausfordert, ist nicht die Folge der Dogmatisierung. Beides, die verstockte Suche nach den 'eigentlichen' Bedürfnissen und ihre Entwertung um der Organisation willen, bedingt sich gegenseitig, hat aber seine Wurzel in dem tatsächlichen Machtverlust der Linken.[14]

By 1972 the student activists had to face the fact that they had attained no power at the base.[15] Whereas they themselves had long since disqualified the superstructure as peripheral and had separated it so rigidly from the base in their praxis, it was no easy task suddenly to find the path of mediation between the two or, indeed, to find the path back to themselves as subjects, acting in integral accord with their own needs and perceptions, and not merely as robots, puppets of political theory.[16] Provided that the participants in the student movement did not want to relinquish their commitment to political activity, they had to rethink their analysis as well as their strategy. The alternative would have been to face a hopeless future predicated on the defeats of the past. This is the context in which the emancipation debate ensued.[17]

The issue of emancipation focused on the individual agents of the protest movement, but not in their objectified capacity as trailblazers for the proletarian revolution or even as supportive fellow travelers in that revolutionary process. The individual activists were, rather, considered victims of alienation on two fronts. There was, of course, their real social alienation as intellectuals. They had, moreover, subjected themselves to the reification of theory. In accordance with that theory, they sought to prove themselves as instruments of revolution rather than transform themselves into revolutionary subjects. Bernward Vesper, in his autobiographical essay <u>Die Reise</u>, speaks of his generation as victimized by the student movement:

> [. . .] wir müssen erst zur totalen Verantwortungslosigkeit zurückfinden, um uns überhaupt zu retten. Die 'Bewegung' vertauscht nur das Ziel, ist aber zur Befriedigung der Bedürfnisse nicht in der Lage. Sie opfert schlimmstenfalls unsere Generation. Aber es geht jetzt darum, die Freiheit hier zu beginnen, d.h. das Ich zu entwickeln. Das ist alles.[18]

Vesper's comments are representative for many, but not for all, who felt that the student movement had denied its own agents their subjectivity and that each individual's specific subjectivity had to be regained. The question has frequently been raised as to whether the "new subjectivity" can be equated with an apolitical "retreat into the private sphere."[19] Does subjectivity mean a renunciation of politics, or is it a necessary prerequisite for successful political praxis? Or is subjectivity a political goal in and of itself? Rudolph zur Lippe's 1974 essay "Objektiver Faktor Subjektivität" is characteristic for the leftist stance on this issue:[20] the problems of the individual rank high in political significance, but only in the sense that their resolution may pave the way for political engagement. "Die individuellen Probleme müssen weitgehend auch individuell verarbeitet werden, aber sie können nur im öffentlichen Sinnzusammenhang produktiv umgewandt werden. Das ist der 'innere Kampf als politische Erfahrung'." Zur Lippe speaks of the production of relationships, thereby declaring as invalid the strict distinction between base and superstructure.[21] "Verkehrsformen sind eine gesellschaftliche Objektivation, und die Produktion von Beziehungen ist deshalb eine politische Strategie." Zur Lippe elaborates on his position that subjectivity must neither be appropriated for consumption by capital nor be subordinated to the goal of the revolution.

> Dann kann Subjektivität nicht wieder mystifiziert werden zur Organisationsleistung des Kapitals oder auch der 'Partei'; und Selbstdisziplin heisst dann rationale Beziehung auf die Bedürfnisse und auf die Erfordernisse der politischen Arbeit. Wir müssen uns die Produktionskraft mühsam befreiender, wenn schon nicht befreiter Beziehungen aneignen.[22]

Important here is the trend to regard subjectivity as a crucial <u>political</u> factor, in spite of any admonitions that it not be reduced to its functional value as a mere tool in the political process of general emancipation.

The concern for subjectivity among leftist intellectuals was, then, not confined to a metaphysical soul-searching for lost individual identity devoid of social ties or constraints. It is the notion of subjectivity as a political factor that manifests itself in the increased interest in and attention to modes of behavior (between individuals and in groups) and patterns of everyday life. It is no coincidence that zur Lippe's article appeared in the issue of <u>Kursbuch</u> entitled <u>Verkehrsformen I/Frauen Männer Linke/ Über die Schwierigkeit der Emanzipation</u>. Six months later followed the <u>Kursbuch</u> issue on <u>Verkehrsformen II/Emanzipation in der Gruppe und die 'Kosten' der Solidarität</u>. The scrutiny of personal relationships was based on the premise that every leftist has to acknowledge the subjective factor and that a strictly individualistic notion of subjectivity would soon find its way to the (non-recyclable) garbage heap of late capitalist society; hence, the collective approach. To enhance successfully the political project, the "new subjectivity" had to consider the demands and pressures of interpersonal contexts in the reproductive sphere.[23] This was not always successful, as the history of Kommune I and II in West Berlin attests. At the end of the 1960's, they were unable to deal with the concrete interpersonal dynamics of the collective living situation.[24] The individual needs of the participants had continued to be subordinated to the action-oriented desires of the group. This obviously represented no qualitative change from the subjugation of subjectivity to the strategic goals of political organizations. The only difference was that now the supremacy of political objectives had expanded its territorial rights.

Abstract, dogmatically applied theories proved to be of as little value in the reproductive sphere as they had been in the students' political work at the base. This experience created a demand for a "Wegkommen von der abstrakten Subjektivität hin zur konkreten Subjektivität. Allgemeiner: die Konkretisierung von gesellschaftlicher Erfahrung, ein neues Vermögen zur Wahrnehmung des Konkreten. Eine weitere Entmythologisierung, nun nicht mehr nur von Religion, sondern auch vom sonstigen Ideologienapparat."[25] This attempt at concretization, designed to escape oppressive abstractions, manifested itself in a variety of ways. One comparable to the interest in interpersonal behavior was the new focus on everyday life.[26] "Die Politik ist ins Leben zurückzuholen und nicht getrennt von der Alltagspraxis der Individuen zu denken; sie geht--wenn überhaupt--davon aus."[27] Sociological studies on everyday life have, in part, been informed by a political realization. By regarding this realm as peripheral to the labor-capital conflict in class society, leftists may have ignored an important factor in workers' lives. The rectification of this oversight might help explain the absence of revolutionary consciousness in the modern-day West German proletariat.[28] Schülein admits this rather begrudgingly in his <u>Kursbuch</u> article, where he describes the alleged retreat into the private sphere as "eine <u>historisch notwendige Konzentration auf die Alltagsprobleme</u>, die bisher politische Praxis behindert und verzerrt haben."[29] Political activists could not be allowed to retreat into an allegedly apolitical sphere of reproduction if they were to change themselves sufficiently to become true participants in the revolution. But everyday life was also considered a potential source of emancipatory strength because it contains elements that are neither ruled nor structured by market forces.[30] "[. . .] diese Diffusität, die Unstrukturiertheit und Brüchigkeit unserer Lebenszusammenhänge [bietet] trotz aller Spezialisierung und Segmentalisierung die Chance, aufzubrechen aus dem Alten [. . .]."[31]

Everyday life is not completely free of market influences, but it does open certain "free spaces" (<u>Freiräume</u>) of experience and fantasy. Alexander Kluge and Edgar Reitz, for example, appeal to such free spaces in their film, "In Gefahr und grösster Not bringt der Mittelweg den Tod."

> Wir stützen uns auf die Eigenschaften im Wahrnehmungsapparat, die sich gegenüber dem sogenannten Erziehungsbewusstsein als unterdrückte Klasse verhalten: Assoziationen, Erinnerungsvermögen, die Bewegungsgesetze der Phantasie, das, was in der gesellschaftlichen Organisation durch Arbeitsprozess und Bildung nicht schon organisiert ist. Wir stützen uns also nicht auf die Dramaturgie der Schulstunde, sondern auf die der Schulpause.[32]

<u>The student movement and theory</u>. Even the orientation towards free spaces of experience and fantasy entails concretization and specificity, a trait it shares with the intensified interest in everyday life, the concern with concrete, real, interpersonal relationships and one's own perceived needs.[33] All these trends represent a reaction against suffocating systems of abstract thought. We may well ask: what has become of theory in the aftermath of the student movement? Oskar Negt summarizes the situation: "In der jüngeren Generation gibt es Tendenzen einer Theoriefeindschaft [...]." Klaus Hartung likewise ascertains and laments the demise of theory.[34] West German leftists' harshly critical reaction to the French "New Philosophers" is indicative both of their vulnerability on the issue of theory and of the crucial significance of theory in leftist praxis.[35] Blaming Marxist theory itself for the atrocities of applied Marxism, particularly as practiced by the Soviet Union, the French philosophers recommend the execution of theory altogether.[36]

Even though the "New Philosophers" may be a specifically French phenomenon, they nevertheless raise questions with which the West German left must also come to terms, at least to the extent that it wishes to adhere to Marxist theory. The existence of the Gulag and the Soviet military action in Czechoslovakia in 1968 are only two political phenomena that have been perpetrated in the name of socialism. The attitude toward theory--any theory, but especially Marxist theory--has become a problem for the West German left. The reception of the French "New Philosophers" is only one indication of that fact. The problematic status of theory also has roots in the Left's own recent history as manifested in the student movement.[37] The dogmatic adherence to rigid theoretical concepts and the enforced hegemony of those concepts had homogenized all experience, all thought.

The painful awakening from the idolatry of the concept raised new doubts about the student intellectuals' own identity, their experience, and even the language in which identity and experience were to be articulated. As long as the supremacy of the concept was unchallenged, these elements had been defined *a priori*, which made life simple and answers clear. But this clarity proved false. Discussing identity and theory in the context of the West German student movement, Peter Brückner declares: "Die Protestbewegung 1966-1969 war auch eine Identitätsrevolte, ihr Bedürfnis nach Theorie mit Prozessen der Identitätsfindung verknüpft. Als Identitätsrevolte ist sie gescheitert."[38] The politically "correct" line had addressed the suffering and alienation which is the lot of the individual in capitalist society, so it could not be argued that individual misery had been ignored. Yet, it was acknowledged in such a way as to prevent the student intellectuals from experiencing their alienation as their own.[39] Their personal torment existed in the neatly defined and clearly prescribed category of alienation in class society. This was a collective concept of individual suffering. At first, it helped the activists to understand their lives, but eventually it became itself a source of alienation. The abstraction of the concept tended to smother the immediacy of emotional experience. Michael Rutschky offers a slightly different, but comparable analysis of the same phenomenon:

> was wir verloren haben in den siebziger Jahren, das kann niemand genau sagen. Was ich als Utopie der Allgemeinbegriffe beschrieben habe, das war ja eigentlich nicht die Überzeugtheit durch irgendeine bestimmte Theorie, eher die unspezifische Hoffnung auf restlose Theoretisierbarkeit, Verallgemeinerung: jeder meiner Impulse sollte ganz unmittelbar eine allgemeine Wahrheit sagen. Und diese Utopie hatte eben ihre finstere Rückseite: jeder meiner Impulse ist tatsächlich etwas Allgemeines, weshalb ich keinen meiner Impulse als meinen eigenen greifen kann.[40]

Brückner's analysis makes an important distinction between theory and abstraction, noting critically that the growing apathy towards theory was accompanied by an insistence on immediacy of experience. "Gemäss dem längere Zeit hindurch geltenden Irrtum, Theorie und theorieförmige Interpretation seien <u>abstrakt</u>, verstand sich dieses Bestehen auf Erfahrungs-Austausch als 'konkret'."[41] Experience may indeed only have the appearance of being concrete, but in the wake of the student movement's encounter with abstract conceptual systems, this appearance was sufficient to attract individuals seeking to find themselves and experience their own reality. Rutschky addresses yet another factor in this insistence on immediacy of experience: "Das vergesellschaftete Individuum löst sich in ein wimmelndes, bedrohliches Reden auf, und das treibt dazu, Selbstverwirklichung, Selbstbestimmung unterhalb der Sprache zu suchen, in der Wahrnehmung, in der Sinnlichkeit, im Körper, zur Not in Schrecken und Schmerz."[42] Since the hegemony of the concept was enforced to no small degree through language, verbal articulation became as suspect as theory itself (or as what was perceived to be theory). This disillusionment with language marks an important connection between Botho Strauss' prose and the West German student movement. The capitulation to non-articulation ultimately has more potential for new forms of oppression than it does for emancipation. As Michael Schneider has pointed out," [. . .] die 'averbale Kommunikation' erscheint der nostalgischen Linken nun als höchste Form der Kommunikation, und just in einer Zeit, da sie eine neue Sprache bräuchte, feiert sie Orgien der Sprachlosigkeit."[43] Klaus Hartung expresses the same sentiment when he notes: "[wir sprechen] nach wie vor zu viele verschiedene politische Sprachen und haben doch nur die eine, nämlich die, die es uns verschlagen hat."[44]

The student movement and history. The insistence on what is perceived to be immediate and concrete has also manifested itself in an obsession with the present. Time is reduced to now, and what is felt in the present moment becomes the criterion with which to ascertain the validity of experience in all its intensity. Since the present moment is thus removed from a complex of moments experienced over time, history is relegated to a rather tenuous standing, to the extent that it remains under conscious consideration at all. An understanding of history implies itself a type of theoretical construct. The historical understanding of one's experience is thus liable to be construed as the subjugation of that experience to the homogenizing process of comprehension.[45] The virulent reaction to the subordination of individual experience to generalized abstractions makes history subject to multiple attack. First of all, the dogmatic line on personal history is rejected as reductive and oppressive because it considers the individual as the predictable product of his or her social circumstances. Secondly, the concern for the immediacy of the present indicates a reluctance to come to terms with the history of the protest movement through any kind of integrative analytical process which would make it possible to build on the failure of the student revolt instead of repressing it. Klaus Hartung poignantly stresses the disastrous consequences of the fact that the West German activists did not come to grips with the history of their own movement as it related--inherently--to the history of their personal lives. Such neglect involved the surrender of an emancipatory project. Hartung places the failure to attain personal and political majority (<u>Mündigkeit</u>) in the broader historical context of post-World War II Germany.

> [. . .] wir mussten unsere Realität von Grund auf neu konstruieren. Es gab keine Anknüpfungspunkte, keine utopische Formel, keine Verwirklichung von Träumen, denn was träumten wir schon--wir als früh gealterte Reali- tätstechniker? Wir mussten unsere Feinde erfinden, um sie zu sehen; wir mussten den Klassenkampf spielen, um die Klassen sichtbar zu machen. Wir waren nicht richtig bei uns selbst, als wir uns selbst zu bewegen anfingen. --Was hier paradox geschildert wird, ist die <u>einfache</u> Konsequenz in einem Deutschland, das von der <u>Geschichte</u> so leer geräumt war wie die Gasöfen nach dem Kriege.[46]

The powerful comparison with which this passage closes in effect indicates a third direction of the attack on history which characterized the end of the student movement. The overemphasis on the immediacy of the present at the expense of any conceptual understanding leaves no room for personal history, for the history of the student movement, or for the history of German fascism--a history which did not terminate in 1945 or 1949 but reaches into the present. Writing in 1959 on the question "Was bedeutet: Aufarbeitung der Vergangenheit?", Theodor W. Adorno characterizes the repression of the past as an objective development of the late capitalist economy of exchange. The authority of the principle of exchange obliterates all historical particularity, and experience becomes interchangeable since it has no history.[47] If this is the case, then the West German student movement's rejection of historical specificity only reflects the blank stare of West German society's structural blindness to history. This implies in turn that the student movement impaired the emancipatory project at least as much as it advanced it. The 1970's faith in the emotions of the individual and in the concreteness of immediate experience[48] could be seen as a last-ditch effort to save the individual from suffocation by conceptual oppression. However, it also runs the risk of acquiescing to the dictatorship of the present moment, a relativism which may be deemed oppressive by virtue of its refusal to acknowledge the very historicity of experience itself. What attitudes toward history become evident after the student movement is, for this reason, decisive. It will figure significantly in our analysis of Botho Strauss' prose in the context of the 1970's.

## IV. THE STUDENT MOVEMENT: LITERATURE

Thus far, we have not addressed the question as to how this relates to literature. Hartung, for one, sees a connection between the literature that arose from the students' experience and their extra-literary failure to learn from their own history.

> Das Selbst, kenntlich zumeist dadurch, dass es sich in politische Diskussionen 'nicht einbringen', in ihnen 'nicht wiederfinden' lässt, wirkt als zitternde Unruhe in der versteinerten Geschichte der neuen Linken. Und es liegt nahe, die linke Literatur in einer geschichtlichen Mechanik eingepasst zu sehen, wonach der Niedergang der revolutionären Hoffnungen einhergeht mit dem Aufgang der Literatur. Gerechter und analytisch fruchtbarer aber scheint mir der weniger weitgehende Schluss zu sein, dass die linke Literatur unseren unglücklichen Umgang mit unserer eigenen Geschichte teilt und wohl auch an ihm teilnimmt.[49]

Hartung was not the only one to point out an absence of history, or to put it another way, an obsession with the present, in the literature to which the student movement gave birth. Recently, Fritz Raddatz observed that history has become a "Negativchiffre" in contemporary West German literature. "Der Umschlag von Angst in Kälte, Inhumanität. Die Suche nach einer anderen Welt treibt Schriftsteller um. Was sie finden: Spuren, Splitter, Reste. Suche erinnert an das Titelwort eines grossen Werks der Weltliteratur--Recherche. Damals galt sie verlorener Zeit; Vergangenheit. Heute und hier gilt sie gestohlener Gegenwart."[50] Peter Beicken characterizes the "new subjectivity" in literature in terms of experience, authenticity, reflection, and the sensitization of reason, but does not discuss the status of history in this literary context.[51] This is understandable since history does not play an explicit role in the works in question. And yet, writing literature is not an act of immediacy capable of capturing the present moment. It may indeed seize the present on some level, but it cannot do so with complete disregard for other dimensions in time, i.e., for history. Helmut Schödel points out this difficulty with reference to Botho Strauss' writings, but his comments are also more generally applicable. Strauss' characters, he argues, are motivated primarily by a sense of loss. "Auch das Gedächtnis wird in solcher Hinsicht zum Problem, weil es die gewünschte Erinnerung verloren hat oder, weil es, im Gegenteil, zu gut funktioniert und auf diese Weise einen Verlust von Gegenwart bewirkt: beispielsweise beim Schreiben."[52] To overlook the presence of history in literature because it is thematically absent is tantamount to blinding oneself to the historical specificity of narrative structures with epistemological ramifications. Rainer Nägele's incisive essay on "Geschichten und Geschichte: Reflexionen zum westdeutschen Roman seit 1965" addresses just this issue. The title reflects the double entendre of the German word Geschichte, meaning both history and story. The two are inextricably linked, Nägele elaborates, as epistemological constructs.[53] It is my contention that Botho Strauss' prose signifies a qualitative challenge to the status of literary language after the West German student movement.[54] It is motivated by the need to bridge the chasm between, on the one hand, immediacy and experience of the present moment (including but not limited to the experience of one's deepest emotions) and, on the other hand, conceptualization, theory, and history (both personal and social). Strauss seeks a language that neither sacrifices the former to the latter nor worships momentary subjective experience at the expense of theory and historical understanding. This is the essence of the challenge voiced in Strauss' prose. To understand the specific nature of this challenge, it will be helpful to consider some texts more explicitly representative of the student movement. An excursion on the theoretical background for this prose will introduce our discussion of the texts themselves.

Theory of literature: Uwe Timm and Peter Schneider. Two of the authors to be discussed here--Uwe Timm and Peter Schneider--also helped formulate a position on literary theory from the vantage point of a student movement thought capable of revolutionizing society.[55] In 1972, Uwe Timm insisted that the purpose of literature should be to make workers comprehend the social forces that dominated their lives and which they had the capacity to change.

> Aufgabe der Literatur wäre es, darzustellen, was der Entfaltung des Menschen zur Betätigung der menschlichen Wirklichkeit entgegensteht, das wäre die aufklärerische Funktion der Literatur, die sie mit der Theorie teilt, zugleich aber könnte sie unmittelbar Phantasie und Emotionen ansprechen--was die Theorie kaum kann [. . .].[56]

This notion of the potential revolutionary function of literature corresponds to the understanding of the student movement as a political vanguard preparing the way for the revolution of the proletariat. Literature could serve this goal, according to Timm. "Die Handlung müsste zentrieren um die Problematik Individuum und Gesellschaft."[57] It is significant that Timm accords plot--and not any notion of subjectivity--greatest significance. Literature as Timm conceives it is a tool with which to elaborate a theoretical insight.

A priori conceptual structures reign supreme, while their political content finds expression in literature. Peter Schneider, on the other hand, took a different position with regard to the revolutionary function of literature: it had none. In 1969, he was willing to acknowledge only an "agitatorische und [. . .] propagandistische Funktion der Kunst." Schneider felt that art in late capitalism could not be protected from being abused to support the system. Although he did not disavow the power of fantasy, Schneider argued against spending that power uselessly in late capitalist art. "Aufgabe der Kunst ist es nicht, die Wünsche künstlerisch zu organisieren, sondern sie aus der Verdrängung hervorzuholen, um sie in ihrer Rohform der Revolution zuzuführen." The task thus outlined for the student movement was to use agit-prop art to promote class consciousness among workers. That is to say, the student movement was called upon, "den vorhandenen Widersprüchen an der Basis durch die Aktionen die revolutionäre Perspektive zu zeigen [. . .]."[58]

For Peter Schneider in 1969, all thought and action was to draw breath from the concept of revolution. Seven years later, he takes a very different position regarding the primacy of the political concept. In an essay "Über den Unterschied von Literatur und Politik", he discusses the relationship between Lenin and Gorki, concluding that his own allegiance now lies with the creative writer whose solidarity with those affected by politics outweighs his loyalty to the party.[59] This implied rejection of the supreme concept indicates a growing concern for the specificity of concrete reality. In an article published in 1976, Uwe Timm likewise assumes a stance that is somewhat different from that put forth in his earlier essays, although it could be argued that the substance is the same and only the frills are different.[60] Indeed, Timm tries to strike a bizarre compromise between the demands for specificity and a persistent allegiance to the abstract concept. He, too, admits that the student movement failed to acknowledge the particular needs of real individuals. Rather than abandon the revolutionary project altogether, Timm attempts to adapt to this new historical situation in two ways. First, he now accords greater respect and significance to literature in the struggle for revolutionary change.[61] Second, he reveals a definite, albeit begrudging openness to the demands of the private individual. One has to read Timm carefully to understand exactly what he means.

> Die erneute Rückbesinnung in der Literatur auf die Probleme und Wünsche des Individuums muss nicht nur --als Folge der inneren Emigration--Beschränkung bedeuten, sondern diese Rückbesinnung kann dort, wo praktische politische Arbeit über Jahre Literatur verhindert hat oder wo diese planmässig der Theorie untergeordnet wurde, durchaus eine Erweiterung in der Aneignung von Wirklichkeit bedeuten.

Further, Timm writes:

> Und diese literarische Entwicklung ist kein Rückzug ins Private, wie einige Kritiker behaupten, denn Individualität meint--richtig verstanden--nicht das Private, das sich vom Gesellschaftlichen abgrenzt, sondern immer auch komplementär die Gesellschaft, mit der das Individuum in einem dialektischen Wechselverhältnis steht.

Timm's very formulations reveal the extent to which he remains indebted to the primacy of the concept. Although he uses the term "dialectical" in the passage cited above, his understanding of literary aesthetics seems very rigid indeed. This becomes pointedly clear when he tries to defend his concept of individualism in literature against the bad individualism of "new subjectivity." (Here again he shows no immunity to popular slogans.)

> Was sich heute als neuester Subjektivismus in der Literatur aufwirft, baut zwischen Individuum und Gesellschaft einen statischen Dualismus auf. Das Leiden und die Irritation des Individuums resultieren nicht aus einer konkreten Gesellschaft, sondern entspringen der Gesellschaft an sich [. . .]. Diesem Rückzug in die Innerlichkeit--und das ist bei Born und bei Struck nicht blosse Attitüde--entspricht im ästhetischen Bereich eine 'Rückbesinnung' auf das rein Literarische.[62]

Timm's conception of acceptable individualism both fails to recognize the particular nature of the aesthetic medium and likewise blinds Timm to his own undialectical understanding of literature which he considers too subjective, a blind spot, as his use of the term "das rein Literarische" shows.

<u>Novels of the student movement</u>. The idolatry of the political concept which characterized the West German student movement left in its wake an acute sense of the seemingly unbridgeable chasm between general abstractions and real individual experience, a state of disunion with literary as well as political consequences. The conflict between theoretical concepts and individual specificity provides a crucial impetus--thematically and stylistically--for a variety of novels born of the student movement. The insistence on immediacy of experience and on specificity of person manifests itself, at least in part, in the call to authenticity. Ursula Krechel has said of this term: "Eine griffige Kategorie, wenn man Wasser mit der blossen Hand schöpfen will und sich die Finger dabei nicht nass machen will."[63] Yet, Peter Beicken designates authenticity as one of the distinct major elements of the "new subjectivity," which he defines as

"Selbsterfahrung auf der Basis autobiographischer Authentizität und fiktionaler Komposition."[64] This linking of authenticity with experience of self, autobiography, and fictional structures actually raises more questions than it answers. One wonders how the dilemma of conceptual domination, threatening the appropriation of individual experience, can be articulated in autobiographical form, which by definition presumes some core of individual identity and synthesis of experience. Krechel comments: "Die authentische Literatur hat [...] Verwandtschaft zu Zeugenberichten, ausgewiesen, verbürgt durch eine einzelne Person, deren Glaubwürdigkeit vorausgesetzt werden muss."[65] The use of the modal here indicates an imperative more forced than real. Krechel writes further:

> Der Schriftsteller als einer, der seinem vorgefundenen Material, dem Wirklichkeitsgehalt in ihm mit äusserster Skepsis gegenübersteht und folgerichtig auch den Leser zur Skepsis gegenüber der Wahrheit der Schriftsteller einlädt. Ich habe in keinem der sogenannt authentischen Berichte, Romane, Zeugenaussagen auch nur den geringsten Zweifel an der Möglichkeit zur eigenen Authentizität gefunden. [...] Wer schreibt, hat recht.[66]

What this implies is that the "authentic" mode, at least as cloaked in autobiographical or even biographical guise, continues to posit reality as essentially intact. The shift in emphasis, from objective reality per se to the subject who perceives it, fails to challenge either the definition of reality or the existence of the subject as such. This is not to say that the subject cannot be depicted as alienated; yet, the autobiographical/biographical mode allows even the alienated subject to be identified as such.[67] Given that the autobiographical thrust to authenticity revolves around the question of individual experience, and given that the very notion of what actually constitutes individual experience has been exploded, it would seem that contemporary autobiographical/biographical narrative structures actually perpetuate the oppression of individual specificity, which they purport to promote.[68] For this reason, it is necessary to look carefully at the aesthetic modes used by authors who strive for authenticity in their struggle with the conflict between concept and experience as borne out by the West German student movement. The works to be discussed here reveal three different, but closely related attempts to address this dilemma. They are: 1) Uwe Timm's Heisser Sommer (1974) and Kerbels Flucht (1980); 2) Peter Schneider's Lenz (1973) and Jochen Schimmang's Der schöne Vogel Phönix (1979); 3) Nicolas Born's Die erdabgewandte Seite der Geschichte (1976).[69] These works merit our close attention, precisely because they bear no aesthetic resemblance to the project which Botho Strauss unfolds. Strauss neither seeks authenticity in the manner pursued by these other authors, nor does the student movement figure thematically in his works. Yet, his works draw breath from the conflict between conceptual systems and individual particularity detailed above.[70] A look at the works by Timm, Schneider, Schimmang, and Born will make it clear why Strauss has chosen a different path.

Uwe Timm: Heisser Sommer and Kerbels Flucht. Uwe Timm's novel Heisser Sommer appeared in 1974 as part of a publishing project called AutorenEdition, first undertaken in 1973 by editors Uwe Friesel, Gerd Fuchs, Richard Hey, and Uwe Timm under the aegis of the Bertelsmann Publishing Company. The literary prorject is outlined programmatically on the inside cover of every AutorenEdition novel:

> Die gesellschaftlichen Probleme sollen anschaulich und unterhaltsam dargestellt werden. Angestrebt wird die realistische Schreibweise. Nicht die Schreibschwierigkeit des Autors angesichts einer widersprüchlichen Realität, sondern die Realität selber ist das Thema der AutorenEdition.[71]

For the moment, we shall overlook the complicated questions raised by the spectre of reality "itself" and address ourselves to the heavily mimetic thrust of this program. "New subjectivity" has been defended as not being "die radikale Ablösung des Engagements durch private Belange, sondern die Konkretisierung des Engagements [. . .]," inasmuch as "die persönliche Konkretisierung verschafft dem kritischen Potential der Literatur die glaubwürdige Wirkung, die dem abstrakten Engagement abging." What is particularly interesting in this defense of "new subjectivity" is the rationalization for the uncritical adaptation of traditional narrative structures. "Das persönliche Engagement ist zwar eine Abkehr vom verbalen Aktionismus früherer Jahre, vor allem aber--jedenfalls in der Wirkungsabsicht der Autoren--unterschieden von der unverbindlich privaten, an biedermeierlichen Eskapismus erinnernden Innerlichkeit, mit der es gerne verwechselt wird."[72] The implication here is that the habitus of literary style is essentially irrelevant to content. In other words, a stylistic focus on the private individual in no way impairs the credibility of the "more-than-personal" content as long as it is clear that the engaged author may be absolved of narcissistic intent. Tellingly enough, the discrepancy between style and content characteristic of the AutorenEdition program and of Heisser Sommer in particular has been the focus of criticism by those who praise the literary medium for its autonomy as well as by those who share Timm's stated emphasis on the revolutionary transformation of objective social conditions at large.

Peter Mosler notes caustically:

> In der AutorenEdition erschien von 1973 bis 1975 jedes Jahr ein 'Roman' (Roman ist anscheinend alles über 150 Seiten) über die Studentenrevolte, ein Buch belangloser als das andere. [. . .] Nicht nur, dass die Autoren die Realität der Studentenbewegung mit einer unverfrorenen Naivität beschreiben, als hätte es nie Zweifel an der Sprache gegeben, nie einen Beckett oder einen Arno Schmidt [. . .].
> Von Spracharbeit sind die Autoren [. . .] offenbar entbunden [. . .].[73]

Lothar Baier criticizes the mimetic faith of the AutorenEdition authors who ignore the extensive diversification of contemporary social life in contrast to nineteenth-century conditions and consequently refuse to recognize: "Was heute nicht mehr geht, das ist: von der Literatur die wahrheitsgetreue, umfassende Darstellung sämtlicher Bereiche der Gesellschaft und im besonderen des proletarischen Lebens verlangen und sich im selben Atemzug auf den Balzacschen Realismus berufen."[74] Baier argues that today's objective social conditions render literary realism à la Balzac or literary theory à la Lukacs impossible. Language is not impervious to the social reality in which it exists.

> Es kann nicht darum gehen, diesem oder jenem Mitglied der 'AutorenEdition' hämisch nachzuweisen, dass er mit seiner Prosa das gesteckte (und unerreichbare, weil falsch konzipierte) Klassenziel nicht erreicht hat, ich finde es nur komisch, wenn diese Autoren großspurig erklären, sich nicht um Lappalien wie Schreibschwierigkeiten zu kümmern, und selbst dann an all den Schwierigkeiten scheitern, denen sie mit blossen Schreibschwierigkeiten den falschen Namen gegeben haben.[75]

In his essay on the complex challenge to contemporary narrative structures, Rainer Nägele singles out AutorenEdition works for their obliviously naive faith in the continued possibility to tell it "like it is." "Mit wenigen Ausnahmen--wozu etwa die einem Konzept des sozialistischen Realismus angenäherte Schreibweise der in der AutorenEdition erscheinenden Romane gehören--integrieren selbst bewusst traditionelle Autoren fast schon routinehaft erzählreflektive Elemente."[76] Nägele also makes reference to the empathetic receptive mode implicit in AutorenEdition writing.[77] The uncritical reliance on empathy with a central character is in turn rejected as an untenable, contradictory stance in Timm's work by Hermann Peter Piwitt, Rolf Hosfeld, and Helmut Peitsch in their essays on literature of the student movement.[78] Regarding Heisser Sommer, Piwitt finds it surprising, "wie sehr erklärt sozialistische Autoren an 'Einfühlungstechnik' und 'Mittelpunktsindividuum' festhalten, obschon sich zeigt, wie wenig Verlass auf sie ist, wenn es darum geht, sich die Realität verfügbar zu machen."[79] This criticism is echoed in Hosfeld and Peitsch, who contend that Timm's stated objective of transforming society is at odds with his mimetic style and the individualistic concept of utopia at its root.[80] A similar analysis is made by Paul Michael Lützeler, who likens the student movement to Expressionism, both movements being essentially existentialist in nature and affirming the "Gleichsetzung der Wandlung des Individuums mit Gesellschaftsveränderung." Whereas Lützeler sees in German Expressionism a revolutionary aesthetic theory and praxis, however, he grants no such status to the novels of the student movement, which he describes as "in erster Linie [. . .] ein literarisch--kulturrevolutionäres Phänomen."[81] For our purposes, what is significant is the consensus among Timm's critics that traditional narrative structures relying on the reader's empathy with a protagonist are both aesthetically as well as politically anachronistic.

What remains to be seen is what Timm's style imports for the concept/experience dichotomy which his novels attempt to address. The absence of a narrative that reflects upon its own terms as well as the relentless faith in the capacity for stable identity--no matter how troubled at times--in the protagonist are both compounded by and accomplice to the dominance of types. Jörg Drews comments on <u>Heisser Sommer</u>: "Realistisch heisst hier die Wiedergabe des Typischen, das um keinen Preis durch die Mittel der Wiedergabe überstiegen werden darf [. . .]."[82] Hosfeld and Peitsch also note the process of typification to which Timm's characters are subjected.[83] Indeed, not only the characters in <u>Heisser Sommer</u>, but also the situations among which they are buffeted are reduced to the common denominator of schematic types. The following summary of the course of the story has essentially the same flavor as the novel itself:

> Die präzis historisierte Entwicklung des Helden Ullrich Krause, aus dessen Blickwinkel erzählt wird, verläuft über verschiedene, die Teile konstituierende Stationen: den 2. Juni 1967 und die Folgen in München; Politisierung im WS 1967/68 im Hamburger SDS bis zur Springer-Blockade; Ausflippen im Sommer 1968 nach dem Scheitern der Anti-NS-Kampagne; Wende durch Betriebsarbeit, gewerkschaftliche Organisierung und Rückkehr nach München. Sie alle verbinden Privatleben (Beziehungen des Helden zu Mädchen, Freunden und Kommilitonen) mit Berufsperspektive und politischem Kampf.[84]

Krause, student of German literature, is depicted as an individual--albeit one void of individual particularity--who becomes radicalized by external events. Moved like an unfinished product on a conveyor belt from one event to the next, he serves as a receptacle for the lessons of content Timm desires the reader to learn. This effectively negates any possibility for specificity of experience. The murder of a student demonstrator on the occasion of the Shah's visit to the Berlin Opera on June 2, 1967, flips the political switch for Krause. From a vaguely dissatisfied, self-centered, uncritical student, he becomes politically enlightened and concerned. "Gleich nach der Demonstration hatte er sich das Buch gekauft und es in der folgenden Nacht gelesen. Persien, Modell eines Entwicklungslands."[85] To make the point perfectly clear, Timm even has Krause cite passages directly from the book (e.g., page 55). An account of a political student assembly takes the form of a series of jemand, einer, einige, viele, and alle, strung together over three pages with the subjunctive of indirect discourse. The account concludes: "Jemand sagt: Das ist ein Lernprozess. Niemand widerspricht" (page 125). Timm obviously intends this verbatim report as a learning process for the reader as well; yet, a learning process by definition requires a subjective agent. Timm neither creates his characters as subjects, nor does he acknowledge the reader as subject. The political discussions in response to the attempt on Rudi Dutschke's life or with regard to the conflicts between the anarchists and the dogmatic Left follow the same pattern (pages 193, 291, et passim). Similarly, Krause discovers that what he considers to be his personal problems are socially determined. The use of the term "leistungsfixiert" to label Krause's problems with finishing his degree has no critical dimension of irony. On the contrary, Timm cites Herbert Marcuse to fatten up his own skeletal concept of <u>leistungsfixiert</u> (page 127). Piwitt's criticism of another <u>AutorenEdition</u> novel thus applies to <u>Heisser Sommer</u> as well: "Die Wahrnehmung versagt [. . .], wo Wahrgenommenes immer wieder quick auf die Höhe definitorischer Satzgegenstände gebracht wird [. . .]."[86] Timm claims to give (over)due attention to the individual but, in effect, only feigns specificity by using an individual case study to demonstrate the applicability of the concept. The concept maintains its sovereign rule.

 The status which Timm accords to plot upholds this regime in a way that is perhaps more spurious because it is less obvious. Timm actually defends plot as the legitimate motivating force in what he considers a realist, utopian novel. Having discussed several novels of the student movement, he claims:

> Neben diesen Beispielen, in denen Utopie thematisch wird, gibt es noch eine weitere Bestimmung, die die realistische Form an sich betrifft. Dieses <u>formale utopische Moment</u> ist in der Handlungsführung eines Romans oder einer Erzählung zu suchen, in dieser Handlungsführung werden <u>Schicksale</u> gezeigt, das heisst, es werden Entwicklungen von Personen dargestellt.[87]

The fact that Timm designates <u>Handlung</u> and <u>Schicksal</u> as the loci for utopian elements in the literature of the student movement, including, presumably, his own works, is most pertinent to our concerns here. Timm reveals in theory and in practice his ideological entrapment in the very pitfall he seeks to avoid. He wishes to demonstrate the individual's ability to change and effect change in society at large.

Yet, the primacy of narrated plot in Heisser Sommer locks the novel and its characters into a pre-conceived conceptual system, which for all intents and purposes denies any possibility for free agency on the part of the literary subjects. The subject so conceived has no epistemological capacity for real choice and remains object, a pawn in Timm's conceptual understanding of history and social change.

The operational subjectivity evident in Heisser Sommer is, as we have seen, not an intended effect, but rather, indigenous to the wasteland of Timm's chosen literary style. Kerbels Flucht, published as late as 1980, is subject to the same aesthetic paradox, even though the reduction of the subject, in this case Christian K., to his didactic value is neither so crude nor quite so obvious. Kerbels Flucht is written partly as a diary; the rest of the story is told by an outside narrative voice. Less naive than Heisser Sommer with regard to the act of writing itself and more critical of the student movement, Timm's later novel is based on the contradiction between an abstract concept and specificity of experience: in this case, the desire for personal emancipation and the feeling of jealousy. Christian's girlfriend disturbs their relationship by taking another lover, and Christian drives his taxi, "wie ein Lebensmüder."[88] The tenor of the novel is pessimistic, again in contrast to the earlier novel. A friend's consolation is small comfort,[89] and Christian ultimately drives his car through a police barrier, is shot, and dies of a perforated lung. It is clear to the reader that he has committed suicide, but one of the leftists from Christian's commune labels his death "ein[en] behördliche[n] Mord" (page 183). This is an indictment of the personal insensitivity Christian's leftist friends show towards his emotional anguish. The conceptual framework in which they think makes it impossible for them even to perceive Christian's emotional need, let alone help him deal with it. And yet, Timm uses Christian, too, for his own purposes. If it were not for the fact that the protagonist dies so unexpectedly, there would be no tension whatsoever to the novel, certainly not as any type of aesthetic experiment and even not in terms of plot or character development. It is that single act of desperation, and it alone, that conveys the depth of Christian's torment. Otherwise, there are only occasional hints of it, in the form of crying jags or violent outbreaks. Timm once again negates individual specificity by the manner in which he appeals to it. Christian and his fellow characters are mere vessels for Timm's --admittedly humane--message to the world, and the plot obscures any hint of a real subject. Timm has learned to be kinder, but the operational subjectivity in his writing still bows to the primacy of the concept.

<u>Peter Schneider: Lenz</u>. Although Peter Schneider's <u>Lenz</u> (1973), like <u>Heisser Sommer</u>, would have to be categorized by Hosfeld/Peitsch and Piwitt as yet another manifestation of "existentialist revolt",[90] it does not reveal the same literary type of operational subjectivity characteristic of Timm's novels. At the same time, <u>Lenz</u> clearly receives its impetus from the concept/experience dilemma of the West German student movement. According to Michael Schneider,

> <u>Lenz</u> verkörpert--und darin liegt seine Berechtigung--
> die Irritation des bürgerlichen Intellektuellen

>       angesichts seiner schlechten Vermassung und Entindividualisierung in den doktrinären politischen Gruppen und Partei-Zirkeln der niedergehenden Studentenbewegung.[91]

Klaus Hartung discusses <u>Lenz</u> as a response to both the anti-authoritarian phase as well as the Marxist-Leninist phase of the student movement. By being first to break with the tradition of not talking about oneself, he argues, it exploded the "Literaturtabu" of the anti-authoritarian movement. The repressive concept of political work in the Marxist-Leninist phase asphyxiated personal experience and rendered the student activists helpless. "Ihre Wehrlosigkeit lag gerade darin, dass sie im Namen politischer Erfahrungen vor politische Ziele sich gestellt fanden, während zur gleichen Zeit der Zugang zu diesen Erfahrungen abgedrückt wurde."[92] And indeed, <u>Lenz</u> has as its theme the experiences of a student activist who runs up against the wall of domination by the concept. He is both victim and perpetrator of this domination, as are his comrades. Realizing this, Lenz suffers from the "Dualismus von sinnlicher Unmittelbarkeit und Theorie."[93] The novel is intended as a damning critique of the primacy of the concept in the West German student movement. In his group for factory activists, Lenz wonders: "Woher kamen die Begriffe der Studenten, aufgrund welcher Eindrücke und Empfindungen war in ihren Gehirnen der Umschlag in Begriffe eingetreten?"[94] The allegedly revolutionary attempt to give every experience its place in a particular conceptual system renders questionable, for Lenz, the concept itself, inasmuch as it leaves all specificity of experience by the wayside, and the persons who should be the subjects of their experience are relegated to a shadow existence behind the rigid wall of concept. Peter Schneider thus addresses one of the crucial experiences of the student movement, which ironically might be termed the loss of experience. Michael Schneider describes Lenz:

> Im Gegensatz zu seinen studentischen Genossen, die vor lauter Ursachen keine Sachen mehr sehen, wendet er seine Aufmerksamkeit wieder auf das scheinbar Nebensächliche [. . .].
> Aus dieser Geste des Erstaunens, des Wiederentdeckens, [. . .], bezieht Schneiders Erzählung ihre poetische Kraft, aus dem unangestrengten Bemühen, die auf den Begriff reduzierte Welt der Erscheinungen wieder auseinanderzuschreiben, ihre stilistischen Schönheiten.[95]

However, Michael Schneider is a bit too hasty in his praise of the aesthetic integrity of his brother's novel. Thematically, Lenz is about the negation of individual experience by the primacy of the abstract concept. And yet, aesthetically, Peter Schneider reduces Lenz' experiences to their generalizable, conceptual typicality. Helmut Kreuzer criticizes the bland narrative style in Lenz:

> Bei Schneider verläuft sich die praktischtheoretische Auseinandersetzung mit der Wirklichkeit [. . .] und die subjektive Anstrengung, eine vorgefertigte Theorie für aktuelle Erfahrungen zu öffnen, in eine linksromantische Reise- und Bohemeerzählung, in der die Versöhnung der erlittenen Widersprüche zwar erzählend mitgeteilt wird, das Erzählen selbst aber nicht wirkungskräftig für den Leser prägt.[96]

It is not, however, merely a question of bland narrative but rather one of aesthetic paradox. The fact that Lenz' rites of passage can all be easily reduced to a generalizable concept effectively undermines Schneider's critique of the dichotomy between abstract concept and subjective experience. The separation from a working-class girlfriend, the experiences in the factory and in the activists' group, the interaction with the student comrades, Lenz' stunted relationship to his own subjectivity and sensuality--these are all rites of passage of the student movement at large, which Lenz typifies. The character becomes the concept: the student who lost himself to conceptual dogma and strikes out to recover his own lived experience. Ultimately, he is supposed to find his way back to himself and to political praxis. Michael Buselmeier faults Schneider for his ultimate reliance on slick conceptual categories. Instead of integrating interior and exterior, image and concept, "[fügt] Schneider der eher diskursiven Beschreibung der adaptierten Bilderwelt die begriffliche Erklärung einfach hinzu [. . .]."[97] Similarly, Hartung characterizes Schneider's language as a mere naming process ("Benennen").

> Es scheint, dass sich die literarisierte Haltung selbständig macht und ihre Prosa in Fahrt gerät, nicht weil sie das herrschende Einverständnis innerhalb der Linken bricht, es verrät oder preisgibt, sondern weil sie sich angesichts der Stagnation und der politischen Perspektivelosigkeit gewisser Ansprüche entledigt weiss.[98]

Unlike Uwe Timm, Peter Schneider does take a strong thematic stance against the primacy of the concept, but the aesthetic reduction of experience to pre-existing, generalizable conceptual categories in Lenz only supports that primacy. "Wo es uns die Sprache verschlagen hat, tut der Lenz den Mund auf und behält recht."[99]

Jochen Schimmang: Der schöne Vogel Phönix. Jochen Schimmang's Der schöne Vogel Phönix, first published in 1979, is a soul mate to Lenz, picking up the strands of the latter and weaving them into the same pattern. Admittedly, Schimmang's tapestry is more desperate in tone than Schneider's, but both works voice the critique of conceptual oppression of lived experience in language that only perpetuates that oppression. Schimmang's book, subtitled "Erinnerungen eines Dreissigjährigen," is in effect a testimony to the non-experience of experience. What he remembers is his own inability to experience his life, and the act of remembering--in this case, the written structuring of these memories--adds no new dimension of experience to that life. The narrator's reflections, in fact, merely reflect, that is to say, affirm the status quo of the character's estrangement from his own experience. This is what the transition from first-person narrative voice to the third-person reference to Murnau (the narrator) conveys, a temporal and emotional distancing that fails to provide any new insight for the character. The creation of such a dimension of experience through literary reflection (<u>Reflexion</u> as opposed to <u>Widerspiegelung</u>) would actually challenge the lament which infuses the book: the character's inability to experience his experience as his own. <u>Der schöne Vogel Phönix</u> is, however, sadly harmonious.

Murnau's alienation from life begins even before his active involvement with the student movement. The first prologue places him on a military base, where he is forcefully relegated to "experiencing" the events of 1968 in an extremely mediated fashion: through reading, radio reports, and gossip. This sets the stage graphically for what will plague Murnau throughout the book, even when he is physically present with persons and at events he would like to be able to experience. Both during military service and school (the subject of the second prologue), reading assumes a positive as well as a negative function for Murnau. It is a form of resistance to his real existence (as a soldier on an isolated military base), and at the same time, it is mediated experience which is not properly his: non-experience. The first-person narrator singles out the role words have played in his life:

> Die Wörter: Von den Kindheitsjahren bis heute haben sie auf meiner privaten Landkarte immer einen riesigen Raum für sich beansprucht. Sie kolonialisierten Gebiete, die eigentlich dem Leben vorbehalten sein sollten, und sie tun es bis heute, so dass bis heute in mir das noch nicht ganz geborene, das potentielle Leben einen zähen antikolonialistischen Kampf gegen diese sanfte, schleichende und doch zugleich terroristische Fremdherrschaft führt. (page 22)

Not only what the narrator says here, but also how he says it is significant. The slick categorization of the dilemma at hand as foreign (conceptual) colonization of experience is itself a conceptual label reminiscent of the recurrent ones the protagonist encounters among the members of his cadre. Of their language--and his own use of it--he is openly critical:

> Ein neues, offensives, aggressives Vokabular wurde geboren. Ständig waren die Genossen damit beschäftigt, etwas in Angriff zu nehmen, etwas voranzutreiben, etwas zu bekämpfen: die Organisation, die Auseinandersetzung, den Klassenfeind. (page 127)

He describes his hearing to be admitted to the cadre as follows:

> Es handelte sich um eine Prüfung, und in die konnte die eigene Geschichte nur eingehen, insoweit sie objektiviert wurde mit analytischen und ironisierenden Mitteln. Ich musste beweisen, dass ich in der Lage war, zu meiner eigenen Geschichte, zu mir selber jederzeit die notwendige Distanz zu wahren. (page 149)

At the same time, the narrator acknowledges the emotional need for acceptance and warmth which prompted many individuals to seek solace in groups whose members effectively denied their individuality (page 130).

Critical as Schimmang is of the "Fremdherrschaft der Wörter," he nonetheless promotes it by writing blandly and generally, even about intimate affairs. For example, on the occasion of the move to Berlin (his dream), he writes:

> Zugleich entfernte ich mich während dieser Fahrt von einem anderen Traum, der mit den langen Briefen aus der Schweiz zaghaft begonnen hatte. Aber erst in den wenigen Wochen vor meiner Abreise, als Angelika endlich freigelassen war aus der Schweiz, fanden wir bei meinen fast täglichen Besuchen in der Wohnung am Tjackleger Fährweg zu jener Zärtlichkeit, die wir bis dahin in unseren Briefen hinter einer Unmenge von Wörtern und Sätzen versteckt hatten. (page 59)

The reader may assume that some tender moments occurred, but Schimmang conveys here only the most generalizable quality of his experience. Another passage on love stories outlines almost programmatically Schimmang's literary endeavor:

> Nehmen wir Liebesgeschichten. Es gibt glückliche Liebesgeschichten und unglückliche. Die eine glückliche Liebesgeschichte gleicht allen anderen. Die eine unglückliche Liebesgeschichte gleicht auch allen anderen. Liebesgeschichten sind ein alter Hut. Was erzählenswert an ihnen ist, scheint nicht die Geschichte selbst zu sein, die allen anderen gleicht, sondern das Detail, der Unterschied, das Autonome, der Schnörkel, das Überflüssige und zugleich Unverwechselbare, das sich nur in dieser Geschichte unterbringen lässt und in keiner anderen. (page 72)

The "I" of this passage goes on to designate Angelika's voice as "das Autonome, das eigentlich Interessante." His attempted description of his lover's voice begins with the assertion that it is impossible to describe. What follows is a half-hearted attempt to describe what has already been classified as "eigentlich unbeschreiblich." Numerous other phrases leave the reader wondering whether Schimmang is being subtly critical of others' language usage or merely careless in his own. Marx is "diese Sache mit dem Mehrwert" (page 109), and the stories told by the workers at a printing company give Murnau "eine Ahnung von dem, was gesellschaftliche Realität ausmachte" (page 209).

It seems particularly odd in a book which deplores the inability of a particular individual to experience his own life free of domination by external, conceptual systems that there are so many pointed reminders that the central character's dull sensation of non-experience is not specific to him, but applicable to many of his generation. His fear of the masses is "keine Eigenart von mir" (page 160), and his experiential impotence is a "Verlust für uns alle" (page 246). The narrator summarizes: "Wie die meisten Leute, die ich kenne, habe ich in den letzten fünf Jahren versucht herauszufinden, wie man einigermassen richtig lebt, und es ist mir bisher nicht gelungen" (pages 280-81; emphasis added). Such references to general applicability are surely intended as an expression of solidarity with fellow victims of the same dilemma, but Der schöne Vogel Phönix only attests to the bond of victimization by rendering all experience interchangeable. Even the inability to experience fully one's own experience is denied any texture of specificity. It is no wonder then that the fear to which the last passage of the book is dedicated remains as amorphous and as menacing as all other generalities in the book. Much like Lenz, Der schöne Vogel Phönix takes a thematic stand against the conceptual petrification of experience, while the form used to articulate that position in fact succumbs to the very dilemma it depicts. Schimmang and Schneider cannot be accused of losing their sense of individual specificity. The problem is that they have never quite found it in the first place.

Nicolas Born: Die erdabgewandte Seite der Geschichte. Nicolas Born's response to the dichotomy between concept and experience as manifested in the student movement differs from the works discussed above in that it takes both a thematic and a structural stand against the subordination of individual existence to neatly structured conceptual systems. Die erdabgewandte Seite der Geschichte, copyrighted in 1976, is infused instead with a radical subjectivity stubbornly, even belligerently irreconcilable with reductive, abstract generalizations. Peter Mosler compares Born's novel to Bernward Vesper's book, Die Reise, of which he notes: "Es erzählt von den Schicksalen des Inneren aus einer Zeit, als die Aufbegehrenden fast nur in den Schicksalen des Äusseren verstrickt waren."[100] Unlike Heisser Sommer, Lenz, or Der schöne Vogel Phönix, Die erdabgewandte Seite der Geschichte contains little explicit reference to what normally constitutes the history of the student movement. Yet, that history is clearly the foil against which--and in response to which--the radical subjectivity of the narrator asserts itself. Klaus Scherpe and Hans-Ullrich Treichel argue that Born's writing, like that of Peter Handke and Botho Strauss, is representative of the so-called new subjectivity in that it depicts what they call a typically bourgeois loss of totality. The tradition of the novel consistently reflects the individual's loss of real (i.e., extraliterary) possibilities for meaningful action in society.[101] Such a streamlined version of the history of the German novel tends to homogenize the historically significant nuances of two hundred years of literary and cultural development; in the particular case in question here, it also overlooks the highly relevant detail that Born's protagonist does not suffer from a loss of totality but quite the contrary, he suffers from too much of it. The book does not bemoan the loss of self and personal identity. It forcefully reveals the intractably rough edges that feel threatened by an oppressive insistence on coherence. This oppression is exercised even by the order of things in the narrator's environment. There is an "unerträgliche Symbolgewalt" in his lover's apartment.

> Hier waren wunderbare, aber für mich unfassbare Zusammenhänge zu bestaunen, eine trickhafte Organisation. Nichts davon durfte ich berühren, obwohl alles nur meinetwegen zusammenpasste. Ich wurde verhöhnt und wäre nun gern Maria mit Krallen durchs Gesicht gefahren. Sie war ja verantwortlich für dieses Arrangement und die Magie, die davon ausging. (page 13)

The coercive symbol of ordered things also takes its toll in the narrator's intensely emotional, frequently brutal involvement with Maria. During his conversations with her, he writes:

> [. . .] nichts fiel mir ein. Es geht immer 'über' irgendwas. Wenn man redet, redet man 'über' irgendwas, wenn man schreibt 'über' irgendwas. Es ist eigentlich nichts. Wie Kommentare zu Friedensverhandlungen. SOLANGE VERHANDELT WIRD, WIRD NICHT GESCHOSSEN. (page 16)

The implication here is that normalcy constitutes a state of war, a fact which our civilized amenities are designed to veil. The "love" relationship between the narrator and Maria is portrayed as a life-and-death power struggle in which the rules of combat are arcane and the casualties severe. Although the narrator sometimes expresses the desire to partake of the apparently normal order of things,[102] he opts for greater and more painful honesty. His physical and psychological abuse of Maria, regardless whatever judgments one might care to make about his behavior, marks a character who refuses to sacrifice the fullness of his emotional contradictions to the desire for progress and personal emancipation. It is precisely this, the underside of his personal history, which demands to be heard in Born's novel. "[. . .] sind wir nicht spätestens dann am Ende, wenn alles erklärt ist, wenn das letzte Geheimnis aus uns rausgewaschen ist wie ein Dreck?" (page 26).

The narrator in turn links the tendency to reduce human behavior to that which can be explained categorically to political developments of the late 1960's.

> Viele unserer Bekannten wurden schnell immer politischer, das hiess erst einmal, dass sie prinzipiell wurden und gewisse Verständigungen abkapselten gegen jeden Zweifel, andererseits, dass sie immer weniger gelten liessen, auch immer weniger Menschen gelten liessen und nach und nach ihre Eigenschaften aufgaben. Die politischen Gruppen griffen auch nach Lasski und mir. Ich fühlte mich manchmal in der Umarmung in den Tropen verseuchter Missionare. (page 46)

Further, in the context of the demonstration in front of the Berlin Opera on the day Benno Ohnesorg was murdered, the narrator reflects:

> Auf halbem Weg zu uns selbst hiess es umkehren, weg von uns; und wir liessen unsere Sachen in der allergrössten Unordnung zurück. Unsere Empfindungen für alles, was uns selbst betraf, legten wir still. (page 48)

Yet, it is not the political objective of progress that the narrator rejects, but rather the policy of abstracting common denominators at the expense of the contradictory details which continue to affect individuals' lives.

> Aber ich wollte ja immer, dass mich noch etwas erreichen sollte, für das ich meinen Körper zur Verfügung stellen konnte, für Gerechtigkeit jederzeit, für Freiheit jederzeit, nur wenn man das genauer haben wollte, wurde es schwierig, einmal gesetzt und schon verloren, aus. So schnell wollte ich mich aber nicht verspielen, dann lieber mit offenen Augen mich langsam mit Widersprüchen vergiften. (page 51)

The stubborn insistence on the contradictory specificity of lived experience also affects attitudes towards writing. While in the hospital for observation, the narrator is asked to write a subjective account of his own condition. He is appalled by this suggestion.

> Ich wollte ja nichts weiter, als eine routinemässige Untersuchung, eine Beobachtung meiner Körperfunktionen; sie aber wollten meine Konflikte in die Hand kriegen, etwas sozial Exemplarisches. (page 121)

Similarly, he argues: "In der Schrift, im Schrecken, würde der Wahnsinn wieder auf einen Sinn zurückgeführt, und unsere Fortsetzungsgeschichten würden auf Papier stehen, als ob sie niemals anders stattgefunden hätten" (page 130). This posture sets Born off in marked contrast to Timm, Schneider, and Schimmang, and also explains why Born's narrator gives us several versions of his relationship with Maria or with Ursel, his daughter, for that matter. The only concession Born makes to the cohesiveness of storytelling is the first-person narrator, who remains coherently contradictory.[103]

Geschichte in Born's title is three-fold: it is the love story, it is the story told, and it is also history itself. Acknowledgment of the contradictions in one implies an acknowledgment of the contradictions in the other two as well. As Born's narrator comments:

> Immer wieder war unsere Geschichte an ihren Anfang zurückgekehrt. Sie war zu unserem Leben geworden,

> sogar zu unserer Öffentlichkeit, obwohl ich mich manchmal fragte, ob sie das Recht hatte, sich derart auszubreiten, aber dann wieder dachte ich, dass Geschichten wie diese die eigentliche Geschichte ausmachen und dass die Weltgeschichte nur die chronische Geschichte ihrer Verwaltung ist. Nicht vor dem Hintergrund einer ruchlosen weltgeschichtlichen Spirale, deren Bewegungen immer enger und unentrinnbarer wurden, spielte sich unsere Geschichte ab, vielmehr vollzog sich das gesellschaftliche Leben, dieser atemlose Stillstand in der Bewegung, vor dem Hintergrund dieser Geschichte. (page 203)

<u>Die erdabgewandte Seite der Geschichte</u> is, then, Born's tribute to a subjectivity radical in its insistence on itself when threatened by the primacy of the concept--be it in the approach to interpersonal relationships, the understanding of history, or in the very telling of tales.[104] Born does not fall prey to the typification of character, experience, or plot which undermined the works by Timm, Schneider, and Schimmang. Yet, this radical defense of subjectivity is undertaken with its back against the wall. It can defend its allotted corner, but it has no place to go. While Born does not delude us with types, neither does he explore potentially new dimensions of experience. His negative defense of radical subjectivity keeps him enslaved to the dichotomy that plagues him. Mosler generally characterizes literature about the student movement as a failed attempt at literary <u>Vergangenheitsbewältigung</u>.[105] To the extent that Born defends the rights of the subject but fails to develop any sense of a space in which it could properly exercise those rights, this novel, too, fails to come to terms with the legacy of the West German student movement.

## V. ADORNO: SUBJECTIVITY AND THE CONCEPT

The literature of the student movement and its theoretical implications are both motivated by and have import for what we have characterized as the domination of lived, subjective experience by abstract conceptual systems. This literature provides a necessary backdrop for understanding Botho Strauss' own, very different approach to the same dilemma. There is, however, yet another pole on the spectrum of German literary phenomena reaching across the last forty years and addressing comparable issues to which Strauss is likewise attracted and indebted, but from which he is ultimately repelled. That pole is the socio-philosophical, aesthetic theory of Theodor W. Adorno.[106] Immediately, one is advised to proceed with caution. The focal terms of our discussion here, "subjectivity" and "concept", cannot by any means be assumed to mean the same thing in the context of Adorno's thought and in the literature discussed above. Nevertheless, it will be argued here that Strauss draws on Adorno's Critical Theory in two major regards: 1) the condemnation of instrumentalized thought (more specifically for Adorno, instrumentalized rationality) that relegates the human subject to object status, and 2) the conviction that the literary work of art is a potential and unique locus for resistance to that instrumentalization. Clearly, the comparison demands differentiation, not least of all because Strauss writes literature and not aesthetic theory. To be sure, this distinction has not kept feuilleton critics from touting one of Strauss' most recent publications, <u>Paare, Passanten</u>, as the definitive refutation of Adorno's thought. Joachim Kaiser proclaims in the <u>Süddeutsche Zeitung</u> (October 14,

1981): "In diesem Buch wird, ohne Verbiesterung und Rechthaberei, die Herrschaft des aufklärerischen, dialektischen, geist-soziologischen Denkens abgetan, beerdigt." Kaiser pronounces further: "Botho Strauss greift weit über das diskursiv-dialektische Denken der Frankfurter Kunstsoziologie hinaus [. . .]," a claim also made by Rainald Goetz in his <u>Spiegel</u> review of <u>Paare, Passanten</u>.[107] The fact that Kaiser once studied under Adorno makes the flip juxtaposition of adjectives which, at least within the framework of Adorno's thought, cannot legitimately be considered synonymous all the more puzzling. Similarly glib is the assumption by both Kaiser and Goetz that the passage in <u>Paare, Passanten</u> in which Strauss suggests we must get by without dialectics sufficiently proves Strauss has refuted Adorno. Even if one were to take Strauss' comments at face value--in itself a spurious procedure for a critic--the passage is in fact much more ambiguous than Kaiser and Goetz would have us believe. It reads as follows:

> Heimat kommt auf (die doch keine Bleibe war), wenn ich in den 'Minima Moralia' wieder lese. Wie gewissenhaft und prunkend gedacht wurde, noch zu meiner Zeit! Es ist, als seien seither mehrere Generationen vergangen.
> (Ohne Dialektik denken wir auf Anhieb dümmer; aber es muss sein: ohne sie!)   (page 115)

Granted, the reference to Adorno is, as Kaiser argues, characterized by both tribute and distance. Yet, the single-sentence parenthetical statement can hardly be construed as a refutation of dialectical thought. Given Adorno's definition of dialectics as "das konsequente Bewusstsein von Nichtidentität,"[108] Strauss' imperative reads more like weary resignation--not to be equated with refutation!--than the

Mut zur Dummheit which Kaiser and Goetz seem to find so laudable.[109]
The voice of resignation also speaks in the following passage, which appears on the page preceding the one cited above:

> Schreiben heisst auch, gegen den individuellen Blick vorgehen, das treffende Detail abwehren. Wir haben zu lange vom Reichtum der Differenz gelebt. Das Grobe und das Gleiche sind das Interessante; das Wirkliche ist das Wenige. (page 114)

This passage is particularly interesting for two reasons. First, it signifies a marked rejection of Strauss' own previous prose oeuvre, which, as will be argued here, constitutes a struggle for the articulation of difference.[110] Second, this abdication of his own project is related to a renunciation of the rigors of Adorno's thought.[111] In the context of the passage just cited, "das Wirkliche ist das Wenige" must be read as an allusion to Adorno's "das Ganze ist das Unwahre"--as Heinz Heller points out, "die [. . .] 'Umkehrung Hegels', die als zentrale These in Adorno's Minima Moralia (1944-49) erschien und in Negative Dialektik (1966) ihre philosophische Explikation fand."[112] Not only does Strauss dismiss the philosophical categories of truth, totality, and difference, he likewise discards his own previous questioning of what constitutes reality.[113] Motivated by the search for "the real"--determined by the crudest common denominator--Strauss here confuses "Überinformation" (page 114) with thought, opting to resist the former by, in effect, renouncing the latter. This type of resistance, however, does not counter but rather succumbs to the victimization of the subject. Indeed, it perpetuates it by accepting surface appearances as real, failing to distinguish between mere variety and critical difference.

It would be misleading, however, to reduce Adorno's influence on Strauss to the more or less explicit references to the philosopher in <u>Paare, Passanten</u>. A much more substantial influence is implicit in the prose works that appeared prior to <u>Paare, Passanten</u>. These are the works in which the struggle against domination by the concept is manifest. As literary works, they also constitute a uniquely literary experiment in subjectivity. We have already discussed the West German student movement's division of human experience in class society into primary and peripheral contradictions. Criticizing the administrability of scholarly research and theory, Adorno also addresses the artificial dichotomy between the allegedly significant and the allegedly peripheral (albeit in a different context from the student movement). A section of <u>Minima Moralia</u> called "Gross und klein" --interestingly enough the title for one of Strauss' plays[114] --contains the following indictment of this dichotomy: "Die Schematisierung nach wichtig und nebensächlich unterschreibt der Form nach die Wertordnung der herrschenden Praxis, selbst wenn sie ihr inhaltlich widerspricht."[115] The same essay goes on to discuss the annihilation of the subject ("<u>Abschaffung des Subjekts</u>") which such a schematic approach to theoretical work effects. "Denkende Subjektivität ist aber gerade, was nicht in den von oben her heteronom gestellten Aufgabenkreis sich einordnen lässt [. . .]." The fate of thought and subjectivity are also at issue in <u>Dialectic of Enlightenment</u>, co-authored by Adorno and Max Horkheimer.[116] They argue that Enlight- enment thought, initially inspired by the promise of humankind's liberation from the forces of nature, ultimately turns back on itself, not liberating humankind but subjugating it instead of the dictates of responsibility. Enlightenment becomes a totalitarian system of equi- valents, whereby everyone and everything alike is defined according to the criteria of calculability and usefulness.[117] "In advance, the Enlightenment recognizes as being and occurrence only what can be apprehended in unity: its ideal is the system from which all and everything follows" (DE, page 6; DA, page 13). In the same vein: "What was different is equalized. That is the verdict which critical- ly determines the limits of possible experience. The identity of everything with everything else is paid for in that nothing may at the same time be identical with itself" (DE, page 12; DA, page 18). The ostensible eradication of difference is effected by a rational system of thought which renounces its emancipatory, subjective capacity for thought and becomes only system. "Thinking objectifies itself to become an automatic, self-activating process; an impersonation of the machine that it produces itself so that ultimately the machine can replace it" (DE, page 25; DA, page 31. See also DE, page 30; DA, page 36). The functionality of Enlightenment thought subjects the indivi- dual particular--not acknowledged as difference--to domination by the general (DE, page 22; DA, page 28). Reason (Vernunft) is described as a tool in this execution of subjectivity, a henchman so totally defined by his work that his being is reduced to the arm that imple- ments the execution. "[Reason] serves as a general tool, useful, firmly directed toward its end, as fateful as the precisely calculated movements of material production, whose result for mankind is beyond all calculation. At last its old ambition, to be a pure organ of ends, has been realized" (DE, page 30; DA, pages 36-37). The concept itself likewise becomes a tool in this process. "Like the thing, the material tool, which is held on to in different situations as the same thing, and hence divides the world as the chaotic, many-sided, and disparate from the known, one, and identical, the concept is the ideal tool, fit to do service for everything, wherever it can be applied" (DE, page 39; DA, page 46). The Enlightenment concept dominates all particulars by reducing them to their common denominator. This domination does not, however, by any means proceed solely in a metaphysical realm of ideal thought. "The universality of ideas as developed by discursive logic, domination in the conceptual sphere, is raised up on the basis of actual domination" (DE, page 14; DA, page 20). Yet, we must be careful not to equate thought per se or even concepts with the concept of and in Enlightenment as critiqued by Horkheimer and Adorno. They themselves make this distinction in their preface.

> We are wholly convinced--and therein lies our petitio principii--that social freedom is inseparable from enlightened thought. Nevertheless, we believe that we have just as clearly recognized that the notion of this very way of thinking no less than the actual historic forms--the social institutions--with which it is interwoven, already contains the seed of the reversal universally apparent today. (DE, page xiii; DA, page 3)118

Even within the system of Enlightenment rationality, which has relinquished the capacity for critical and, hence, emancipatory thought, Horkheimer and Adorno ascribe to the concept a certain truth content, inasmuch as it bears witness to the annihilation of the subject.

Thought which denies this is illusionary: "All mystic unification remains deception, the impotently inward trace of the absolved revolution" (<u>DE</u>, page 39; <u>DA</u>, page 46). The concept, "as the self-consideration of thought that in the form of science remains tied to blind economic tendency, allows the distance perpetuating injustice to be measured" (<u>DE</u>, page 40; <u>DA</u>, page 47).

The truth content of the concept is, however, extant in the realm of philosophical thought. In the realm of art, the concept figures only as lie, as petrified substantiation of the status quo. The notion that the authentic work of art alone is truly capable of resisting "the mere imitation of that which already is," thereby rendering it different from the conceptual knowledge of philosophy, is articulated in <u>Dialectic of Enlightenment</u>[119] and reiterated and elaborated in Adorno's <u>Ästhetische Theorie</u>, published posthumously in 1970.[120] When Adorno claims, "die fortschreitend sich entfaltende Wahrheit des Kunstwerks ist keine andere als die des philosophischen Begriffs" (<u>ÄT</u>, page 197), we should bear in mind that the concept in philosophy cannot be equated with the concept in art.[121] To be sure, language, as both the medium of the concept and the material medium of the literary work of art, infuses the apparently subjective literary work of art with objective content (<u>Gehalt</u>) and social reference.[122] Since no word and no concept means the same thing within the work as outside it, however, what becomes decisive is the objective form of the literary work; the form of an authentic work of art precludes its transcription into the terms of discursive thought.[123] The authentic work of art, then, is both subjective and objective, autonomous and social at the same time.[124] The autonomous work of art is that which does not duplicate the status quo but resists the hegemony of that which is. Yet, this very resistance binds the work of art to the concrete social condition which its negative difference indicts. This tension between autonomous art and society is in fact the social component in the work of art. For Adorno, art maintains its social and aesthetic integrity by resisting instrumentalization. Art that serves a social function has no social truth value.[125] "Gesellschaftlich an der Kunst ist ihre immanente Bewegung gegen die Gesellschaft, nicht ihre manifeste Stellungnahme." Here again the social truth content of autonomous art resides in autonomous form--where shattered subjectivity is housed--and not in discursive content. Adorno is adamant on this point. "Das künstlerische Subjekt an sich ist gesellschaftlich, nicht privat. Keineswegs wird es gesellschaftlich durch Zwangskollektivierung oder Stoffwahl."[126] The rejection of thematic content as something which neither challenges the status quo nor is capable of resisting its own instrumentalization and which is, therefore, inappropriate to art in advanced industrial society is also at the heart of Adorno's response to Sarte's famous essay in favor of engaged art.[127] Adorno asserts in "Engagement" that autonomous works of art are most political, "wo sie politisch tot sich stellen." It is significant that Adorno characterizes autonomous works of art as "Erkenntnis als begriffsloser Gegenstand."[128] This ascribes to them an inherent truth content as articulated in their form--the objective manifestation of subjectivity--and at the same time designates that truth content incapable of discursive conceptualization. <u>Es lässt sich nicht auf den Begriff bringen</u>.

Adorno's socio-aesthetic theory is clearly not compatible with the literature of the West German student movement, even though both may be said to be motivated by the fate subjectivity has suffered at the hands of the concept. Adorno's theory is, of course, a response to the totalitarianism of fascism and of the developing mass culture industry, while the concern for subjectivity in the post-dogmatic phase of the student upheaval is a response to the history of that movement. Although the different historical constellations which gave rise to these phenomena should not be overlooked, there are certain legitimate points of comparison, even where the comparison is marked by contrast. Literary representatives of the student revolt such as Timm seek to resurrect subjectivity in order to put it to work for the class struggle. This operational approach to subjectivity not only instrumentalizes it, it also fails to question the intactness of subjectivity in the first place.[129] Even Schneider and Schimmang, who want to salvage subjectivity from instrumentalization, surrender any semblance of it to the primacy of the concept. And Born's radical subjectivity speaks from an identifiable narrative center that sees itself as a challenge to the primacy of the concept but, in fact, only exists alongside it. This reminds us of Adorno's comments in 1954 regarding the truth content of the traditional narrative voice used in twentieth-century prose: there is none. "Zerfallen ist die Identität der Erfahrung, das in sich kontinuierliche und artikulierte Leben, das die Haltung des Erzählers einzig gestattet."[130] Further:

> Etwas erzählen heisst ja: etwas <u>Besonderes</u> zu sagen haben, und gerade das wird von der verwalteten Welt, von Standardisierung und Immergleichheit verhindert. Vor jeder inhaltlich ideologischen Aussage ist ideologisch schon der Anspruch des Erzählers, als wäre der Weltlauf wesentlich noch einer der Individuation, als reichte das Individuum mit seinen Regungen und Gefühlen ans Verhängnis noch heran [. . .].[131]

Along these lines, one could argue that Born's protagonist, by claiming to have a particular voice, already lives a lie. More fundamentally, however, Adorno's socio-aesthetic theory is incompatible with the literature of the student movement because of the unique capacity for truth and social reponsibility which the former accords to art.[132] Pained and unruly witness to the annihilation of subjectivity, authentic art is at the same time its last vestige, its hope for a qualitatively different future. The literature of the student movement, by its nature, denies the autonomy of art and, more particularly, of literary language.

## VI. THE REALISM DEBATE: UWE TIMM AND JÖRG DREWS

We shall see that Botho Strauss, while attributing to literature a unique potential for challenging the domination of the subject, does not share Adorno's notion of aesthetic autonomy. The specific manner in which Strauss distances himself from Adorno's aesthetic theory in turn has bearing on the porous sense of realism manifest in the author's prose. Before elaborating on the particulars of Strauss' prose, however, we should like to draw brief attention to a debate on realism between Uwe Timm, representative of the student movement literature, and Jörg Drews, literary critic and scholar. The debate is included as a series of essays in an anthology bearing the title

<u>Realismus--welcher? Sechzehn Autoren auf der Suche nach einem literarischen Begriff</u>.[133] All the essays here revolve around the question of the continued relevance of realism as a concept for the discussion of contemporary literature. Drews considers it an anachronism,[134] while Timm insists on its continued validity as both a stylistic method and a criterion for aesthetic judgment. It is not surprising that Adorno figures so significantly as a point of tension in this debate, more explicitly for Timm than for Drews, whose position Timm virtually equates with that of Adorno. The key issues of the debate include the depictability (<u>Anschaulichkeit</u>) of abstract (social, economic, political) conditions for extraliterary reality, the functional effect of literature on that reality, and the nature of literary language. Citing Marx, Timm will concede only that language constitutes consciousness;[135] he steadfastly refuses to delve into the specific complexity of literary language. What is important, he argues, is plot, content, the fate of identifiable individuals: "keine linguistischen Sprechblasen."[136] For Timm, the utopian function of literature is not only to depict the existing reality of class society as changeable, but also to make it clear to the reader just what it is that needs to be changed. Realistic literature as Timm defines it constitutes an alternative vision to the status quo,[137] a vision capable of contributing to the transformation of the given. Since Timm does not question the application of traditional class analysis to contemporary society, the acceptance of literary content at face value, or the viability of integral subjective identity in literary characters, he has no doubts that literature--by which he means its

ostensible content--can be checked against extraliterary reality in order to determine its truth value; he speaks of the "Überprüfbarkeit" of literature.[138] This posture on Timm's part effectively denies literature any cognitive potential specific to its own medium. It also allows Timm to fault both Adorno and Drews with mechanically reproducing and supporting the status quo by not allowing for the agency of the human subject. For this failure, he even accuses Adorno of "executing history".[139]

Although there are certainly differences in how Adorno, Timm, and Drews assess extraliterary reality and its capacity for change, what is crucial here is the stance on literary language. It is precisely in their insistence on the specifically literary nature of language in literature that Adorno and Drews posit hope for human subjectivity. Drews finds, for example: "Die Betätigung von Phantasie, die Realisation von Freiheit der Sprache, erobert in der Auseinandersetzung mit klischierter, verdinglichter Sprache--das scheint mir vor allen Inhalten und jenseits aller Inhalte das Element von Utopie zu sein." Or: "Die schärfste Negation aller Utopie, etwa bei Beckett, kann den stärksten Appell zur Veränderung einer Welt bergen, die die utopische Dimension abzuschneiden scheint."[140] Both the status of human subjectivity and that of literary modes are seen as infused with history. For this reason, Drews argues, as Adorno does in "Standort des Erzählers im zeitgenössischen Roman," that nineteenth-century realism is no longer appropriate to literature in advanced capitalist society. "Ganz Wesentliches lässt sich gar nicht mehr anschaulich erzählen, und auf jeden Fall sind genau jene Erzählverfahren notwendig geworden, gegen die der Ruf nach einem neuen Realismus sich wendet, die er als elitär, dekadent, überkompliziert, abseitig-experimentell verschreit." In keeping with his classification of literary realism as an anachronism in our time, Drews concludes: "Die Forderung nach einer Re-Simplifizierung der Literatur zu einer realistischen sollte als unrealistisch eingestellt werden." Not only is realism anachronistic as a literary style, it also constitutes a lie. "Der Wunsch nach einer realistischen Literatur läuft weitgehend auf den Wunsch nach einer Entlastung von der ganzen Bürde der Erkenntnisse hinaus, die das naive Erzählen immer schwieriger machen."[141] The fact that Drews and Adorno do not equate language in literature with extraliterary language does not by any means imply that they consider literature impervious to extraliterary influences. On the contrary, literature partakes of extraliterary conditions without necessarily succumbing to them. Drews rebukes Timm: "Wer [. . .] von der verdinglichten und entfremdeten Welt sprechen will und nicht reflektiert, dass Sprache heute ein Teil eben dieser Welt ist, dessen literarisches Produkt wird selbst unmittelbar und im schlechten Sinn die Male der Entfremdung tragen."[142]

There are, to be sure, differences between Drews and Adorno, even if they are not apparent to Timm. When Drews argues, for example, that literature is not the place to effect political enlightenment,[143] he implies acceptance of the division of labor that designates the extraliterary sphere as the proper place for political work. This leads Timm to reproach Drews for merely defending his rights as a member of a privileged class.[144] Timm would not make the distinction, but when Adorno and Horkheimer discuss the fate of subjectivity in the context of the advanced division of labor,[145] it is with a much greater sense of tragedy. Aesthetic autonomy becomes --much more acutely than in Drews' essay--the last bastion of possible human subjectivity. "Kunst vermag einzig noch durch konsequente Arbeitsteilung hindurch ihre humane Allgemeinheit irgend zu realisieren: alles andere ist falsches Bewusstsein."[146] For our discussion of Strauss and West German prose of the 1970's, however, it is not as significant to ascertain that Drews is not Adorno as it is to note that the 1975 debate on realism between Timm and Drews revolves around a familiar axis. Drews refers to the realism debate between Brecht and Lukacs;[147] Timm refers to Adorno, who in his own turn also deals with Brecht and Lukacs at numerous points in the development of his aesthetic theory. Timm and Drews do not provide new insights on an old topic under changed conditions. Despite the fact that Drews does not maintain a traditional formalist position, both parties argue in terms of content versus form, the unique dictates of the literary medium versus its socio-aesthetic autonomy. Timm looks at reality in the Federal Republic and sees only class society; he offers no nuances for the 1970's that might lend some fresh color (if not cogency) to his arguments. Drews does not make the same mistake. Yet, while his arguments <u>remind</u> us of Adorno, they lack the sociophilosophical framework that gave Adorno's theory its historical foundation and weight. The conclusion from all this would seem to be that the antinomies which ultimately structure the debate between Timm and Drews in stale repetition of debates gone by are no longer appropriate to literature of the 1970's. In fact, Rainer Nägele has concluded just that in a different context.[148] "Geht es noch um den Realismus?" dismantles the dichotomy between formalism and realism in the debate on modernism. Nägele does in fact shed new light on an old topic: Lukacs' concept of realism and his aesthetic categories of the general and the particular. Nägele contends that Lukacs was so enamored of nineteenth-century bourgeois realism that he used it as a criterion to judge all other art. It is Lukacs' "bourgeois nostalgia" and not his aesthetic categories per se which lead to this blind spot. Nägele argues against the insistence on objectivity in today's literature for the following reasons:

> Die Insistenz auf Gegenständlichkeit in der Literatur kann in der jetzigen gesellschaftlichen Situation nur die ohnehin bestehende Verdinglichung der Verhältnisse verstärken und den Blick auf die formierenden und deformierenden Interrelationen verwehren. Die Gefahr einer funktionslosen Formalisierung liegt dabei allerdings nahe.

As Nägele sees it, the question formulated in terms of either/or does not allow for a meaningful answer. The aesthetic categories of the general and the particular have continued validity today, but we must find new ways in which to discuss the manner of their mediation. The old terms of the discussion are no longer appropriate.

> Das Problem ist nicht, wie manchmal kurzschlüssig argumentiert wird, dass es heutzutage in der Realität keine Vermittlung gäbe. Natürlich ist das Einzelne vermittelt mit seinem Ganzen, natürlich gibt es einen Vermittlungszusammenhang zwischen meinen partikulären Erfahrungen und dem Aktienmarkt. Das Problem ist eines der Darstellungsweise der veränderten Vermittlungsform.[149]

The emphasis here is on the <u>changed</u>.

## VII. BOTHO STRAUSS AND THE PRINCIPLE OF DIACHRONIC LONGING: BETWEEN ADORNO AND THE STUDENT MOVEMENT

Earlier in this chapter, we noted the loss of faith in conceptual paradigms once thought capable of explaining the general--loosely defined as objective reality--in a meaningful, coherent way. If this occurs simultaneously with the loss of faith in even the identifiability of the particular--in this case, the individual subject--then the situation does indeed call for a new understanding, not only of the mediation between the general and the particular, but of the general and the particular themselves. It is the premise here that Botho Strauss' prose is based on this dual configuration of ambiguity. Michael Zeller's "Versuch, zehn Jahre westdeutscher Literatur in den Blick zu nehmen" uses the word Ausdrucksnot to characterize the general plight of West German literature after the student movement: atrophy of form.[150] The destruction of traditional models had, Zeller argues, left in its wake a lack of aesthetic orientation. Zeller concludes from this that the perspective of the first person, the I, had to be retrained and reasserted in literary endeavors.[151] Whereas Ausdrucksnot can truly be considered a fundamental impetus to Strauss' prose,[152] Strauss' treatment of the phenomenon renders it much more complex than Zeller would have us believe it generally is. The word itself, so closely reminiscent of Atemnot, connotes for Strauss more than a renewed search for literary models. The potentially fatal inability to express oneself threatens survival itself. This is the cultural malaise designated by Strauss' prose; it involves more than merely getting back to the business of producing literary texts. Even more significantly, Strauss questions the very perspective of the I, the reinstatement of which Zeller ascertains in post-movement literature. The failure to recognize that Strauss does not accord his protagonists the status of individuals with an identifiable core has led a variety of critics to the false conclusion that his characters retreat into and defend the inner sanctum of their narrowly defined individuality. Hans Wolfschütz, for example, claims in his entry on Botho Strauss for the <u>Kritisches Lexikon zur deutschsprachigen Gegenwartsliteratur</u> that Strauss' writings, bearing "alle Zeichen von Melancholie und Resignation einer als nachrevolutionär erfahrenen Zeit," see the "Aktionsraum des Individuums in den Bereich seiner Erinnerungen, Sehnsüchte und Phantasien abgedrängt [. . .]."[153] Klaus Scherpe and Hans-Ullrich Treichel, on the other hand, compare Strauss with Handke and Born, noting "Ich-Verlust und Persönlichkeitsschwund" as the common denominator. Yet, rather than discussing the three authors in detail, they make the sweeping connection between "Ich-Verlust" and "Totalitätsverlust," the latter being the essence of the novel throughout history and of "new subjectivity" in our time.[154] Regardless how generally valid such historical connections and comparisons may be, the conclusion from this that the experience of loss of reality is transformed into the "literarischen Gestus der unbedingten Verweigerung von Realitätserfahrung jenseits des eigenen Erfahrungshorizonts" falsely implies--at least for Strauss --that there <u>is</u> an identifiable horizon of experience for the individual to retreat behind. Helmut Schödel, discussing Strauss' early works, defines Strauss' "aesthetics of loss" as one which essentially welds disparate parts back together through memory.[155] There is a grain of truth in Schödel's notion of the tension between disparate parts, but there is no welding of discordant parts in Strauss' prose, least of all in "Marlenes Schwester" and "Theorie der Drohung," where the characters exist in an oppressive, draining relationship to each other.[156]

It is true that Strauss' prose manifestly rejects all abstract, preconceived systems that claim to comprehend either reality or the individuals that live in it. Strauss has even gone so far as to reject Marxism in the form of Bloch's "principle of hope" as too positive an insistence on the world making sense.[157] Yet, there would seem to be a contradiction here. While Strauss is opposed to conceptual systems, he is at the same time opposed to "Polaroid-Lyrismus" which abrogates meaningful connections and interrelationships (<u>Zusammenhänge</u>).[158] If abstract systems can be faulted with oppressive domination and even silencing of difference, of that for which the system does not allow, then <u>Ausdrucksnot</u> does not indicate the atomistic co-existence of unrelated particles. Rather, in the context of Strauss' work, it implies the need--albeit not necessarily its satisfaction in reality--for meaningful interconnections as vital to human survival. Interviewing Strauss, Zacharias claims: "Die Zerstörung des Subjekts, die Auflösung der Grenzen zwischen Innen und Aussen, zwischen Du and Ich, zwischen männlich und weiblich. Davon handeln alle seine Erzählungen."[159] To this Strauss responds: "Die Auflösung dieser Grenzen ist zugleich Gefahr und Chance." This one sentence essentially outlines the aesthetic principle of Strauss' prose.

The disruptive challenge to oppressive conceptual systems--including those which define what constitutes the individual--entails the danger of drowning in the relativistic quagmire of unrelated particles. Yet, the failure to challenge such systems means surrender to them. Disruptive challenge is in fact the prerequisite, albeit not the guarantee for qualitatively new visions that would restore the living dimensions to experience. This would necessitate making connections that are not linear and hence not even open-ended, but open-edged: porous.[160] The partner to <u>Ausdrucksnot</u> in this literary endeavor is the principle of diachronic longing ("das diachrone Verlangen"). This principle is cited in <u>Die Widmung</u> in apposition to writing, "die Schrift,"[161] but it has much broader applications. It is the aesthetic principle for which Strauss' statement on the dissolution of boundaries has prepared us. We have seen that the West German student movement left behind a specific void--a wasteland between subjective experience of the moment and generalized conceptual systems. Strauss' prose seeks to fertilize that wasteland by making the boundaries fluid in all directions. Diachronic longing presumes the living tension of desire and need between discordant (non-identical) elements. Its manifestations are manifold, in keeping with Strauss' rejection of oppressive linear systems of conceptual domination. Perhaps the most obvious locus for diachronic longing is between two individuals. In fact, Strauss has a predilection for main characters who function as pairs: two sisters, a male writer and a female patient in a mental hospital, a man and the lover who has left him, and a father and his daughter.[162] The separateness of the components of these pairs is not always clear or even constant. That is to say, the state of the individual is in flux. Diachronic longing, moreover, ties the self, which seeks to know itself (its identity), to the experience of emotions. Likewise, diachronic tension exists between experience and the language in which it seeks articulation. Both thematically and aesthetically, the need to mediate between language and the experience of the present is central to Strauss' prose. No less important is the mediation between the present and the past. The present moment strives to connect with its past, thus allowing, on the personal level, for biography; on the social and national level, this allows for history as a lived experience. Both individual history (biography) and social history constitute theory to the extent that they make connections establishing meaning. Diachronic longing, however, precludes theory as an abstract system of conceptual domination.

Diachronic longing in the context of the written word likewise manifests itself on a variety of levels. The act of writing is both externalization of self--as when Richard Schroubek writes his first clear word: his name[163]--and a re-appropriation of self as well--as when Schroubek writes his journal entries.[164] It constitutes a tension that both acknowledges difference and makes connections between disparate parts. By the same token, the numerous allusions throughout Strauss' prose to literary works by other authors manifest a diachronic longing between Strauss' writing and the broader literary tradition on which he draws.[165] There exists, at the same time, diachronic longing among the four prose works by Strauss under discussion here. When studied together, these works demarcate the rise and fall of a literary project: the articulation of the aesthetic principle of diachronic longing. It has been argued that the recurrent literary motifs in Strauss' work and the references to other literary texts serve to establish a nexus of meaningful connections which Strauss finds lacking in reality.[166] This is only partially true. Rather, they are an extension of the principle of diachronic longing, which encompasses more than the tension between components of the literary tradition. Diachronic longing also entails tension between literature--in this instance, Strauss' prose--and extraliterary reality. Strauss' specifically literary attempt, first to depict and then to challenge the domination of lived experience by the concept harks back to Adorno's aesthetic theory. Although the aesthetic principle of diachronic longing is not communicative or discursive (i.e., does not yield a core of information or a message that could be reproduced independently from the text), it is nonetheless referential. Any given component refers to and struggles with something outside itself--actively, not *ex negativo*. This renders it incompatible with Adorno's aesthetic theory of autonomous art. For Strauss, the particular--to the extent that it is discernible at all--actively seeks connection with the collective. Whether Strauss' prose is successful in this mediation is not presently at issue, but the striving is what motivates Strauss' literary project, both as thematic essence and aesthetic principle.

## VIII. BOTHO STRAUSS AND HIS CRITICS

The few existing attempts to analyze Strauss' work critically and systematically acknowledge some individual aspects of the principle of diachronic longing to varying degrees while drawing the general conclusion that the author's oeuvre functions as a closed system of negation, one without hope.[167] Gerd Michels, for example, undertakes a hermeneutic analysis of Die Widmung in which he discusses the crisis of the narrative voice and the story that no longer lends itself to narration.[168] The particular, having no sense of past or tradition, has no meaning. "Auch das Einzelne ist nun nicht mehr Ausdruck des Allgemeinen: weder bestätigt ein von sich aus sinnvoller Zusammenhang dieses, noch kann die Tradition, in der der Sinnzusammenhang verlorengegangen ist, das Einzelne stützen." The self, having no contours, seeks to establish its own meaning through the act of writing. "Die Schrift bleibt ihm der Balken im Meer, an den sein gefährdetes Ich sich noch klammern kann [. . .]." and "Nur noch das Schreiben schützt Richard vor dem Verlust jeglicher Geschichtsverbindlichkeit [. . .]." Michels concludes from this that Strauss' protagonist occupies a "Position der Negation" only: "von hier aus führen keine Wege zu einem Happy-End."[169] From a different analytical perspective, Gerhard vom Hofe and Peter Pfaff draw the same conclusion. Their book, Das Elend des Polyphem, discusses subjectivity in the works of Thomas Bernhard, Peter Handke, Wolfgang Koeppen, and Botho Strauss in the aesthetic-political context of the historical notion of ontological subject, the mediation between the individual and the general being "ein problemgeschichtlicher Progress in der fortschreitenden Reflexion, welche die Literatur ist [. . .]."

> Nun scheint [. . .] zu den Erfahrungen der Existenz eine Abhängigkeit zu gehören, wie sie fundamentaler nicht vorzustellen ist: nicht nur können wir nicht allein sein; wir können auch allein nicht sein. Insofern zählt der Bezug auf ein Anderes als den Grund des Selbstseins unter die existentialen Schemata, die auch das Verhältnis zu einem transzendentalen Absoluten, den Glauben, strukturieren. Aus diesem einzigen Prinzip der erotischen Transzendenz jedenfalls lässt sich die Mannigfaltigkeit der Fabel und Situationen in den Geschichten und Dramen von Botho Strauss entwickeln.

Vom Hofe and Pfaff articulate this ontological dilemma in the terminology of salvation theology and conclude: "Die verlorene heilsgeschichtliche Hoffnung ist eine Obsession auch von Botho Strauss, sie strukturiert sein Werk." His "Widerlegung der Romantik" draws on the Romantic tradition of transcendental love but denies art's continued capacity to attain that transcendence. "Eigentlich ist die Einsicht in die Unmöglichkeit der Kunst deren letzte nachromantische Apologie."[170] From yet another perspective, Michael Schneider also makes the link between Strauss' work and what Schneider calls "Negativ-Romantik."[171] Schneider tells us that he is less interested in analyzing Strauss' aesthetic structures than in criticizing the "climate of decay and hopelessness" which permeates Strauss' writing and which no longer accords love any positive capacity for change.[172]

> Botho Strauss darf als der ästhetisch avanciertteste Vertreter jener neuen Negativ-Romantik gelten, der sich die Literatur der siebziger Jahre zunehmend verschrieben hat; einer Romantik, die ihre Leser in immer neuen Versionen das Fürchten und Frösteln lehrt, indem sie, Verfechterin eines neuzeitlichen Entropie-Gesetzes, den 'Kältetod' und die angebrochene 'Eiszeit der Gefühle' in geradezu apokalyptischen Bildern zu beschwören sucht.[173]

What Michels, vom Hofe/Pfaff, and Schneider share despite their very different critical perspectives is their assessment of the overriding function of negativity in Strauss' work. I shall argue that the principle of diachronic longing precludes the closure of negativity, since it presumes active, that is to say, open, non-finite interplay between non-identical elements. None of these elements can be rigidly defined or clearly distinguished from the others inasmuch as they all live in the symbiotic realm of interaction. Whether Strauss' prose is consistently true to this principle is another question altogether. Indeed, it is not. The principle of diachronic longing is most clearly and most hopefully at work in Die Widmung, which more than any other individual piece forms the core of Strauss' prose oeuvre. The two earlier works laid the groundwork for the project it articulates, and Rumor marks the renunciation of that project. Tellingly, Paare, Passanten has a markedly different stylistic format from any of the other prose works. The development of the literary project manifest in "Marlenes Schwester," "Theorie der Drohung," Die Widmung, and Rumor will be traced in detail in the chapters to follow here. A final chapter will discuss its aesthetic and epistemological implications in the context of post-World War II German literature.

Notes: Chapter I

[1] See Marcel Reich-Ranicki, "Gleicht die Liebe einem Monolog?", Frankfurter Allgemeine Zeitung (September 10, 1977), and Martin Roda Becher, "Poesie der Unglücksfälle: Über die Schriften von Botho Strauss," Merkur, 32(1978), Nr. 6, 625, for the two opposing viewpoints I have paraphrased here.

[2] "Marlenes Schwester" was first published in Neue Rundschau, 85 (1974), Nr. 1, 68-84. It was later published together with "Theorie der Drohung" in Botho Strauss, Marlenes Schwester: Zwei Erzählungen (Munich: Hanser, 1975), followed by Die Widmung: Eine Erzählung (Munich: Hanser, 1977) and Rumor (Munich: Hanser, 1980). A very early (1963) and extremely short allegorical prose piece by Strauss, Schützenehre: Erzählung (Düsseldorf: Eremiten-Presse, 1975), will not be discussed here inasmuch as it has no bearing on the literary project outlined in the four works which provide the focus for this study. Strauss' most recent prose publication, Paare, Passanten (Munich: Hanser, 1981), will be given some attention in this chapter. Its marked stylistic deviation from the four preceding works, however, only underscores the end of the aesthetic experiment manifested in the four earlier works.

[3] The Radikalenerlass of 1972 unleashed a pack of legal and atmospheric furies with a voracious appetite for anything remotely resembling leftist sympathies. The terrorist activities of the Red Army Faction were used to polarize public opinion and implement increasingly repressive policies of professional proscription, censorship, and general surveillance. For a relatively brief but informative account of these phenomena, see "Notes and Commentary" in Telos, 34 (Winter 1977-78), 121-147, with contributions by Jay Rosellini, Oskar Negt, and Jack Zipes.

[4] The original use of the term Tendenzwende in the early to mid 1970's actually referred to a broader political trend towards the restoration of conservative ideals and policies. It was the topic of a conference held in Munich in 1974 at the Bavarian Academy of Arts, the proceedings of which have been published as Tendenzwende?: Zur geistigen Situation der Bundesrepublik, ed. Clemens Graf Podewils (Stuttgart: Klett, 1975). For discussions of this trend, see Martin Greiffenhagen, "Der gewendete Zeitgeist: Ueber den neuen Konservatismus der siebziger Jahre," Stuttgarter Zeitung (October 19, 1974), and Rolf Zundel, "Tendenzwende--mehr als Einbildung: Den Konservativen regnet es Sterntaler in die Schürze," Die Zeit (December 13, 1974). See further Der bürgerliche Rechtsstaat, ed. Mehdi Tohidipur (Frankfurt/Main: Suhrkamp, 1978), p. 136ff.; Jürgen Habermas, "Einleitung," Stichworte zur 'Geistigen Situation der Zeit', ed. Jürgen Habermas (Frankfurt/Main: Suhrkamp, 1979), I, 17, and Joachim Hirsch, Der Sicher-

heitsstaat: Das 'Modell Deutschland', seine Krise und die neuen sozialen Bewegungen (Frankfurt/Main: Europäische Verlagsanstalt, 1980). It is on the secondary capacity of Tendenzwende, used to designate shifts on the Left, that I focus here. David Roberts notes the two-fold thrust of Tendenzwende in "Tendenzwenden: Die sechziger und siebziger Jahre in literaturhistorischer Perspektive," Deutsche Vierteljahrsschrift, 56 (June 1982), No. 2, 290-313.

[5]This has been argued in places too numerous to cite here. The point has obvious implications for the critical debate on the periodization of contemporary literature, one which shows some structural similarities to the debate on the alleged "zero hour" in German literature after World War II. Since the term Tendenzwende is used to categorize works as either political or apolitical, Rainer Nägele notes the following: "So fragwürdig in der Praxis der Literatur die Oppositionsreihe als Alternative ist, muss sie doch zunächst anerkannt werden als konkreter Faktor der Literaturdebatte der letzten Jahrzehnte, deren historische Wurzeln zurückreichen in die Anfänge der Moderne." Rainer Nägele, "Geschichten und Geschichte: Reflexionen zum westdeutschen Roman seit 1965," Deutsche Gegenwartsliteratur, ed. Manfred Durzak (Stuttgart: Reclam, 1981), p. 237.

[6]One article on Strauss' play "Gross und klein" rejects the label of Tendenzwende, claiming for this drama instead a sense of social realism. See Gisela Erbslöh and Hans Burkhard Schlichtung, "Offener Hermetismus und Theater des Alltäglichen: Über 'Gross und klein' von Botho Strauss," Spectaculum 33: Vier moderne Theaterstücke (Frankfurt/Main: Suhrkamp, 1980), pp. 312-317.

[7]See, for example, Peter Mosler, "Die Kunst ist die Umkehrung des Lebens," Aufbrüche, Abschiede: Studien zur deutschen Literatur seit 1968, ed. Michael Zeller (Stuttgart: Klett, 1979), p. 44. The biographical data on Strauss are sparse. Born on December 2, 1944, in Naumburg/Saale, he attended the universities of Cologne and Munich, where he studied theater, German literature, and sociology. From 1967 to 1970, he was a contributing editor for the journal Theater heute. Since then he has been involved, both as playwright and director, in numerous theatrical productions at the Schaubühne (formerly am Halleschen Ufer) in West Berlin, where his emphatically private life style has earned him the reputation of being a recluse.

[8]Hans Wolfschütz, "Botho Strauss," Kritisches Lexikon der deutschsprachigen Gegenwartsliteratur, ed. Heinz Ludwig Arnold (Munich: edition text und kritik, 1978), II, n.p.

[9]The notion of language as oppressor is nothing new. Consider, for example, Oswald Wiener's statement: "in wahrheit ist definition natürlich ein instrument der politischen unterdrückung, sie nimmt dem wort die möglichkeit des meinens," in Die Verbesserung von Mitteleuropa: Roman (Reinbek bei Hamburg: Rowohlt, 1969), p. XXIII. Beyond

this basic premise, however, Strauss' and Wiener's efforts to liberate language have little in common.

[10]There seems to be consensus on this point, although there are differences of opinion as to when exactly each new phase begins and how it is to be evaluated. For a discussion of the student movement in the Federal Republic, see the following: Gerhard Bauss, <u>Die Studentenbewegung der sechziger Jahre in der Bundesrepublik Deutschland und West Berlin: Handbuch</u> (Cologne: Pahl-Rugenstein, 1977); Gerd Langguth, <u>Die Protestbewegung in der Bundesrepublik Deutschland 1968-1976</u> (Cologne: Verlag Wissenschaft und Politik, 1976); <u>Literatur und Studentenbewegung: Eine Zwischenbilanz</u>, ed. W. Martin Lüdke (Opladen: Westdeutscher Verlag, 1977); Peter Mosler, <u>Was wir wollten, was wir wurden: Studentenrevolte--zehn Jahre danach</u> (Reinbek bei Hamburg: Rowohlt, 1977); and Peter Rühmkorf, <u>Die Jahre, die ihr kennt: Anfälle und Erinnerungen</u> (Reinbek bei Hamburg: Rowohlt, 1972).

[11]This is not to underestimate the political significance of the women's movement, citizens' action committees, or the anti-nuclear movement. Whereas the rise of these movements (and others) may be related to failures of the student movement, they cannot, however, be classified as subsidiary elements of a broader student movement.

[12]Several terms that figure prominently in the discussion to follow may require some elaboration for those readers unfamiliar with the vocabulary of orthodox Marxism. Thoughts or deeds reflect politically "correct" consciousness if they adhere to the fundamental postulate that capitalism is predicated on the exploitation of the working class and only the proletariat can and will ultimately effect true revolution. Systematic efforts to change society along orthodox Marxist lines constitute a political "praxis," which distinguishes between the "base" and the "superstructure" as spheres of social life. "Base" refers to the material forces of production, which are credited with determining all other aspects of life. "Superstructure" connotes the realms and institutions of thought, culture, law, religion, politics, philosophy, and the like; these are considered subordinate to the base. The distinction between base and superstructure corresponds to that between the "productive" and "reproductive" spheres, the latter essentially echoing the dictates of the former and including such things as interpersonal relationships and family life. The classification of the student activists as "bourgeois" in this context indicates their exclusion from the revolutionary class of the proletariat and membership in a class whose real interest allegedly lies in maintaining the status quo.

I use these terms in my discussion of student movement politics in order to illuminate the contradictions inherent in the activists' own strategy and vocabulary, contradictions which they themselves ultimately could not ignore.

[13]Klaus Hartung, "Versuch, die Krise der antiautoritären Bewegung wieder zur Sprache zu bringen," <u>Kursbuch,</u> 48(June 1977), 18,

puts it succinctly: "Die soziale Realität wurde aufgelöst in ein Feld von Haupt- und Nebenwidersprüchen." See also page 16 of the same essay.

[14]Hartung, "Versuch," p. 21. It will be argued in this study that the effects of dogmatization are of greater consequence than Hartung indicates here.

[15]Rolf Hosfeld and Helmut Peitsch attribute this failure to the inherent existentialist nature of the student movement. See their essay, "'Weil uns diese Aktionen innerlich verändern, sind sie politisch': Bemerkungen zu vier Romanen über die Studentenbewegung," Basis, 8(1978), 92.

[16]See Michael Schneider, "Von der alten Radikalität zur neuen Sensibilität," Kursbuch, 49(October 1979), 174-187.

[17]See, for example, Lothar Binger, "Kritisches Plädoyer für die Gruppe," Kursbuch, 37(October 1974), 3, and Rainer Paris, "Befreiung vom Alltag?" Kursbuch, 41(September 1975), 111. The phrase "emancipation debate" has become something of a colloquialism. It refers to the general discussion following the demise of the organized student movement as to new ways for the individual to seek emancipation from traditional political and social constraints. Its emphasis particularly addressed the realm of personal relationships.

[18]Bernward Vesper, Die Reise: Romanessay (Jossa: März, 1977), p. 34.

[19]The 1970's issues of the journals Basis, kürbiskern, Kursbuch, and Literaturmagazin contain numerous articles on this question.

[20]Rudolph zur Lippe, "Objektiver Faktor Subjektivität," Kursbuch, 35(April 1974), 1-35. See also Johann August Schülein, "Von der Studentenrevolte zur Tendenzwende oder der Rückzug ins Private: Eine sozialpsychologische Analyse," Kursbuch, 48(June 1977), 109-117.

[21]See my comments on the terms of orthodox Marxism in note 12.

[22]Zur Lippe, see pp. 13, 25, 26, and 34-35.

[23]Even the maintenance of the concept of "reproductive sphere" versus "sphere of production" does of course partake of the dichotomy previously established between essential and peripheral contradictions, a dichotomy which "new subjectivity" implicitly challenges, depending of course on how it is conceived.

[24]For a detailed account of this, see Raoul Hübner's essay, "'Klau mich' oder die Veränderungen von Verkehrsformen: Anstösse der Studentenbewegung," Literatur und Studentenbewegung: Eine Zwischenbilanz, ed. W. Martin Lüdke (Opladen: Westdeutscher Verlag, 1977), pp.

219-247. See also Lawrence Baron et al., "Der 'anarchische' Utopismus der westdeutschen Studentenbewegung," Deutsches utopisches Denken im 20. Jahrhundert, ed. Reinhold Grimm and Jost Hermand (Stuttgart: Kohlhammer, 1974), p. 127.

[25]Hübner, p. 244.

[26]There have been many studies on this topic in recent years: Erving Goffman, Rahmen-Analysen, trans. Hermann Vetter (Frankfurt/Main: Suhrkamp, 1979); Lothar Hack, Subjektivität im Alltag: Zur Konstitution sozialer Relevanzstrukturen (Frankfurt/Main: Campus, 1977); Agnes Heller, Das Alltagsleben: Versuch einer Erklärung der individuellen Reproduktion, trans. Hans Joas (Frankfurt/Main: Suhrkamp, 1975); Henri Lefèbvre, Das Alltagsleben in der modernen Welt, trans. Annegret Dumasy (Frankfurt/Main: Suhrkamp, 1972); Henri Lefèbvre, Kritik des Alltagslebens, trans. Hans Jacob, 2nd ed. (Munich: Hanser, 1976); Thomas Leithäuser, Formen des Alltagsbewusstseins, 2nd ed. (Frankfurt/Main: Campus, 1979); Thomas Leithäuser et al., Entwurf zu einer Empirie des Alltagsbewusstseins (Frankfurt/Main: Suhrkamp, 1977); Materialien zur Soziologie des Alltags, ed. Kurt Hammerich and Michael Klein (Wiesbaden: Westdeutscher Verlag, 1979); Rainer O. Neugebauer, Alltagsleben: Zur Kritik einer politisch-historischen und didaktischen Kategorie (Frankfurt/Main: Haag und Herchen, 1978); Arno Plack, Philosophie des Alltags (Stuttgart: Deutsche Verlags-Anstalt, 1979); Alfred Schütz and Thomas Luckmann, Strukturen der Lebenswelt (Frankfurt/Main: Suhrkamp, 1979); Hans Thurn, Der Mensch im Alltag: Grundrisse einer Anthropologie des Alltagslebens (Stuttgart: Enke, 1980). See also Kursbuch, 41 (September 1975), which is dedicated to the topic of everyday life.

[27]Paris, p. 112.

[28]Gunther Weimann, doctoral candidate at Washington University, discusses this point in his dissertation in progress on Max von der Grün.

[29]Schülein, p. 112.

[30]For a detailed analysis of the emancipatory potential of experience that is not structured by market forces, see Oskar Negt and Alexander Kluge, Öffentlichkeit und Erfahrung: Zur Organisationsanalyse von bürgerlicher und proletarischer Öffentlichkeit (Frankfurt/Main: Suhrkamp, 1972).

[31]Karl Markus Michel, "Unser Alltag: Nachruf zu Lebzeiten," Kursbuch, 41(September 1975), 40.

[32]Alexander Kluge and Edgar Reitz, "In Gefahr und grösster Not bringt der Mittelweg den Tod," Kursbuch, 41(September 1975), 70.

[33] The very nature of needs is itself subject to debate. See, for example, Agnes Heller, The Theory of Needs in Marx (London: St. Martin, 1976) and Ferenc Fehér, "The Dictatorship Over Needs," Telos, 35(Spring 1978), 31-42. Jacquelyn Zita, a doctoral candidate in the Department of Philosophy at Washington University, is currently completing a dissertation on authentic versus artificial needs.

Specificity refers to the physiognomic detail which renders a particular experience the individual's own, distinct from all others.

[34] Oskar Negt, "Nicht das Geld, Wotan ist das Problem/Der jüngste Aufstand gegen die dialektische Vernunft: die 'Neuen Philosophen' Frankreichs," Literaturmagazin, 9(1978), 44; Klaus Hartung, "Versuch," pp. 42-43. In his essay "Neue Subjektivität: Zur Literatur der siebziger Jahre in der Bundesrepublik Deutschland," Deutsche Gegenwartsliteratur, ed. Manfred Durzak (Stuttgart: Reclam, 1981), p. 79, Helmut Kreuzer also mentions theory's precarious standing in the 1970's. Most recently, Tilman Spengler discussed the current aversion to theory in terms of a "Liebe zu überschaubaren Verhältnissen." See Tilman Spengler, "Der Bauch als Avantgarde--über den aufrechten Niedergang der Theorie," Kursbuch, 65(October 1981), 188. Spengler makes the following comment on the status of theory in "the movement": "Dass die Bewegung--mit nur ganz wenigen Ausnahmen--theorielos sei, darin stimmen Aktivisten und Theoretiker überein. Ungleich verteilt ist nur der Schmerz, den diese Aussage zufügt. So recht betroffen scheinen davon im Augenblick nur die Theoretiker zu sein, denn für 'altlinke Hirnwichser' gibt es in der Bewegung zwar kein Berufsverbot, doch erst recht keine Planstellen" (p. 180). (For a more detailed discussion of the contemporary non-dogmatic movement, see Autonomie oder Getto? Kontroversen über die Alternativbewegung, ed. Wolfgang Kraushaar [Frankfurt/Main: Verlag Neue Kritik, 1978].) For a multidisciplinary response to the troubled status of theory--"'wer traute sich noch eine Theorie des gegenwärtigen Zeitalters zu?'" (Habermas)--see Stichworte zur 'Geistigen Situation der Zeit', ed. Jürgen Habermas, 3rd ed., 2 vols. (Frankfurt/Main: Suhrkamp, 1980). Of particular interest is Wolf-Dieter Narr's essay, "Hin zu einer Gesellschaft bedingter Reflexe" (II, 489-528), in which he discusses the seemingly paradoxical relationship between the increasingly rapid influx of informational data and the ostensible erosion of communicative structures (pp. 502-503) in the context of the urgent need for better theory (p. 514), understood as process appropriate to our times (pp. 523-524).

[35] See, for example, Literaturmagazin, 9(1978), entitled "Der neue Irrationalismus" and dedicated entirely to this phenomenon.

[36] For some elaborations on this position, see "Notes and Commentary" in Telos, 33(Fall 1977), 93-122.

[37] See Hartung's article "Versuch, die Krise der antiautoritären Bewegung wieder zur Sprache zu bringen" for a detailed, critical account of the movement. Gerhard Bauss has written a longer, informa-

tive account of the West German student movement (see note 10), but his DKP bias prevents him from addressing the issues which are pertinent to this study.

[38] Peter Brückner, "Über Krisen von Identität und Theorie," Kursbuch, 1(1978), 39. In an interview with Harald Wieser, Oskar Negt also discusses the issue of identity among the Left. See Oskar Negt, "Interesse gegen Partei: Über Identitätsprobleme der deutschen Linken," Kursbuch, 48(June 1977), 175-188.

[39] Brückner, p. 39.

[40] Michael Rutschky, Erfahrungshunger: Ein Essay über die siebziger Jahre (Cologne: Kiepenheuer & Witsch, 1980), p. 263.

[41] Brückner, p. 47.

[42] Rutschky, p. 263.

[43] Michael Schneider, "Von der alten Radikalität," pp. 184-185.

[44] Klaus Hartung, "Die Repression wird zum Milieu: Die Beredsamkeit linker Literatur," Literaturmagazin, 11(1979), 52.

[45] As Michael Rutschky puts it, "Eine Erfahrung machen heisst, wie unerwartet den Augenblick finden, in dem eine Geschichte zu Ende ist und von diesem Ende her formuliert werden kann" (Rutschky, p. 265).

[46] Klaus Hartung, "Über die langandauernde Jugend im linken Getto: Lebensalter und Politik--Aus der Sicht eines 38jährigen," Kursbuch, 54(December 1978), 187.

[47] Theodor W. Adorno, "Was bedeutet: Aufarbeitung der Vergangenheit?", Erziehung zur Mündigkeit: Vorträge und Gespräche mit Hellmut Becker 1959-1969, ed. Gerd Kadelbach, 5th ed. (Frankfurt/Main: Suhrkamp, 1977), pp. 19-28.

[48] A phenomenologist would argue this formulation is a contradiction in terms. I am inclined to agree.

[49] Hartung, "Die Repression wird zum Milieu," pp. 54-55. This essay discusses Peter Schneider's Lenz (Berlin: Rotbuch, 1973); Peter Chotjewitz' Die Herren des Morgengrauens (Berlin: Rotbuch, 1979); Inge Buhmann's Ich habe mir eine Geschichte erzählt (Munich: Trikont, 1977); and Bernward Vesper's Die Reise (Jossa: März, 1977).

[50] Fritz Raddatz, "Angst-Literatur," Die Zeit (August 7, 1981).

[51] Peter Beicken, "'Neue Subjektivität': Zur Prosa der siebziger Jahre," Deutsche Literatur in der Bundesrepublik seit 1965, ed. Paul Michael Lützeler and Egon Schwarz (Königstein/Ts.: Athenäum, 1980),

pp. 164-181. A clear understanding of this "new subjectivity" as a literary phenomenon is highly elusive. Most simply, it connotes a renewed emphasis on the problem of the individual versus the predominance of objective social concerns. Certainly, it reflects the Tendenzwende discussed at the beginning of this chapter. Yet, the phrase is applied so broadly as to erase any contours that might render it useful for this study. Rather than try to wrestle with this mercurial journalistic label, I have chosen to discuss Strauss' prose on terms I find more fruitful.

[52] Helmut Schödel, "Ästhetik des Verlusts: Zur Literatur des Botho Strauss," Theater heute, 17(1976), Nr. 13, 104. The same article may also be found in Spectaculum 26: Acht moderne Theaterstücke (Frankfurt/Main: Suhrkamp, 1977), pp. 298-303.

[53] Rainer Nägele, "Geschichten und Geschichte: Reflexionen zum westdeutschen Roman seit 1965," Deutsche Gegenwartsliteratur, ed. Manfred Durzak (Stuttgart: Reclam, 1981), pp. 234-251. See especially p. 245. For historical and philosophical analyses of historical narrative, see the essays collected in Geschichte: Ereignis und Erzählung, ed. Reinhart Koselleck and Wolf-Dieter Stempel (Munich: Fink, 1973). While this volume does not address the problematic of fictional narrative, it does contain an article by Eberhard Lämmert "Zum Wandel der Geschichtserfahrung im Reflex der Romantheorie," pp. 503-515.

[54] In the article just cited, Nägele asserts: "Sprache nicht bloss als Darstellungsmittel, sondern als Organisationsprinzip der Wirklichkeit, als potentielle und reale Gewalt, ja als das Subjekt schlechthin, das spricht, beherrscht thematisch und formal die wichtigsten Romane des vergangenen Jahrzehnts" (p. 247). Apparently, Nägele does not count Botho Strauss among the most important authors of the 1970's; he is not mentioned at all in Nägele's article.

[55] See Uwe Timm, "Peter Handke oder sicher in die 70er Jahre," kürbiskern (1970), Nr. 4, 611-621; "Realismus und Utopie," kürbiskern (1975), Nr. 1, 91-101; "Sensibilität für wen?", kürbiskern (1976), Nr. 1, 118-122; "Zwischen Unterhaltung und Aufklärung," kürbiskern (1972), Nr. 1, 79-90; Peter Schneider, "Die Phantasie im Spätkapitalismus und die Kulturrevolution," Kursbuch, 16(March 1969), 1-37.

[56] Timm, "Zwischen Unterhaltung und Aufklärung," p. 86.

[57] Timm, "Zwischen Unterhaltung und Aufklärung," p. 87. It seems almost superfluous to note that Timm ignores here both the real reading habits of real workers as well as the question of reception aesthetics. Indeed, as a writer of fiction, Timm seems to be oblivious to the demands of the aesthetic medium. This will be discussed in greater detail later.

[58] Schneider, "Die Phantasie," pp. 29, 30 and 35.

[59] Peter Schneider, "Über den Unterschied von Literatur und Politik," Literaturmagazin, 5(1976), 198.

[60] Uwe Timm, "Über den Dogmatismus in der Literatur," Kontext, 1(1976), 22-31.

[61] Here Timm seems to float with the tide of uncritical categorization which is quick to characterize literary developments in the late 1960's and early 1970's as beginning with the "Tod der Literatur"--as allegedly proclaimed in the by now infamous Kursbuch, 15(1968), including pivotal articles by Hans Magnus Enzensberger, Karl Markus Michel, and Walter Boehlich--and ending with the journalistic slogan "Jetzt dichten sie wieder!"

[62] Timm, "Über den Dogmatismus," pp. 24-25. The references in this last passage are to Nicolas Born, author of Die erdabgewandte Seite der Geschichte (Reinbek bei Hamburg: Rowohlt, 1976) and Karin Struck, who is best known for Klassenliebe (Frankfurt/Main: Suhrkamp, 1973).

[63] Ursula Krechel, "Leben in Anführungszeichen: Das Authentische in der gegenwärtigen Literatur," Literaturmagazin, 11(1979), 80.

[64] Beicken, p. 170. Helmut Kreuzer also finds: "In der Tat gehört das autobiographische Genre zu den florierenden schon seit Anfang der siebziger Jahre. In ihm kann sich der Authentizitätsanspruch des Dokumentarismus mit dem neuen Rückbezug auf das eigene Ich verbinden." See Kreuzer, "Neue Subjektivität," p. 79.

[65] Krechel, p. 82.

[66] Krechel, p. 86.

[67] I do not mean to obscure the differences between autobiography and biography, but to emphasize the notion of continuity of personal history to both.

[68] In an essay on "Selbsterfahrung und Neue Subjektivität in der Lyrik," Akzente, 24(February 1977), Nr. 1, 89-90, Jörg Drews makes a related point but does not elaborate beyond the following: "[. . .] es scheint, als sei die Erzählung von fiktiven Gestalten und Situationen oft--und nach wie vor--eine viel günstigere Form, gerade radikal individuelle und subjektive Erfahrungen niederzulegen" (p. 89), and "Lyrik als Ich-Aussprache und autobiographischer Roman oder Autobiographie verbürgen ja noch keineswegs die Mitteilung wirklich unschematischer, spezifischer Subjektivität" (pp. 89-90).

[69] Uwe Timm, Heisser Sommer: Roman (Munich: Bertelsmann/Autoren-Edition, 1974); Kerbels Flucht: Roman (Munich: Bertelsmann/Autoren-Edition, 1980); Peter Schneider, Lenz: Eine Erzählung (Berlin: Rotbuch, 1975; originally published in 1973); Jochen Schimmang, Der

schöne Vogel Phönix: Erinnerungen eines Dreissigjährigen, 3rd ed. (Frankfurt/Main: Suhrkamp, 1980; originally published in 1979); Nicolas Born, Die erdabgewandte Seite der Geschichte: Roman, 3rd ed. (Reinbek bei Hamburg: Rowohlt, 1979; originally published in 1976).

[70] David Roberts in fact cites Die Widmung as one example of Neue Subjektivität literature, in which the characters experience their own lack of true individuality. See Roberts, "Tendenzwenden", p. 300, fn. 26.

[71] Although the AutorenEdition was not solely a literary project, only its literary objectives will be discussed here.

[72] Hinrich C. Seeba, "Persönliches Engagement: Zur Autorenpoetik der siebziger Jahre," Monatshefte, 73(Summer 1981), Nr. 2, 142, 148-149, and 153.

[73] Peter Mosler, "Die Kunst ist die Umkehrung des Lebens," Aufbrüche, Abschiede: Studien zur deutschen Literatur seit 1968, ed. Michael Zeller (Stuttgart: Ernst Klett, 1979), p. 45.

[74] Lothar Baier, "Kinder, seid doch einmal realistisch! Über den Putschismus in der Literatur," Realismus--welcher? Sechzehn Autoren auf der Suche nach einem literarischen Begriff, ed. Peter Laemmle (Munich: edition text + kritik, 1976), p. 121.

[75] Baier, p. 125.

[76] Nägele, p. 238. Alluding to Adorno's essay on Lukacs, Ralf Schnell referred to this phenomenon in Timm's work as "erpresste Versöhnung" during a lecture held at the Free University of Berlin on July 3, 1981.

[77] Nägele, p. 244.

[78] Rolf Hosfeld and Helmut Peitsch, "'Weil uns diese Aktionen innerlich verändern, sind sie politisch': Bemerkungen zu vier Romanen über die Studentenbewegung," Basis, 8(1978), 95-126, and Hermann Peter Piwitt, "Rückblick auf heisse Tage: Die Studentenrevolte in der Literatur," Literaturmagazin, 4(1975), 35-46. In his content-oriented discussion of the AutorenEdition project in "Langer Marsch und kurzer Prozess: Oppositionelle Studentenbewegung und streitbarer Staat im westdeutschen Roman der siebziger Jahre," Horst Denkler also makes passing reference to AutorenEdition's conventional narrative style. See Der deutsche Roman und seine historischen und politischen Bedingungen, ed. Wolfgang Paulsen (Bern/Munich: Francke, 1977), 9. Amherst Colloquium, p. 132.

[79] Piwitt, p. 39.

[80] Hosfeld and Peitsch, p. 116.

[81] Paul Michael Lützeler, "Von der Intelligenz zur Arbeiterschaft: Zur Darstellung sozialer Wandlungsversuche in den Romanen und Reportagen der Studentenbewegung," Deutsche Literatur, ed. Paul Michael Lützeler and Egon Schwarz (Königstein/Ts.: Athenäum, 1980), pp. 128-131.

[82] Jörg Drews, "Wider einen neuen Realismus," Realismus--welcher?, p. 162.

[83] Hosfeld and Peitsch, p. 118. Bernward Vesper writes that there is no such thing as a typical (exemplarisch) biography and that there never has been, "aber die Jahrhunderte der Repräsentativsysteme konnten das nicht wahrnehmen." Die Reise, p. 51.

[84] Hosfeld and Peitsch, p. 117.

[85] Timm, Heisser Sommer, p. 54. Further references to this work will appear parenthetically in the text.

[86] Piwitt, p. 43. Piwitt says this of Roland Lang's Ein Hai in in der Suppe, another AutorenEdition production.

[87] Uwe Timm, "Realismus and Utopie," Realismus--welcher?, p. 146.

[88] Kerbels Flucht, p. 161.

[89] "In dieser kalten Zeit kann man nur überwintern mit viel Geduld und Bescheidenheit" (p. 180).

[90] Hosfeld and Peitsch, p. 108 ff., and Piwitt, passim.

[91] Michael Schneider, "Die Linke und die Neue Sensibilität," Die lange Wut zum langen Marsch: Aufsätze zur sozialistischen Politik und Literatur (Reinbek bei Hamburg: Rowohlt, 1975), p. 329.

[92] Hartung, "Die Repression wird zum Milieu," pp. 53 and 54.

[93] Hosfeld and Peitsch, p. 109.

[94] Lenz, pp. 28-29.

[95] Michael Schneider, "Die Linke und die Neue Sensibilität," p. 319.

[96] Kreuzer, "Neue Subjektivität," p. 88.

[97] Michael Buselmeier, "Nach der Revolte: Die literarische Verarbeitung der Studentenbewegung," Literatur und Studentenbewegung: Eine Zwischenbilanz, ed. W. Martin Lüdke (Opladen: Westdeutscher Verlag, 1977), p. 171.

[98] Hartung, "Die Repression wird zum Milieu," p. 56.

[99] Hartung, "Die Repression wird zum Milieu," p. 58.

[100] Mosler, "Die Kunst ist die Umkehrung des Lebens," p. 45.

[101] Klaus R. Scherpe and Hans-Ullrich Treichel, "Vom Überdruss leben: Sensibilität und Intellektualität als Ereignis bei Handke, Born und Strauss," Monatshefte, 73(Summer 1981), Nr. 2, 193 and 200. Scherpe and Treichel speak of the "experience of the loss of experience" (p. 200). As I tried to indicate in my discussion of Lenz (p. 34), however, the very capacity to experience anything, even the loss of experience, is under attack in contemporary West German prose. The failure to acknowledge this twist in the notion of experientiality weakens Scherpe's and Treichel's analysis.

[102] See, for example, pp. 20 and 117.

[103] Ralf Schnell, lecturing at the Free University of Berlin on July 3, 1981, characterized the existence of a narrative voice at one with itself as a fundamental contradiction in a novel which otherwise depicts a breakdown in subjectivity. If one reads the novel, however, not as a collapsing of subjectivity but as a radical insistence on a very vibrant subjectivity, then the narrative voice does not appear incongruous with the rest of the novel.

[104] This relentless insistence on a sometimes brutally radical subjectivity is reminiscent of Rolf Dieter Brinkmann's Keiner weiss mehr (Cologne/Berlin: Kiepenheuer & Witsch, 1968), but milder. The sex and everyday life of Brinkmann's protagonist are embodiments of alienation. He--and the reader--are constantly struggling against the overwhelming physical presence, not of conceptual systems, but of things (including human bodies). Brinkmann's character does not even have the solace of self. Every thing is his oppressor, and other people (particularly women) function as things as well, as a typical passage demonstrates: "Sie stand unbeweglich vor ihm zurückgewichen am Spülstein. Nichts. Es war nichts. Verrückt. Jede Anstrengung war umsonst. Er war nicht durchgekommen. Es war schon zu spät. Nach eins. Und das Licht war trüb. Sie hatte die Schüssel gespült, in der sie morgen früh den Brei für das Kind anrühren würde. Ein sauberer Teelöffel lag daneben. Und daneben stand die Packung Griess. Einfache Sätze. Aber jeder Satz war falsch. Er dachte sich durch sie hindurch. Nichts." (p. 117)

[105] Mosler, "Die Kunst ist die Umkehrung des Lebens," p. 40.

[106] Russell Berman calls Adorno's aesthetic theory "a camouflaged social theory in self-imposed exile." See his critical analysis of the problematic Marxist aspects of Adorno's aesthetic theory in Berman, "Adorno, Marxism and Art," Telos, 34(Winter 1977-78), 158.

107Rainald Goetz, "Im Dickicht des Lebendigen," Spiegel, 43 (October 19, 1981), 235.

108Theodor W. Adorno, Negative Dialektik, Gesammelte Schriften (Frankfurt/Main: Suhrkamp, 1973), VI, 17.

109Peter von Becker reads Strauss' parenthetical imperative "als ein zweifelsgewisses Heilungsbegehren, gedacht mit tiefverwundetem Kopf," against the background of what von Becker terms "die unwiderruflich letzten Tage der Menschheit." Von Becker rightly concedes the "Raum zum Staunen und Wünschen" informing Strauss' aesthetic reflection but wrongly implies this posture is identical to Adorno's. The failure to analyze in any detail Strauss' aesthetic project accounts for this misleading simplification. See Peter von Becker, "Die Minima Moralia der achtziger Jahre: Notizen zu Botho Strauss' 'Paare Passanten' und 'Kalldewey, Farce'," Merkur, 36 (February 1982), Nr. 2, 153-155.

110Even Rumor, which bears marks of resignation similar to those manifest in Paare, Passanten, is ultimately shaped by the struggle for articulation of difference. In the later work, the struggle no longer figures at all.

111Close to the end of Paare, Passanten, Strauss describes the time he saw Adorno from a distance at a cafe in Venice: "[. . .] ich war sicher, nur er könnte es sein, von dem ich soviel in mich hineingedacht hatte" (p. 204). Strauss' turning away from Adorno is thus entirely compatible with his renunciation of his own work (which, however, does not imply that his initial enthusiasm for Adorno rendered his own work fully congruous with that of the philosopher). The paragraph on p. 204 concludes with a reference to Adorno's death in Sils Maria--for Strauss, a "death in Venice," so to speak. If Adorno's death in 1969 marks the end of the struggle against barbarism for Strauss, then he must see his own work, in retrospect, as a parody of culture. Fortunately for Strauss, his critics do not note the distinction.

112Heinz Heller, "Literatur im Zeichen der Rezession, Neuen Linken und 'Tendenzwende'," Sozialgeschichte der deutschen Literatur von 1918 bis zur Gegenwart (Frankfurt/Main: Fischer, 1981), p. 655.

113This questioning is particularly evident in Die Widmung.

114Botho Strauss, Gross und klein: Szenen (Munich: Hanser, 1978). Peter von Becker likewise notes the source for Strauss' play in his review of Paare, Passanten and Kalldewey, Farce. See Peter von Becker, "Die Minima Moralia der achtziger Jahre," p. 156.

115Theodor W. Adorno, "Gross und klein," Minima Moralia: Reflexionen aus dem beschädigten Leben, Gesammelte Schriften (Frankfurt/Main: Suhrkamp, 1980), IV, 139-141.

116Max Horkheimer and Theodor W. Adorno, Dialectic of Enlightenment, trans. John Cumming (New York: Herder and Herder, 1972). The German edition, Dialektik der Aufklärung: Philosophische Fragmente (Frankfurt/Main: Fischer, 1969), was first published in 1944 by the Social Studies Association, Inc., New York. Quotations will be taken from the English text, but references will be given for both Dialectic of Enlightenment (abbreviated DE) as well as for the 1969 edition of Dialektik der Aufklärung (abbreviated DA).

117See especially Horkheimer and Adorno, DE, pp. 6-7 and 24; DA, pp. 12-13 and 31.

118What Cumming has translated as "the notion of this very way of thinking" reads in the German as "der Begriff eben dieses Denkens."

119DE, pp. 18 and 19; DA, pp. 24 and 25.

120Theodor W. Adorno, Ästhetische Theorie, ed. Gretel Adorno and Rolf Tiedemann, 2nd ed. (Frankfurt/Main: Suhrkamp, 1974), suhrkamp taschenbuch wissenschaft 2. Further references to this work will be abbreviated as ÄT.

121Adorno's statement in ÄT that no concept remains unchanged in the work of art (p. 186) is reminiscent of his claim in his 1962 essay "Engagement" that indeed no word remains unchanged by its entry into a work of art. See "Engagement," Noten zur Literatur (Frankfurt/Main: Suhrkamp, 1965), III, 111.

122Theodor W. Adorno, "Rede über Lyrik und Gesellschaft," Noten zur Literatur (Frankfurt/Main: Suhrkamp, 1963), I, 85.

123ÄT, pp. 205 and 251.

124See ÄT, pp. 253, 335, 345, and 518.

125"Soweit von Kunstwerken eine gesellschaftliche Funktion sich prädizieren lässt, ist es ihre Funktionslosigkeit." ÄT, pp. 336-337. This conviction also underlies Adorno's critiques of Georg Lukacs' stance on realism and Jean-Paul Sartre's position on engaged literature. See Adorno, "Erpresste Versöhnung," Noten zur Literatur (Frankfurt/Main: Suhrkamp, 1963), II, 152-187, and "Engagement," Noten zur Literatur (Frankfurt/Main: Suhrkamp, 1965), III, 109-135, respectively.

126ÄT, pp. 336 and 343. See also p. 341.

127Jean-Paul Sartre, Qu'est-ce que la littérature? (Paris: Gallimard, 1948).

128Adorno, "Engagement," p. 133 and 135.

[129]This brings to mind Adorno's open letter to Rolf Hochhuth (Frankfurter Allgemeine Zeitung of June 6, 1967): "Sie sträuben sich heftig gegen die Annahme, 'dass der Mensch in der Masse kein Individuum mehr sei', so als ob, wer darauf deutet, dazu beitrüge, während die Entwicklung es dahin brachte." See "Offener Brief an Rolf Hochhuth," Kritik: Kleine Schriften zur Gesellschaft, 2nd ed. (Frankfurt/Main: Suhrkamp, 1973), p. 136.

[130]Theodor W. Adorno, "Standort des Erzählers im zeitgenössischen Roman," Noten zur Literatur (Frankfurt/Main: Suhrkamp, 1963), I, 62.

[131]Adorno, "Standort des Erzählers," p. 63.

[132]For a critical account of the reception of Adorno's ÄT by the student movement itself, see Peter Uwe Hohendahl's recent article, "Autonomy of Art: Looking Back at Adorno's Ästhetische Theorie, German Quarterly, 54(March 1981), Nr. 2, 133-148. Hohendahl joins Peter Bürger (Theorie der Avantgarde) in seeing Adorno's aesthetic theory historically, as "limited to a specific period of European art" (Hohendahl, p. 146), but goes further than Bürger by pointing out that Adorno's ultimate reliance "on a Hegelian model of history in which all strands relate to one single center [. . .] seems to blind him with respect to the divergence of artistic trends and movements" (p. 147). For another historical critique of Adorno's theory which also touches on Adorno's relationship to the student movement, see Susan Buck-Morss, "The Dialectic of T. W. Adorno," Telos, 14(Winter 1972), 137-144.

[133]Realismus--welcher?, pp. 137-183. Timm's essay "Realismus und Utopie" was first published in kürbiskern (1975), while Drews' essay "Wider einen neuen Realismus" first appeared in Merkur (1975). Timm's rejoinder to Drews in Realismus--welcher? is entitled "Von den Schwierigkeiten eines Anti-Realisten"; Drews' final word in the same volume is called "Ein paar notwendige Anmerkungen zu Uwe Timms 'Realismus und Utopie'."

[134]See especially Drews, "Wider einen neuen Realismus," pp. 153, 157, and 163.

[135]Timm, "Von den Schwierigkeiten," p. 172.

[136]Timm, "Realismus und Utopie," p. 146.

[137]See Timm, "Realismus und Utopie," p. 148, and "Von den Schwierigkeiten," p. 176.

[138]Timm, "Von den Schwierigkeiten," p. 177.

[139]Timm, "Realismus und Utopie," p. 144. See also the same essay, p. 142, and "Von den Schwierigkeiten," pp. 167 and 174.

[140] Drews, "Ein paar notwendige Anmerkungen," pp. 183 and 180, respectively. Drews shares here Adorno's admiration for Beckett. See Adorno, "Versuch, das Endspiel zu verstehen," Noten zur Literatur (Frankfurt/Main: Suhrkamp, 1973), II, 188-236.

[141] Drews, "Wider einen neuen Realismus," pp. 156-158. Drews' rebuttal of Timm sounds much like Adorno's criticism of Hochhuth.

[142] Drews, "Ein paar notwendige Anmerkungen," pp. 180-181.

[143] Drews, "Wider einen neuen Realismus," pp. 157-158.

[144] Timm, "Von den Schwierigkeiten," p. 170.

[145] See, for example, DE, pp. 29-30 (DA, p. 36): "[. . .] the more the process of self-preservation is effected by the bourgeois division of labor, the more it requires the self-alienation of the individuals who must model their body and soul according to the technical apparatus. This again is taken into account by enlightened thought: in the end the transcendental subject of cognition is apparently abandoned as the last reminiscence of subjectivity and replaced by the much smoother work of automatic control mechanisms." See also DE, pp. 21-22 and 39-40 (DA, pp. 28 and 46-47).

[146] Adorno, ÄT, p. 349.

[147] Drews, "Wider einen neuen Realismus," p. 153 ff.

[148] Rainer Nägele, "Geht es noch um den Realismus? Politische Implikationen moderner Erzählformen in Roman," Der deutsche Roman und seine historischen und politischen Bedingungen, ed. Wolfgang Paulsen (Bern/Munich: Francke, 1977), 9. Amherst Colloquium, pp. 34-53.

[149] Nägele, "Geht es noch um den Realismus?", pp. 43, 45, and 50.

[150] This essay is his introduction to Aufbrüche, Abschiede: Studien zur deutschen Literatur seit 1968, pp. 5-13.

[151] Zeller, "Versuch," pp. 8 and 10.

[152] The word itself actually appears in Die Widmung (p. 9); the phenomenon of Ausdrucksnot can, however, be traced through all four prose works to be treated here in the chapters to follow.

[153] Ed. Heinz Ludwig Arnold (Munich: edition text + kritik, 1978), II, no pagination.

[154] Scherpe and Treichel, "Vom Überdruss leben," pp. 189 and 200.

[155] Schödel, "Ästhetik des Verlusts." See footnote 52.

[156] My particular understanding of this relationship will be discussed in greater detail in the second chapter here.

[157] In an interview with Dieter Bachmann, "Das Ende der Liebe: Lektüre des Schriftstellers Botho Strauss und eine Begegnung mit ihm, nebst Sätzen aus seinem Werk," <u>TagesAnzeiger</u> [Zürich] (June 9, 1979), p. 10. Strauss allies himself here with the "New Philosophers" in France.

[158] See his interview with Carna Zacharias, "Jeder Mann ist auch eine Frau," in the <u>Münchener Abendzeitung</u> (November 11, 1977).

[159] Zacharias, Bachmann (p. 8), and Hans Bertram Bock, in "Das Leben als Abschied," <u>Nürnberger Nachrichten</u> (May 14/15, 1977), all speak of women or the male-female tension as central to Strauss' work. I find the argument that Strauss writes about the female psyche rather shallow. I am more inclined to view whatever male-female dynamic there is in Strauss' work as only one of several polarities of tension that structure his prose. I shall not, however, discuss it in terms of male and female categories.

[160] This recalls Strauss' early praise of Michel Foucault's <u>L'archéologie du savoir</u> for its strain to multiply meaning and not to unify it. See Botho Strauss, "Versuch, ästhetische und politische Ereignisse zusammenzudenken: Neues Theater 1967-70," <u>Theater heute</u>, 11(1970), Nr. 10, 61. One very intriguing and potentially fruitful aspect of Strauss' work which I am unable to develop here is Strauss' particular reception of contemporary French philosophy and cultural theory. Reviewers occasionally make passing reference to influence by Foucault or Lacan, but I am aware of only two critical essays in which a more detailed analysis is attempted. They are Eric Bolle's "Subjektiviteit van de mislukking: Over de prozateksten van Botho Strauss" and Paul Cobben's "Foucaults begrip van de waanzin als inspiratie-bron voor Botho Strauss." Both articles may be found in <u>Botho Strauss Symposium 9.2.1981 - 5.4.1981: Dokumentatieboek</u> (Amsterdam: CREA, University of Amsterdam, 1981), CREA-Dokumentatieboek Nr. 7, pp. 78-81 and 87-103, respectively. Bolle uses Derrida's notion of <u>différance</u> to analyze Strauss' texts, which, he finds, evidence a Lacanian opposition between presence and absence and posit writing as a substitute for that which is absent. Bolle argues, however, that Strauss is in the process of breaking with this tradition and moving closer to Derrida's understanding of the text. Cobben, on the other hand, concentrates on Strauss' work in terms of Foucault's break with the traditional Hegelian concept of the subject and his analysis of madness in Western civilization. While both essays make fascinating, insightful connections, they also tend to overlook the intricate structural contradictions and complications in Strauss' texts. This does not by any means discredit the fundamental hypothesis that there is a considerable French influence on Strauss, but it does forbid reading Strauss as a more or less direct, literary transcription of contemporary French philosophy, linguistics, or literary theory. Neither would a

detailed analysis of this influence necessarily be confined to Foucault, Lacan, or Derrida. A look at French surrealism--as several reviewers have noted--or even, I suspect, Jean Baudrillard would probably also prove rewarding.

161 Die Widmung, p. 83.

162 In "Marlenes Schwester," "Theorie der Drohung," Die Widmung, and Rumor, respectively.

163 Die Widmung, p. 18.

164 The act of writing also figures thematically in "Theorie der Drohung," but not in "Marlenes Schwester" or Rumor. Strauss as author remains nonetheless involved in the act of writing. Hence, diachronic longing is implicit in these two works as well.

165 These allusions are most explicit in Die Widmung, where many works and authors are cited by name; yet, they are also implicit in the other prose works. The most obvious allusions--to German Romanticism--are cited frequently in reviews. The most detailed analysis of Strauss' connection to Romanticism to date can be found in an essay by Gerhard vom Hofe and Peter Pfaff entitled "Botho Strauss und die Poetik der Endzeit," in Das Elend des Polyphem: Zum Thema der Subjektivität (Königstein/Ts.: Athenäum, 1980), pp. 109-131. Strauss' literary allusions to works by Max Frisch will be elaborated on in the last chapter of this discussion of Botho Strauss' prose. Helmut Schödel, "Ästhetik des Verlusts," p. 105, draws a cursory comparison between "Theorie der Drohung" and Frisch' Stiller.

166 Schödel, "Ästhetik des Verlusts," p. 105.

167 One exception to this is an article on Strauss' drama, in which Dieter Kafitz ascertains "doch ein[en] Hoffnungsschimmer." See Kafitz, "Die Problematisierung des individualistischen Menschenbildes im deutschsprachigen Drama der Gegenwart," Basis, 10(1980), 93-126. Another exception is Sybrandt van Keulen's "Het realisme van Botho Strauss," Botho Strauss Symposium, pp. 65-68.

168 Gerd Michels, "Skeptische Melancholie: Zu Botho Strauss' Die Widmung," Textanalyse und Textverstehen (Heidelberg: Quelle & Meyer, 1981), pp. 145-168.

169 Michels, pp. 154, 155, 162, and 166.

170 Vom Hofe and Pfaff, pp. 3, 26, 113, 117-118, and 127-128. Their particular analysis of Strauss' prose, which does not include a discussion of Rumor, allows them to see a smooth development from "Theorie der Drohung" to Die Widmung. They argue, however, that the thrust of "Theorie der Drohung" is to establish difference for the ultimate purpose of transcending it (p. 123) and that Die Widmung

draws the logical conclusion from the failure to establish that difference (p. 124). I would argue instead that the earlier piece voices the struggle for articulation of difference in a world of ambiguity that fails to acknowledge difference. Difference, then, is not to be transcended but articulated <u>as difference.</u> The transition to <u>Die Widmung</u>, as I see it, is that this piece presumes the existence of difference but seeks meaningful connections of mediation, not transcendence.

[171] Michael Schneider, "Botho Strauss, das bürgerliche Feuilleton und der Kultus des Verfalls: Zur Diagnose eines neuen Lebensgefühls," <u>Den Kopf verkehrt aufgesetzt oder Die melancholische Linke: Aspekte des Kulturzerfalls in den siebziger Jahren</u> (Darmstadt/Neuwied: Luchterhand, 1981), p. 257.

[172] Michael Schneider, "Botho Strauss," pp. 236, 234, 250 and 241.

[173] Michael Schneider, "Botho Strauss," p. 257.

Chapter II

"MARLENES SCHWESTER" AND "THEORIE DER DROHUNG": AMBIVALENCE

I. "MARLENES SCHWESTER"

Two words paradigmatically indicate the paradoxical symbiosis which is the thematic and structural crux of Botho Strauss' first longer prose piece: "Marlenes Schwester."[1] Each component of the title reaches out to some other--one by virtue of the possessive and one by virtue of its substantive reference. The protagonist of the text is indeed not Marlene's sister but in fact the relationship between the two women. Marlene's sister derives all identity from her younger sibling. The narrator grants her no proper name.[2] Indeed, she is horrified at the thought of a name proper to herself. When a stranger introduces himself by name, her response is one of shock and confusion: "'Was heisst das? Was ist das für ein Ausdruck?' Dann glaubte sie, ihre eigene Stimme zu vernehmen. 'Ich?'--sie fuhr zusammen und erwachte . . . Ich bin Marlenes Schwester" (MS, page 14). Marlene, by contrast, does have a name of her own, as do a number of other figures: Julien, Michel, Max, Bertrand, Mr. and Mrs. Holzer. The precarious existence of Marlene's sister is also evident in other ways. Unlike the characters with names, she is afflicted with a disease which debilitates and threatens to destroy her. At the same time, this very disease is, paradoxically, a lone manifestation of health, a physical acknowledgment of and rebellion against the diseased state of emotionlessness to which Marlene's sister is repeatedly urged, most frequently but not solely by Marlene.[3] A young communal farmer, noting the sister's depression, asks her if she is not afraid that her feelings might belong to a chapter of social history that has long since been surpassed (MS, page 25). The sister's aversion to emotional atrophy amounts to an insistence on her own illness, which she knows to be fatal. Her situation is one of Ausdrucksnot, that potentially fatal inability to articulate oneself. She is not only financially "vollkommen mittellos" (MS, page 8), but also void of expressive capability. She contemplates the ocean, seeking "nach dem verschollenen Ausdruck für ein Gefühl, das älter war als die Menschheit" (MS, page 10). Her disease manifests this quest as well, the diachronic longing for an expression of the love she feels for Marlene: "Sie lockt mich" (MS, pages 12 and 13). The articulation of this love would at the same time be an articulation of identity for Marlene's sister. It is telling that this articulation is achieved, if at all, only in the negative terms of a physical disease which is itself not without paradox. Ambivalence permeates the text, just as disease invades the body of Marlene's sister. Thematically, the emphasis is on ambivalence of identity. Although not completely absent, the ambivalence of language plays a much lesser role here than in Strauss' later works. As will be shown, ambivalence structures the symbolism as well as the narrative time of this prose text. First, however, one must take a closer look at the relationship between the two sisters, since all ambivalence in the text emanates from it.

Marlene's sister, thirty-eight and ill, and Marlene, twenty-nine and physically healthy, are spending their summer holidays together. After arguing all night, they decide to separate in Nîmes. Marlene forces her sister to promise not to attempt any further contact.

> Das Leben der Schwester neben dem ihren, in dieser schwirrenden Zwei-Personen-Wahn-Welt, so hatte sie gesagt, liefe unabänderlich auf die Unterdrückung, die Zerstörung ihrer eigenen, ohnehin schmächtigen Existenz hinaus. 'So lieb du es auch meinst mit mir.' (MS, page 15)

The two sisters do not see each other again until Marlene's sister arrives at the Holzer residence, where the Holzers are drinking to their newly adopted daughter: Marlene.

> In einem Augenblick von tiefer Geduld erkannten die beiden Schwestern ihre neugeborene Fremdheit. Marlene brach den Blick ab und sagte übermütig: 'Ich bin jetzt die Tochter von Herrn und Frau Holzer.' Ihre Schwester konnte nichts mehr sehen und sank bewusstlos zu Boden. (MS, page 38).

Marlene subsequently offers to allow her sister to move into her commune on one condition: she must abandon her "übergrosse Zuneigung" for Marlene and adopt "jene ebenmässigen Gefühle" characteristic of the commune. "'Ja', sagte Marlenes Schwester ängstlich, 'ich will es versuchen'" (MS, age 38). Marlene, the named one, has everything under control, with the single exception of her sister's love for her. The intensity of this emotion threatens the lethargic equilibrium of Marlene's existence. At the same time, her sister cannot survive without Marlene. There are repeated images of their mutual dependence and inseparability. Their seating position in a taxi is "ein letztes Bild von müder, naturergebener Unzertrennlichkeit" (MS, page 15); Julien conjures "die leibhaftige Undenkbarkeit ihrer Trennung" (MS, page

20); Marlene's sister imagines herself and Marlene "tot geborgen aus der Lawine, geborgen! . . . in der Umarmung vereist" (<u>MS</u>, page 26). Marlene's physical absence does not make her any less of a determinant in the older sister's identity. Marlene's sister says of herself: "Ich lebe für eine Abwesende" (<u>MS</u>, page 19). She listens to the stories Julien has created for Marlene, exchanges the contents of her suitcase with those of Marlene's when the latter is not looking, and wears Marlene's dress, "wie eine Selbstmörderin im Karnevalskostüm" (<u>MS</u>, page 18). While Marlene cannot tolerate her sister's emotional exhuberance and the ill woman cannot exist without Marlene, neither can she exist with her, for co-existence means the destruction of that part of herself which renders her different: her intense emotions. Paradoxically, that which comprises her difference is also dependent on Marlene, her other, for whom she feels such a strong emotional bond. Neither woman can fully survive with or without the other. It cannot even be argued that Marlene could exist without her sister, since that would be possible only in that community of emotional atrophy in which her person has no distinguishing characteristics. Under such circumstances, personal identity becomes a non-issue: there are no criteria for ascertaining or developing it. Marlene's sister is appalled by this, as she is by Julien's depiction of the "Wundertüten-Wirtschaft," in which consumers are provided with surprise products, around which they organize their activities. This economy was introduced, Julien relates,

> 'um den Begriff und das Gefühl des Bedarfs abzuschaffen, um statt dessen die Freude am freien Zufall, die Erfindungsgabe und das Improvisationstalent zu wecken

> und zu fördern. Wenn also jemand Nägel und Brot bekam, dann beschäftigte er sich eine Zeitlang mit dem Zimmern und dem Brotessen. Bekam er jedoch Zündhölzer und hatte von einer früheren Sendung zufällig noch Zigaretten, so beschäftigte er sich eine Zeitlang mit dem Rauchen.'
> (MS, page 23)

This barely disguised caricature of capitalist planning is a vision of horror for Marlene's sister. The loss of a sense of need and the ability to articulate that need means the loss of self, the destruction of identity. Her love for Marlene is

> vielleicht der letzte gesellschaftliche Ort, den ich passiert habe, sehr entlegen schon, [. . .]; sehr entlegen schon, aber immer noch ein Ort der Sprache, der Verständigungs- und Gefühlsarbeit. Und jetzt? Ich habe den Höhenweg gefunden, auf dem meine Spur sich verliert. (MS, page 18)

It is no coincidence that Strauss makes the association here between the inability to articulate diachronic longing for another person with the disappearance of self. Marlene's sister is obsessively concerned with keeping her shoes on, even in death (MS, pages 9 and 12). They are, after all, what leave traces of her physical presence: all the more important, given the progressive decay of her body. "Sie trat mit der Fußspitze auf einen vorgewölbten Stein und zog die heisse Augustluft ein. Die Schuhsohle ächzte wie unter einer Gewichtszunahme" (MS, page 7). The strain on the shoe sole caused by the intake of air is a subtle but pointed reminder of the fragile, if not dubious physical state of the woman ridden with disease; the air inhaled weighs at least as much as the body it enters. Indeed, corporeality, disease, and death are the recurring motifs which define the essence of Marlene's sister.[4] Since she exists only in a state of symbiotic --or perhaps, and more appropriately, parasitic--tension with Marlene, the relationship itself is predicated on the absence or presence of disease. Whereas Marlene can mock "'[d]as Gekörpere'" (<u>MS</u>, page 13), her sister <u>is</u> "das Gekörpere." Her body is not only the voice of her suffering, it also functions as an epistemological organ. By acknowledging pain, it knows experience; its decay paradoxically attests to its life. This notion is not peculiar to Botho Strauss. Adolph Muschg characterizes Fritz Zorn's cancer as an epistemological organ (<u>Erkenntnisorgan</u>). "Es ist der Tod zu Lebzeiten, gegen den Z. protestiert und dem er das einzige entgegenhält, was er <u>wirklich</u> erfahren hat: dass es ein Leben--ein gepeinigtes, unvollständiges, aber immerhin ein Leben--vor dem Tode geben <u>muss</u>; wenn es nicht anders geht, ein Leben im Sterben, als Agonie."[5] Claudia Kalasz comments that Strauss' insistence on suffering connotes a negation of the loss of experience, an insight fully congruous with Michael Rutschky's more general comments about the articulation of experiential hunger in the 1970's.[6] The older sister's kneecaps "think" (<u>MS</u>, page 21). Her vomiting attacks connote the confrontation with and exorcism of evil (<u>MS</u>, pages 12 and 18), and the muscular contractions of her intestines are likened to birthing labor. Her diseased body and its functions mark the woman's participation in lived human experience. Even her experience of loss of identity is voiced in biological terms. She describes her own dissolution in terms of "grenzenloser Zellteilung" (<u>MS</u>, page 21), and Julien's faith in the indivisible bond between the two sisters is that in "eine lebendige Konstruktion des Zusammenhalts, die euer gemeinsames Leben wie eine biologische Spur, wie ein Kind, wie das Netz einer Spinne erzeugt hat [. . .]" (<u>MS</u>, page 20). The paradox of the sister's illness is not only that it is an indication of her participation in life, a healthy response to the carriers of disease that attack her body. Likewise paradoxical is the fact that although she suffers from a terminal disease, she is denied knowledge of the traditional definer of all human experience, that which renders life meaningful: death.[7] Helmut Kreuzer has referred to the frequency with which death figures in contemporary literature.[8] Botho Strauss complicates the issue in "Marlenes Schwester" by refusing the terminally ill woman her death: the ultimate denial of human experience.

> Häufig beklagte sie jetzt, dass ihr die Gewalttat nicht durch den Sinneszauber einer Euphorie, wie er angeblich den natürlich Sterbenden zuteil wird, erleichtert würde. Von allen Qualen erlöst, so hiess es, und diesen Zustand hätte sie wirklich gern am eigenen Leib gespürt. (MS, page 9)

Defecation is likened to birthing, but the child in the diseased body is death, and it is never actually given birth. "Den Tod wie ein Kind im Leibe nähren, grossziehen, aber niemals herauslassen" (MS, page 10). Wearing Marlene's Mexican dress, the sister is compared to a suicide victim, but one "im Karnevalskostüm" (MS, page 18). The one time she actually contemplates suicide, the dramatic action ends in a less than fatal sneeze. This occurs while the two sisters travel separately. Marlene's sister imagines Marlene has died in an accident, a thought which completely negates the significance of her own diseased life, "wie komisch umsonst ihr eigener Tod" (MS, page 36).

> Und fast hätte sie jetzt im Jähzorn, in blinder gegen sich selbst gerichteter Mordlust gehandelt. Sie führte die Pistole zum Mund und legte die Mündung auf die

> Lippen; doch plötzlich, als fühle sie den späteren
> Pulverstaub in der Nase kitzeln, musste sie laut niesen.
> Wie? Was war das? Ein Witz? Ein Kind? Ein
> pathetischer Irrtum? . . . Ich habe es nicht erkannt.
> (<u>MS</u>, page 36)

This mildly comical diversion from death is not quite so amusing when seen in contrast with the successful suicide of S..[9] The interaction between S. and his pistol has clearly sexual connotations. He woos her (<u>die Pistole</u>) as a lover.

> Und tatsächlich, sie erhörte ihn, sie gab ihm nach.
> Ihr dunkler, warmer Lauf schmiegte sich an seine Lippen
> und drang sanft in seine Mundhöhle. Dort richtete er
> sich stolz auf und entlud sich mit einem kurzen gewaltigen Stoss ins Hirn. Der tote S. soll, als man ihn
> fand, recht stillvergnügt ausgesehen haben [. . .].
> (<u>MS</u>, page 13)

Here, in an orgasmic burst of energy, the generically female pistol plants the seed of death in S.' mouth, where the seed bears fruit: S. does in fact die. (The generically male part [<u>Lauf</u>] of the female whole [<u>Pistole</u>] enters and impregnates the generically female parts [<u>Lippen</u> and <u>Mundhöhle</u>] of the male whole [<u>der S.</u>], with the end result that the male conceives and the child born is death.) The traditional center does not hold; yet, neither is there a new center to replace it.

The fact that Marlene's sister cannot even conceive death coincides with the paradoxical ambiguity of her disease and of her relationship with Marlene. The ramifications of Strauss' ambivalent death imagery are further elaborated by the vampire society, Julien's account of which is not merely a tale within a tale. As will be seen, the vampire society actually determines the plot cycle of "Marlenes Schwester" itself.[10] Just as the relationship between the two sisters—and not the two women as individual characters—provides fundamental thematic and structural tension in the text, so too does the vampire society have significance only in its interplay with the life Marlene's sister tries to lead. The threat of her fatal disease is contrasted with the "Scheintod" (MS, page 31) of the vampires. Marlene's sister is both appalled and threatened by the tale, particularly when she learns that Michel, the last remaining member of the vampire commune, has been released from prison and is likely to seek a new circle of friends (MS, page 33). On the two occasions when Julien actually introduces the ill woman to Michel, her response is seemingly illogical: "Sie richtete sich auf, zu Tode erschrocken, und starrte Michel an. Das ist also das Ende, dachte sie, das Ende beginnt" (MS, pages 12 and 39). It does seem odd that a woman facing real death would be "frightened to death" and think of "the end" when confronted with the prospect of eternal life. Her reaction appears, however, completely logical if we recall that the fatality of her disease is what marks her participation in life, her insistence on the struggle for her identity. The integration into the vampire society means the end of that struggle, the end of emotional intensity, and the end of need that demands articulation. It is no coincidence that Marlene's sister suffers from a blood disease and an "inexplicable" one at that (MS, page 24). While speaking with Marlene, who remains cool and unruffled, it is the "blood in her ears" and the flush in her face that indicate the sister's physical and emotional turmoil (MS, page 19). The bond between the two sisters is an affinity of blood. Marlene's sister muses on Marlene's blood:

> Marlenes Blut trinken. Unsere Blutverwandtschaft auf-
> frischen. Eine Schwester verliert man doch nicht, wie
> einen Mann, wie einen Kerl, aus dem Leben. Eine
> Schwester ist eine angeborene Lebensgefährtin. (MS,
> page 17)

Yet, the two sisters do not actually meet until Marlene reaches the age of puberty at thirteen, a fact which lends some cogency to the notion that Marlene's sister is her own double.[11] They do not share the emotional bond of common experience--self-alienation?--but only the affinity of blood. In fact, the visual image in the taxi scene of the two women's inseparability is immediately followed by Marlene's angry announcement that her menstrual blood has arrived prematurely (MS, page 15). The affinity of blood is one of which Marlene wants no part. Its intensity threatens the security of her emotional atrophy. Marlene's desire to participate in the vampire society thus makes sense, as does her sister's aversion to it. Such a community demands the sacrifice of blood, in this case, a sacrifice of person.

> Wie im Schlaf, wie in einer zweiten Natur entschwanden
> ihnen die aufsässigen Gefühle und Bedürfnisse, die das
> soziale und körperliche Leben des vereinzelten Bürgers
> üblicherweise beherrschen, vor allem das Wollustgefühl
> und das Ungleichheitsgefühl lösten sich in nichts auf.
> Denk dir nur: eine Liebe ohne Begehren, gewaltlos, nur
> diese glühende Leidenschaft, einander unablässig zu
> beobachten, aus wechselnden räumlichen Entfernungen.
> (MS, page 29)

Ironically enough for a society of vampires, the members are not bound by any affinity of blood such as that which draws Marlene's sister to the younger woman. Rather, the vampires are inextricably bound in an affinity of coincidence (MS, pages 28-29). The original members meet as strangers when they all witness the same airplane crash. "Das gemeinsame Erlebnis der Verkehrskatastrophe lockte sie immer wieder zusammen" (MS, page 29), Verkehrskatastrophe connoting both modern technology and interpersonal relationships. Like the consumers in the Wundertüten-Wirtschaft, the vampires survive by eradicating any personal needs or desires. The perceptible alienation between the two sisters on the occasion of Marlene's adoption is the prerequisite for the older sister's acceptance into the vampire community. The renunciation of need becomes the renunciation of self, since all needs are severed from any subjective agent and hence become both interchangeable and manipulable. The insurance system which makes the vampire society possible--"Hin und wieder wurde gestorben, wenn das Geld knapp wurde" (MS, page 32)--is described as the "'Stützkorsett des Kapitalismus'" (MS, page 33). The security here is of the system and not of any individual that would be identifiable as such. It is, of course, significant that the affinity of coincidence that binds the members of the vampire society to each other becomes an affinity of blood: they feed off each other's blood for prolonged existence. This affinity, predicated on the draining of emotional need and articulation, is the contemporary fate of the affinity of blood which Marlene's sister feels for Marlene. The sister's reaction to a pictorial series of human accidents and catastrophes is revealing in this context. Most of the drawings depict "altmodische Unglücksfälle" (MS, page 34) which do not particularly horrify the diseased woman.

> Aber am Schluss der Serie befand sich ein alarmierendes Foto: ein schlafendes oder ohnmächtiges Mädchen lag auf einer Rolltreppe und ihre langen, hinter dem Kopf ausgebreiteten Haare mussten im nächsten Augenblick, wenn sie nicht sofort aufwachte, in den Schlitz zwischen der letzten Schwelle und dem Abtritt gezerrt werden und

> dann mitsamt der Kopfhaut abgerissen werden . . . 'Marlene! Hilfe!' Sie schrie mit tierischer Gewalt; doch als sie davon erwachte, hörte sie eben noch den Nachklang des merkwürdigerweise ganz ruhig ausgesprochenen Wortes 'Hilfe', als sei ihr Schrei auf dem Weg vom Traum zum Mund von einem dämpfenden Filter zu einer teilnahmslosen Gesprächsbemerkung abgeschwächt worden. (<u>MS</u>, page 35).

The emotional intensity characteristic of Marlene's sister thus belongs to a bygone era.[12] In today's world as Strauss depicts it, this intensity persists only as a diseased reminder of the need for personal identity. And even that reminder--the articulation of disease--is threatened. The technology of our age is oblivious to its human victims, who themselves are not conscious of this victimization, but the voice with which she tries to articulate this consciousness is continuously stifled, albeit not successfully silenced altogether.[13]

Discussing love and cannibalism, Sigmund Freud associates the consumption or physical appropriation of the love object with the negation of its existence as other; he designates this phenomenon as ambivalent.[14] Julien's vampire society clearly fits this description, with regard to both emotional and physical states. The metaphor of ambivalence is also reflected in a variety of other physical states. Marlene's sister is frequently depicted in a state of sleep or half-sleep, constantly on the gray edge between life and death. This is a manifestation of her inability to die, even though she longs for that clarity: "Marlenes Schwester sehnte sich nach dem grossen Schlaf, der unsichtbar macht. Sie fand jedoch nur einen flachen, nervösen Schlummer [. . .]" (<u>MS</u>, page 16). This ambiguous physical state is likewise linked to another physical property, that of shadow. The first page of the text tells us: "Ein wenig später glitt sie, erschöpft, entmutigt, zurück in den Halbschlaf. Mein Schattengelände, ich döse und staune . . ." (MS, page 7). Marlene's sister not only drifts like a nameless shade between this world and the next. She is also confined to the shadow of Marlene's existence.[15] Yet, as we might expect by now, shadow in Strauss' work is not shadow as we presume it to be. The sister is not only corroded by disease. Figuratively, since she exists as a shadow figure to Marlene's presence, the older woman is also denied any physical presence that is properly her own. Even her disease is predicated on Marlene's response to her emotionality. Yet, if the ill woman's physical presence is threatened by corrosive bacteria, then Marlene's presence or existence is likewise put into question. For, if her body casts no shadow, what proof does it have of its own existence? One could of course argue that the sun does not shine in Strauss' text and consequently everything appears as omnipresent, amorphous shadow. And yet, even if we assume that Marlene's sister is consumed by such general atmospheric shadow, we are still faced with the negation of any physical object capable of casting shadow. Logically, however, there can be no shadow without the object that casts it.[16] The omnipresence of shadow destroys that which calls shadow itself into being. This menacing physical ambiguity also comes in sound.

> Der gestaute Atem unterdrückte zuweilen vollständig das Gehör. Dann taumelte sie inmitten der bildüberströmten Lautlosigkeit, von der es in einer Julienschen Wunschgeschichte hiess, dass sie eines kommenden Tages, ausgehend natürlich von China, sich über alle Länder und Meere ausbreiten werde, wie eine feine Äthermasse, die sich sanft und schalltötend auf die Erde niedergesenkt

hat. 'Eine Epoche der natürlichen Lautlosigkeit, in
der es keine Totenstille mehr geben wird, eine Zeit wie
die Katzen, wie die Fahrräder und wie die Schlafwandler, wo die Menschen fiepen werden wie die Fledermäuse
. . .' (MS, page 37)

As "märchenhaft klar" as Marlene speaks, her sister hears only chaos. "Je angestrengter ich ihr zuhörte, um so beunruhigender und doppelsinniger wurde alles, was sie sagte" (MS, page 19). This formlessness is oppressive. "Das Stimmenmeer im Kopf, die Summe der mich bevölkernden fremden Stimmen--das bin ich, obwohl ich mich nicht mehr darin erkenne" (MS, page 21). Contrast this to the passage in which the ill woman longs for the soothing amorphousness of the ocean:

Und sie hasste nichts so sehr wie diese fahrigen, überreizten Gedächtniszustände, wenn ihr das Leben in tausend Fetzen um die Ohren flog. Wenn doch nur das Meer käme . . . (MS, page 9)

Here the ocean promises temporary relief from the torment of unrelated particles of past: the lack of connection offends the principle of diachronic longing. Julien indicates the same dilemma when, upon hearing of the sisters' separation, he asks how they intend to divide up the past between them (MS, page 20). There can be no sense of personal identity without a sense of personal history. Kalasz makes the association in Strauss' work between the inability to establish meaningful connections through integrative remembering, on the one hand, and hopelessness, on the other.[17] It is the same lack of personal continuity in the Wundertüten-Wirtschaft that horrifies Marlene's sister.[18]

The metaphors of ambivalence which abound in "Marlenes Schwester" manifest, as we have seen, ambivalences of identity. At the same time, there is some focus on the ambivalence of language, which figures both symbolically as well as structurally in the text. The ill sister's attitude towards language is no less paradoxical than her disease. This is not surprising, given our identification of her diseased body as both organ of articulation and witness to its failure. Language, the traditional medium of articulation, holds both promise and danger for Marlene's sister. Language, written as well as spoken, is likened to physical movement upon the earth. This movement, in its capacity to be traced, is oppressive for Marlene's sister: "das von ihr verfluchte Gehen, das, wie eine Schrift, sich in die Räume und Landschaften zeichnet, für jeden Lümmel aufschlussreich, so unleserlich sie auch zu gehen versucht" (<u>MS</u>, page 11). By the same token, Marlene's sister tries to disturb the "legibility" of spoken language in the form most commonly held to be understandable: everyday language usage. "Sie verunstaltete die natürliche Ordnung ihres Körpers, sie veralberte die geläufigsten Wörter der Alltagssprache, erfand neue, unsinnige hinzu. 'Jetzt gehen wir aber esseln'" (<u>MS</u>, page 11). This emphasis on not being understood first seems illogical given the woman's tormented need for articulation of self. Yet, it is precisely the generality of that which is so readily understood which denies her individuality and reduces her essence to the common denominator of existing categories. Dreaming of herself reading a novel, Marlene's sister hears the muffled voices of a people striving for articulation. "Geträumt wie ich lese, lese, lese. Auf den Buchseiten aber entsteht ein gedämpftes Volksgemurmel. Seine gesammelte Leserschar spricht aus dem Roman und erörtert ihn flüsternd" (<u>MS</u>, page

13). This form of written language, in which human voices strive however unsuccessfully for articulation, is contrasted with the oppressively methodical language of written texts. The sister's fear of such oppression invades her dreams.

> Ja, bin ich denn ein Buch? Sie wachte auf und kämpfte mit dem Zweifel an ihrer leibhaftigen Gegenwart. Doch bereits ihr erster Augenaufschlag hatte sich eingeschrieben in die Weltgeschichte des Augenaufschlags. Von nun an konnte sie keinen Gedanken mehr fassen, keine Beobachtung anstellen, die nicht sofort zu Notizen einer alles überwachenden Geschichtsschreibung wurden. Sie drohte in einem grenzenlosen Serienwerk der historischen Wissenschaften zu verschwinden, in dem die Kulturgeschichte der Wahrnehmungen und des Schmerzempfindens, der Lust und des Trostes, der Nervosität und des Gähnens, des Flüsterns, des Wartens, des Türeschliessens, des Händefaltens usw. aufgezeichnet stand und fortwährend in unzähligen Ergänzungsbänden erweitert und revidert wurde, obendrein begleitet von einer philosophischen Geschichte des dem Serienwerk zugrundeliegenden Denkens in ähnlichem Umfang. (MS, pages 25-26)

The historical text outlined here is hardly the one which we are accustomed to reading.[19] To understand this passage, we must again call to mind that Marlene's sister's body is her organ for articulation of self. What is missing in the "Weltgeschichte des Augenaufschlags" is the individual context which gives that articulation experiential significance. The ontological yawn cancels the particular experiential value of the individual one. The former is a synchronic phenomenon, while the latter is experientially diachronic. There is no love in the ontological whisper. Whereas the love for Marlene was once a locus for language as both personal understanding and emotional articulation, the diseased sister is now left with "das wilde unsinnige Gedankengestöber" (MS, page 18). The loss of love, that principle of diachronic longing, goes hand in hand with the loss of articulation. This is underscored by Julien's reaction to the news that the two sisters have separated: "Wie wollt ihr je wieder trennen, was ihr miteinander gesprochen und empfunden habt?" (MS, page 20). This Biblical allusion to the integrity of the (divine) word only delineates more clearly the loss of that integrity, be it in promise or in fact.[20]

The language of narrative time and of narrative voice in "Marlenes Schwester" indicates both ambivalence of historical time and historical agent, as well as the refusal to capitulate totally to that ambivalence. Julien's stories, we are told, usually take place in some future time; yet, Marlene insists they be narrated in a past tense (MS, page 22). This inversion of traditional chronology challenges the validity of temporal concepts, that is to say, of history itself. Similarly, the obvious linear chronology of Strauss' text, which could be summed up in three phases (joint travels, separation, and ultimate reunion) is undermined by two elements which structure the actual cyclical temporality of the text. The passage where Julien introduces Marlene's sister to Michel, the founder of the vampire commune in which Marlene invites her to participate, appears verbatim twice in the text (MS, pages 11-12 and page 39). The reader's chronological confidence is not challenged the first time when Marlene's sister, "zu Tode erschrocken," thinks the end has begun. When the same passage is repeated at the conclusion of the text, however, the reader is told in essence that the end has repeated beginnings. The three-part chronology mentioned above now appears as elemental repertoire, while the events which comprise that repertoire, by implication, know infinite repetitions.[21] Just as Marlene's sister cannot know death, neither can the text know chronological progression. The other structural element supporting this argument is a single sentence. "Sie versuchte es noch einmal" is repeated four times (<u>MS</u>, pages 7, 14, 21 and 39). As the second sentence of the text, it seems to reflect on the one preceding it: "Das gütige Leben, dachte sie, das gütige Leben" (<u>MS</u>, page 7). It does not become clear, however, just what "das gütige Leben" is until towards the end, when Marlene offers to let her sister join the vampire community of emotional neutrality. "'Ja', sagte Marlenes Schwester ängstlich, 'ich will es versuchen'" (<u>MS</u>, page 38). The "good life" thus becomes one that actually occupies the amorphous realm somewhere between life and death. The fact that the text closes with the ill woman's repeated attempt to accept the atrophy of personal identity and history does two things. On the one hand, it stresses the repetition of her attempts, thereby partaking of the temporal ambivalence which torments her and structures the tale. On the other hand, the fact that she must repeatedly try again attests to her continued resistance to her integration into the society of vampires. If she ever actually succeeded in accepting that fate, her attempt to do so would be superfluous. Comparable to the diseased body which neither heals nor dies--an inverted manifestation of health--the repeated efforts to accept "das gütige Leben" demonstrate both temporal ambivalence as well as the resistance to it. By the same token, the narrative voice of "Marlenes Schwester" neither fully negates nor fully accepts the particularity of the ill woman's voice.

The neutral, third-person narrative voice predominates, reinforcing the air of dispassionate impersonality that pervades the text. Yet, the first-person voice of Marlene's sister does assert itself from time to time. This particular combination can be read in terms of the ambivalence of identity characteristic of Marlene's sister--unable to assert itself consistently--but it can also be read in terms of her continued struggle for personal articulation: her voice does not disappear totally from the contours of the text. Yet another element of the narrative voice disturbs the reader's confidence in the understandability of plot or the identifiability of person. At one point, two questions are asked that have no apparent reference to the surrounding text. Neither do they give any clear indication as to their narrative source. "Wie? Liegt Staub auf dem Wasser?" (MS, page 10) is like one of the many murmuring voices Marlene's sister cannot clearly distinguish; it, too, stands unmediated in the text. It also indicates the existence of another level of perception that cannot be grasped in accounts of what the characters said, did, or thought. It is a voice that refuses systematization and at the same time, clearly haunts the text. A similar interrogative voice speaks at the conclusion of the passage describing the imagined suicide attempt: "Wie? Was war das? Ein Witz? Ein Kind? Ein pathetischer Irrtum? . . . Ich habe es nicht erkannt" (MS. page 36). The "I" of this last sentence, however, gives us additional information. It is not, as might be suspected, the first-person voice of Marlene's sister. Rather, it is the only place in the text where the narrator speaks in the first person. This is a crucial juncture. Where traditionally the reader could expect some narrative authority, the narrative voice here in fact confesses ignorance and uncertainty.[22] The narrator thus undermines his own authority of perception. Albeit not total, the hegemony of ambivalence thus permeates all textual dimensions.

## II. "THEORIE DER DROHUNG"

As in the case of "Marlenes Schwester," the title of Strauss' second major prose piece speaks paradigmatically for the text itself.[23] "Theorie der Drohung" implies the structural complexity of the text. It is at the same time the title of the publication we read, the title of a psycho-literary study which the first-person narrator undertakes, and the title of a right-wing propaganda piece on the nature of mass strikes. This multiple identity of title clearly raises the question of authenticity of authorship and language. While the specific nature of this question as Strauss poses it will be delineated more clearly later, it should be noted here that "Theorie der Drohung" is also thematically a carefully chosen title, the explication of which bears many resemblances to "Marlenes Schwester." The two substantives seem to stand in semantic opposition to one another but are surprisingly linked by the genitive article. <u>Theorie</u> by itself indicates a system of conceptual categories designed to explain some phenomena of human experience. In conjunction with <u>Drohung</u>, it implies the domestication or neutralization of a threat, the source of which remains for the moment undefined. The genitive article is, however, a subtle but pointed reminder that the theory in question cannot or does not totally neutralize the threat. If it did so, it would effectively obliterate its own subject; void of content, it would reduce itself to a theory of no thing, existing in a vacuum, negating its own telos and, hence, its own existence. Here again, we are confronted with the tension of ambivalence which figured so significantly in "Marlenes Schwester." Strauss continues to develop his notion of ambivalence in "Theorie der Drohung" thematically with regard to personal identity and structurally by virtue of symbolism, narrated time, and a reflective narrative mode. "Theorie der Drohung," unlike "Marlenes Schwester," also accords the ambivalence of the writing process and the literary institution a pronounced and crucial role in its own composition. A meaningful discussion of the ambivalence in "Theorie der Drohung" will, however, necessitate a brief recapitulation of the ostensibly chronological plot, the retelling of which seems simple enough. The first-person narrator, a writer who remains unnamed and speaks only as "I," receives a phone call one wintry day from his acquaintance, Dr. W..[24] The latter, director of a psychiatric clinic, has a female patient named Lea who cries constantly and desperately for the narrator by name. W. convinces the narrator to see the woman, who claims they lived together as lovers from 1968 to 1970, during which time the narrator maintains he lived with S., who subsequently left him for a dentist in Copenhagen. Although he denies all knowledge of Lea, the narrator allows her to move in with him and be his constant companion while he researches and writes, first about other authors and then about Lea. Lea and the narrator travel to England together, where she unexpectedly encounters her former lover, Don, a political radical who had gone underground without a trace. Upon their return home, Lea gradually disappears; on his way to Copenhagen to see S., the narrator finally discovers that he has assumed Lea's physical appearance. It is telling that this chronological account of "the story" reveals virtually nothing about "Theorie der Drohung." This is true not only because it adheres structurally to the principle of narrative linearity, but more importantly because it assumes the identity of one character is clearly distinguishable from another. This erasure of the tension of ambivalence which binds the characters together as a single constellation negates the essence of the text.

Indeed, it is extremely difficult, and misleading, to attempt any discussion of individual characters, since they function only in dynamic interaction with each other. The situation is somewhat more complicated in "Theorie der Drohung" than in "Marlenes Schwester," where the paradoxical symbiosis spanned two poles. "Theorie der Drohung" draws on the tension among three primary poles: the narrator, Lea, and S.. The narrator's response to S.' desertion, he informs us, consisted of continuous reading and forceful forgetting (TD, pages 56 and 66). Lea, on the other hand, whom the narrator claims not to know, remembers everything about S. and the narrator together. Lea remembers in great detail things which the narrator only vaguely recalls and serves as a memory bank on the subject of S..

> Nun [. . .] war Lea eingetroffen, eine Unbekannte, Fremde, hatte mit ihren energischen und akkuraten Erfindungen (und mithilfe ihres blauen Notizbüchleins voller 'Gedächtnisstützen') die Autorenschaft über meine Zeit mit S. übernommen und schrieb sich unbeirrbar an die Stelle meiner verlorenen Freundin, die keine Spur hinterlassen hatte oder eben doch vielzuviele

>  Spuren, als dass die sich zu einer einheitlichen
>  Schrift hätten festigen können. (TD, page 67)

Curiously, Lea remembers everything about S. and her relationship with the narrator but has no idea who S. is. She is baffled by the suspicious narrator's constant references to S. in his attempt to prove that Lea is a fraud. The apparent contradiction in her exasperated "S. . . . S. . . .! Immer diese S.! Wer soll denn das bloss sein?" (TD, page 68) is actually quite logical if one accepts the identity of S. and Lea. If Lea embodies or is S., then to acknowledge S. as existing independent of herself would amount to an admission of self-alienation. It is significant that the voice of alienation speaks through the narrator; he is the one who distinguishes between S. and Lea. The interpretation of "Theorie der Drohung" advanced by vom Hofe and Pfaff is informed by psychoanalytical concepts applied to the ontological subjectivity of post-Romantic literature. The Orpheus-Eurydice tale serves them as a model. Identifying S. as the id (Es) and Lea as literature, they contend "Lea ist S. in literarischer Modifikation, ist eine literarische Replik, durch die der Autor als neuer Orpheus sich S. wieder ins Gedächtnis bringt [. . .]."[25] The id in Lacanian terms, they argue, finds productive articulation in literature. Reading the conclusion of "Theorie der Drohung" in terms of the narrating author actually becoming Lea, they find that the text attests to its own impotence.

>  Sich in Lea vertiefend, ist [der Erzähler] eine literarische Existenz geworden. In solcher Vereinigung von Gedanke und Bild, Sehnsucht und Ziel erweist sich freilich auch in der Insubstantialität der wiederkehrenden poetischen Eurydike die Ohnmacht der Kunst an irgendetwas ausser an sich selbst zu rühren.[26]

Although I would disagree with this conclusion as well as with the equation of Lea with literature per se, it is certainly true that S. can be read as *Es*. Indeed, psychoanalysis as a cognitive theory of personal identity contributes certain basic concepts which are pivotal in "Theorie der Drohung." Psychoanalytical theory is at the same time subject to critical reproach and, at times, inversion.

Having noted the paradoxical symbiosis between Marlene and her sister, which allows neither one to exist as "I" without the other, the reader is surprised by the firm assertion of the first-person narrator in "Theorie der Drohung." It seems that individual contours here are more clearly defined. Yet, the "I" in "Theorie der Drohung" is not only first-person narrator but ego (*Ich*) as well. As the latter, it is threatened by the id. "Das Es ist der Ort der Leidenschaften, es ist weit ins Somatische geöffnet und kann das Ich genauso bedrohen wie die Aussenwelt."[27] As Freud describes it, the ego operates on the basis of perception, while the id functions according to instinct. The ego reigns with reason over the passions of the id comparable to the manner in which an equestrian reins in the animal force of the horse.[28] The ego's function is to organize and synthesize and hence to dominate and subdue the chaos of passion.[29] Effecting sovereignty over the id is, in turn, a function of psychoanalysis itself. "Das Ich entwickelt sich von der Triebwahrnehmung zur Triebbeherrschung, vom Triebgehorsam zur Triebhemmung. [. . .] Die Psychoanalyse ist ein Werkzeug, welches dem Ich die fortschreitende Eroberung des Es ermöglichen soll."[30] "Theorie der Drohung" in fact inverts this process. The initial description of Dr. W. clearly implies a critique of psychoanalysis as oppressive in its monopolistic system of personal cognition.

> Ein Mensch, dessen Existenz die meine von jeher bedrückt und überschattet hat, weil er mir ähnlich und dabei doch in allem weit überlegen ist, es immer schon war, und heute erst recht, wenn er mir zu verstehen gibt, dass er mich viel gründlicher kennt als ich selbst es je vermöchte und dass einzig seine Behandlung imstande wäre, mir die Augen über mich zu öffnen. (TD, page 45)

The Ich-narrator in "Theorie der Drohung" seeks to dominate and subdue the pain caused by S. (her desertion) by reading and forgetting as much as possible about her. Yet, S. (as Es) never actually appears in the text, and the threat she poses takes its most immediate form, oddly enough, in Lea, first described as "eine junge Frau, die schreit" (TD, page 45). The narrator experiences Lea's threat in her uncanny capacity to remember his past (with S.) and in her unrestrained body movements. He notes the "Unordnung ihrer Glieder" (TD, pages 49-50), responding to her body language with theory designed to cloak and control his own fear.

> Jedenfalls bildete ich mir [. . .] die eine oder andere theoretische Meinung über die wilde Darbietung, um ihren unmittelbaren sinnlichen Einwirkungen nicht völlig schutzlos ausgeliefert zu sein. In Wahrheit bekam ich's mit der Furcht zu tun, der blosse Anblick der Hysterika könne gleichsam eine infektiöse Übertragung auf mich auslösen. (TD, page 51)

The fact that so much attention is paid to Lea's corporeality--her body language, her physical presence, and its ultimate disappearance--can best be understood in light of Freud's theory of the unconscious attaining consciousness. "[. . .] bewusst werden kann nur das, was schon einmal bw Wahrnehmung war, und was ausser Gefühlen von innen her bewusst werden will, muss versuchen, sich in äussere Wahrnehmungen umzusetzen. Dies wird mittels der Erinnerungsspuren möglich." I should like to juxtapose this passage from the essay on the ego and the id with one from Freud's essay on the unconscious: "In Wirklichkeit tritt nun eine Aufhebung der Verdrängung nicht eher ein, als bis die bewusste Vorstellung sich nach Überwindung der Widerstände mit der unbewussten Erinnerungsspur in Verbindung gesetzt hat."[31] Seen as a link between ego and id, Lea thus becomes the externalized perception of that which the narrator has repressed (forcefully forgotten) about S..[32] She is necessary to attain consciousness of his own past. Strauss gives us very early indications that Lea and S. are, on some level, one with the narrator. The first line of the text tells of the narrator's renewed conversation with himself: "Aufgewacht aus tiefem Lesen, vom unruhigen Rhythmus der Zeilen zum Reden gebracht, der Mund halb noch im Dunklen, so wendet sich nun das wieder aufgenommene Selbstgespräch dem ersten Kalendertag des Winters zu" (TD, page 43). The surrounding landscape, heavy with snow as yet unmarked by any tracks, is likened to an "offenes weisses stumpfes Nichts" (TD, page 43). The narrator makes the first tracks in the snow, indeed, when he leaves his house to go see (perceive) Lea. The snowy landscape can thus be likened to the unarticulated self, the denial of the id, the failure to remember. The encounter with Lea is the first step towards renewing the dialogue with S..[33] Lea is thus not merely a threat to the narrator's calm, rational, forgetful existence. She is also the key to a reunion with his repressed instincts and past experience; in other words, she embodies the hopeful promise of non-alienated identity. This explains the narrator's initial ambivalent response to the young woman who cries out for him. He feels first pleased and then threatened when he hears about Lea's case (TD, pages 45-47), and he finds her physical gestures "ebenso anziehend wie verletzend" (TD, page 50). Not coincidentally, he is reminded of his own literary sketches entitled "'Notizen zur Wunschangst'" (TD, pages 46-47). The ambivalent compound pointedly entwines unrestrained desire and fear of wish fulfillment. Inverting the notion, however, that the ego conquers the id that threatens it, the narrator in "Theorie der Drohung" is threatened most seriously by the denial both of his desire and of his fear. The "I" in this case rejects consciousness, and the id refuses to let him forget. The ego does not conquer the id with the aid of psychoanalysis. Instead, the id defiantly insists on speaking its voice.

The narrator's resistance to memory is great. Realizing the danger that acknowledging his past with S. would pose, he decides to protect himself by believing that Lea is a liar (TD, page 66). Her lies comprise a system of entrapment against which he feels he must protect himself.

> Dieses harmonische System sich unendlich fortzeugender Lügen, in dem alles sich aufklärte und zu einer lückenlosen Beweiskette verband, war durch nichts zu erschüttern oder in Frage zu stellen; es war ganz einfach das 'System Lea', das sich völlig gleichberechtigt neben anderen Aussagesystemen behauptete. (TD, page 68)

This is not the final word on Lea's perception of the past; it is merely the narrator's particular interpretation at a given point. It is an interpretation prompted by fear.  By categorizing Lea's account of their shared past as a system just like any other, he uses theory to neutralize or deaden the specific threat of his own experience. The point at which this changes and resistance gives way to acceptance is linked to a shift in the narrator's posture concerning the writing process.  Up until this point, the narrator and Lea represent opposing possibilities for language and literature.  Since the two characters are in fact one constellation, their positions can be seen as exemplifying the ambivalence of the writing process as mapped out in the text.  The initial encounter with Lea causes the narrator to note the connection between her insanity and his attempts to articulate himself in writing.  He comments on the difference between the integral specific identity of Lea's body language and the interchangeable, generalizable non-identity of the written word, which is after all his medium.  This theoretical distinction does not, however, prevent him from recognizing his affinity with the insane woman.

> (Was uns schreckt, sagte ich mir daraufhin beflissen, kann unmöglich das ganz Andersgeartete oder das sogenannte Abnorme sein, sondern stets nur das wesentlich Verwandte im Zustand seiner extremsten Erscheinungsform. Zweifellos las ich in Leas Verrücktheit sofort das Schreckensgleichnis auf meine eigenen qualvollen Versuche, mich schreibend auszudrücken.) (<u>TD</u>, pages 51-52)

Thus, he both recognizes himself in her and at the same time distances himself from her, in this case with a theoretical observation. Throughout the first four sections of the text, the narrator pursues distance as opposed to self-recognition.  Lea proclaims: "Was wir einmal gelesen haben, [. . .] steht nicht mehr in den Büchern" (<u>TD</u>, page

69), tears out every page she reads, and throws it away. This reading habit emphasizes the living dimension of interaction between text and reader. The narrator, on the other hand, confesses to writing in order to establish something fixed and stable outside himself. "Ich wollte um mich herum etwas Festgelegtes und persönlich Signiertes schaffen, das man mir nicht eines Tages wieder ausreden und streitig machen konnte" (TD, page 70). The logical extension of this stance is in effect the written text as alienated self. This is in fact the content of a sentence which the narrator finds in one of his old, forgotten texts: "'Ich bin nirgendwo auf der Welt etwas Fremderem begegnet als einem von mir zustandegebrachten Aussagesatz'" (TD, page 73). Yet, for the time being, he fails to draw the consequences from this. He writes in order to protect himself from what he terms "Leas Lügendiskurs" (TD, page 70). The major study he undertakes is likewise characterized by flight from Lea. Absorbed in his research, he no longer concerns himself at all with her. "Sie war jetzt schon so gut wie nicht mehr vorhanden" (TD, page 76). Even the onset of her illness once he actually begins to write--the coincidence is not accidental--is not sufficient to make him acknowledge that part of himself embodied by Lea (TD, pages 77-78). Spurning her in a manner reminiscent of the divine warning to Lot prior to his departure from Sodom and Gomorrah, he says: "'Dreh dich nur um, Lea, und sieh wieder hinaus. Alle Wege führen nun fort von dir'" (TD, page 76). Lea, like Lot's wife, wants to and does look back and remember. Here, however, it is the narrator who bears the curse of non-memory.[34] The narrator's flight from Lea as flight from his own identity is echoed in his approach to his study, to which he gives the title "Theorie der Drohung." Hypothesizing, in contrast to Freud, that writing is a function of a primary instinct and not a cultural product of sublimation (TD, page 74), he plans the following:

> Meine bevorstehende Studie, soviel stand bereits fest, würde sich mit jenen riskanten Grenzfällen des Schreibens beschäftigen, in denen eine luststeigernde Angst und eine angsterzeugende Lust zur höchsten Bedrohung des schreibenden Autors führen, untersucht an zentralen Texten und Selbstzeugnissen der von mir bevorzugten Autoren. (TD, page 73)

First to fall prey to the researcher's unbridled enthusiasm is Freud himself, to be followed by Friedrich von Hardenberg (Novalis). Yet, the research project is doomed. While the narrator believes he is finally articulating his own voice, he discovers, much to his chagrin, that his text is rife with plagiarism (TD, pages 79-81). Vom Hofe and Pfaff read this as a reference to the ontological "Zirkel von Subjektivität und Literatur, in dem nach einem Anfang zu fragen, vielleicht gar nicht sinnvoll ist."[35] Martin Roda Becher is closer to the truth when he writes:

> So wird in dieser Erzählung der Mythos vom Individuum, das sich an der Idylle des freien Schriftsteller- und Gelehrtentums nährt, von innen heraus zerstört. Die positive Bewertung des Schreibens als ein Akt der Selbstfindung wird schlagartig entleert und durch die Ironie des Plagiats umgewandelt.[36]

What both of these opinions overlook, however, is the twofold nature of the image of literary writing as developed around the relationship between the narrator and Lea. Although he sets out to research writing as a function of a primary instinct, he fails to acknowledge his own instincts and the role they play in his writing. This is why he must, necessarily, plagiarize. He has not found his own voice but stifled it by ignoring Lea, who speaks to him with the voice of his past, the one shared with S.. It is no coincidence that he cries out in desperation for Lea's help when he realizes his plagiarism (<u>TD</u>, page 82). She rises to the occasion from her sickbed. "Und in diesem Augenblick wusste ich, dass ich als Autor nur eine Chance hatte: ich musste über Lea schreiben. Jedes andere Thema würde unvermeidlich immer wieder zu gestohlenem Schreiben führen" (<u>TD</u>, page 82).

Musing somewhat anxiously on Lea's detailed knowledge of their allegedly shared past, the narrator tells us:

> 'Ich'--ich war die ständige Pointe dieser nicht geheueren Witze, ich war aller meiner Rätsel Lösung. Aber diesmal nicht, diesmal kam es ganz anders. (<u>TD</u>, page 86)

This is no casual indication of confusion on the narrator's part. It is, rather, a sign of recognition that the "I"--the organizing, dominant ego that has hitherto governed his life and his writing--is no longer the key to survival or the discovery of a voice he can properly call his. The last sentence of the above quotation is, first of all, a reference to Lea--the image of his repressed past which he must integrate into his own voice. Here we recognize the principle of diachronic longing, this time applied to the writing process. The ambivalence of the two possibilities for writing as embodied by the <u>Ich</u>-narrator and Lea is exemplified in the notion of <u>Verflüchtigung</u> (evaporation, gradual disappearance) and <u>Verscheuchtsein</u> (a state of banishment). These terms appear frequently in relation to the narrator's texts and to Lea's physical presence or lack thereof. The narrator's study on "Theorie der Drohung" addresses the author's sense of disappearing as he writes (TD, page 73). The old text he finds which concludes with the recognition of alienation from his own sentences also discusses the loss of individual contours in the act of writing:

> 'Was ich auch schreibe, es schreibt über mich. Ich schreibe unaufhörlich den Fremden, der mich bedroht. Was ich schreibe, weiss, wer ich bin, weiss auch Bescheid über mein künftiges Ende, und jedermann kann in meinem Geschriebenem lesen über mich, wie die alten Weiber im Kaffeesatz, nur ich nicht. Ich nicht, ich kann es nicht lesen; versiegelt die Bedeutung, übersehen die Warnungen in jeder Zeile. [. . .] Aber dann, am Ende, vermischt sich ohnehin alles, das Erkennen und das Beschriebene zu einunddemselben Geräusch vom regenüberströmten Papier im Sommerwind. (TD, pages 72-73)

He speaks of losing his countenance (and likewise his vision, Gesicht) to his text (TD, page 71). The same problem poses itself even when he writes about Lea.

> Ich schreibe über Lea und werde, Satz für Satz, unerbittlich verfolgt von der endgültigen Auflösung alles bisher von mir über Lea Geschriebenen. Es ist, als liefere diese Geschichte sich ein Kopf-an-Kopf-Rennen mit ihrer eigenen Verflüchtigung. Ich bin jedenfalls darauf gefasst, am Ende, nachdem ich die letzte Linie am äusserst letzten Buchstaben gezogen haben werde, eine spurlos verschwundene, vollständig verblasste Erzählung zu hinterlassen. (TD, page 55)

The loss of Lea's history with its textual articulation represents the danger, albeit not the foregone conclusion, of writing as self-alienation. Lea's curse upon the narrator when he spurns her presence ambivalently conveys both positive and negative aspects of this threat:

> 'Ich wünschte, das allerletzte Kapitel deiner Arbeit würde nur vom Verscheuchtsein handeln. Wie du von deinem Geschriebenen verscheucht wirst [. . .].' (TD, pages 76-77)

This curse is in fact fulfilled. As the narrator writes about Lea, she gradually vanishes from his sight. The last remnant of her actual physical presence which he perceives outside himself are two fingertips spreading dead flies on a piece of buttered bread, which then disappears into an invisible mouth (TD, page 100). Lea does not, however, vanish altogether. Her physical appearance, the narrator finds, has been displaced onto his person. It is important to note that the narrator does not actually become Lea; he sees himself as her, but with his own eyes and not hers. Thus, the external perception of his repressed past ceases to exist in externalized form. Likewise, it is not until the narrator decides to write about Lea that she begins to speak in the voice of the first person (TD, page 82). This turning point marks an approximation of the two figures. Lea gains entrance into the narrator's person, just as she does to his memories (TD, page 53). Yet, this does not mean *a priori* that the narrator's future textual efforts will be free of self-alienation. What they will be is the expression of diachronic longing between the conscious self and its repressed passions and memories.

> Und jetzt, da ich mit dem letzten Abschnitt meiner Arbeit beginne, der zweifellos vom Verscheuchtsein handelt, wie Lea es beschworen hatte, jetzt weiss ich, dass sie den Sirenenrufen ihres Beschriebenwerdens nicht widerstehen konnte; ihr Körper, zusammenstürzend, kraftlos, aufgelöst zu Schrift, hat sich ganz in meine Obhut begeben, und so, mit mir vereinigt, hat sie auch mich zu einem anderen gemacht, dessen unentwegtes Schreiben nichts anderes zu erreichen sucht, als uns wieder zu teilen, die alte Trennung wiederherzustellen--damit wir uns wieder sehen können! Deshalb nur schreibe ich noch und werde immer weiter schreiben bis zum letzten Seufzer meiner Erinnerung. (TD, page 96)

The separation that allows renewed perception is not, as vom Hofe and Pfaff argue, the establishment of difference per se through literature,[37] but the invocation of repressed instincts and repressed time out of the depths of darkness into the clarity of self-knowledge. The writing process thus becomes a living manifestation of diachronic longing within the writing subject. The agony of this task is reflected in the narrator's virulent response to the last and only vestige of Lea's presence: the smell of her perfume. It creates not only a continued presence, but also a present time which makes it virtually impossible for the narrator to write his past.

> Und doch fühlte ich mich in dieser neuen Nähe, die fast einer Durchdringung gleichkam, nicht recht wohl, nein, ich fand sie sehr bald ganz unerträglich. Sie behinderte meine Arbeit. Sie unterband die Ausflüge meiner Erinnerung, denn dieser starke Geruch schuf eine unausweichliche, betäubende Gegenwart, die mir das Weiterschreiben schliesslich unmöglich machte. (TD, page 101)

This passage testifies to the struggle between the desire to gain control over the past by giving it textual form and the persistent demand of the repressed present to be heard as well. The fact that the narrator cannot write dead memories--the easy textualization of Lea-- and sets out for an unmediated reunion with S. manifests, not the guarantee, but the living hope implicit in a literature of diachronic longing: between author and unknown self of the present, on the one hand, and personal history of that self's past, on the other. The narrator's appropriation of Lea's outward appearance in "Theorie der Drohung" is not the end of art;[38] it is proof that the narrator has accepted the challenge of diachronic longing.

As in "Marlenes Schwester" love also belongs in the realm of diachronic longing in "Theorie der Drohung." It is his love for Lea that effects a qualitative change in the narrator's writing and brings him closer to self-knowledge; he no longer feels the need to protect himself against what he has previously termed her discourse of lies.

> Jetzt war ich mir ganz sicher, dass ich über Lea schreiben würde; und zwar nicht mehr, um mich gegen ihre Lügen zu schützen, sondern weil das Gefühl, Lea zu lieben, nichts anderes war als das Gefühl, ein Buch zu beginnen. (<u>TD</u>, page 93)

The principle of diachronic longing embodied in love extends, however, to more than the author's inner self. This brings us to the second implication of the "I" no longer being the solution to all its puzzles (see <u>TD</u>, page 86). The first was found in Lea; the second can be found in Don, Lea's radical lover, characterized repeatedly as "der ganz Andere" in contrast to the narrator. The narrator himself tells us that it is Lea's love for Don and himself that creates an indivisible bond between the two men.

> Der ganz Andere als ich wäre ich schon immer gerne selbst gewesen, und Lea kannte nun so einen, hatte ihn sogar geliebt wie mich, und dadurch auf unauflösliche Weise mit mir verbunden. (<u>TD</u>, page 91)

If the constellation between the narrator, Lea, and S. details the ambivalence of both identity and writing, then Don can reasonably be expected to contribute another dimension to this constellation. Lea's account of her history with Don (<u>TD</u>, pages 88-90) locates that history, not only in relation to the narrator's history with S., but also in relation to developments around the West German student movement as outlined in the first chapter of this study. According to her account,

Lea left the narrator in 1970 in order to be with Don, one of the leading activists in the British student movement. Her encounter with political work coincides precisely, the narrator informs us, with S.'s abandonment. These parallel developments have as their background a third: the onset of the dogmatic phase of the student movement. Lea says of her work with Don: "[. . .] ich hatte ziemlich schnell gelernt, mich kampfgerecht auszudrücken, und war bald noch geschickter darin als er" (TD, page 89). When political circumstances dictate that Don abandon Lea and go underground, she is tortured by interrogators seeking Don's whereabouts. Once released, Lea searches for him herself but to no avail. "[. . .] er hatte überhaupt keine Spuren hinterlassen" (TD, page 89). Fearing Don has disappeared from her forever, she has a nervous breakdown. This is actually the starting point of "Theorie der Drohung," when Lea desperately cries out for the narrator. S. (Es) deserts the narrator (Ich) at the same time that Lea, who will later become the voice of the past, learns to express herself in terms described as **kampfgerecht**. This is, in nar- rated form, the alienation of person and of language inflicted by the dogmatic adherence to and insistence on fixed conceptual categories that failed to allow for the living dimension of human experience. It reflects, too, the literary debates divided along the lines of political texts versus individualistically-oriented (bourgeois) literature. Lea's crying out for the Ich-narrator--at one point Lea is even referred to as "ich-süchtig" (TD, pag 53)--is in fact the reinstatement of the principle of diachronic longing that would reunite the narrator,

S., and Lea as one author living and writing in diachronic relationship to his inner self and his past and would, moreover, include the element of Don, that which integrates the diachronic extension to "we." Don represents an historical phase that was disastrous in its ultimate deadening of radical subjectivity, but the political element of human community remains a necessary component of any truly emancipatory text. Lea's apparent rejection of Don after their reunion in England is misleading. The narrator's reaction to this is revealing:

> Ich dachte, jetzt redet sie mir aber ganz schön nach dem Mund. Aber weshalb tat sie es? Vom ganz Anderen als ich war nun keine Rede mehr, Don war wie nie erlebt. (<u>TD</u>, page 93)

What Lea rejects in Don is the political language that failed. The locus of the new (hoped for) language that would be subjective and collective at the same time is not found in Lea, but in the narrator, the author who struggles between past and present, between theoretical systems and lived experience. The ambivalent possibilities of political language are underscored by the narrator's discovery of the right-wing propaganda brochure that bears the same title as his study on writing as a function of instinct and as the Strauss text we read.

> Es war mir klar, dass ich diesen höhnischen Zufall als Anspielung auf die unausweichliche Totalität des politischen Bedeutens begreifen musste, der sich selbst der abgeschiedenste Gedanke, die einfachste Nervenanspannung nicht zu entziehen vermögen.
>     Nicht dass ich je daran gezweifelt hätte: ich meine übrigens sogar, aus der Grundthese meiner Studie: kein Text existiert, der nicht Mehr über seinen Autor schreibt, als dieser von sich aus sagt; kein Text, der nicht Mehr zu verstehen gibt, als der Autor selbst darunter verstanden hat--ich meine, daraus folgt, dass dieses Mehr eines Textes in erster Linie von einer politischen Lektüre erschlossen werden kann. (<u>TD</u>, page 94)

Political meaning is omnipresent; it is the responsibility of the subjective agent--in this case, the reader--to establish specific meaning that enhances understanding as opposed to nullifying it. The text always exists in a network of which it is part but not whole. Political reading thus harbors danger (abrogation of specificity) as well as hope (specificity in a living network of collective meaning). The awkward American in London voices the need for this type of hope:

> sie seien in letzter Zeit alle ein bisschen schüchtern geworden, es sei so etwas wie eine Übergangszeit, jetzt würde von allen Leuten fast nur noch Musik gehört, und es wäre besser, wenn jemand wie Don da sei, der einem ein paar frische Gedanken ins Hirn bläst; denn wenn man selbst, für sich allein anfinge nachzudenken, da käme doch nur ein Spleen heraus, und mit so einem einzelnen Spleen liefe ja heute schon fast jeder herum. (TD, page 84)

It is no capricious coincidence that Strauss then has the American inquire as to Ernst Bloch's health. Strauss develops the notion of diachronic longing as a principle of hope through which the individual lives in a political network of collective subjectivity. The transition period the American describes is characterized by individuals who try to survive as monads. The 1970's, scarred by deficient paradigms, invoke the restoration of the political element of diachronic longing as well. The fear and confusion that accompany the gaps between paradigms are reflected in an eighteenth-century phenomenon the narrator calls "Teatrauma." His interest in this phenomenon dates back to his time with S. but, tellingly, remains forgotten until Lea provides him with the details. The joint study, entitled "'Teatrauma-- Ein Beitrag zur Geschichte der Gefühlskultur im vorgoetheschen Weimar'" (TD, page 61), dealt with "eine noch unerforschte Sinnesverwirrung" (TD, page

62) that befell the members of Anna Amalia's court in 1774. On the precipice between their familiar feudal order and a budding bourgeois public sphere, they develop a critical, neurotic fear of their own behavior.

> Sie wurden nämlich von der grotesken Schreckensvorstellung geplagt, nichts mehr, auch die abgeschiedenste und intimste ihrer Verrichtungen nicht, sei vor den Augen der anderen, vor dem Blick einer total und in sich grenzenlos gewordenen Öffentlichkeit geschützt. Sie fühlten sich immerzu und überall auf dem Theater agieren, unablässig beobachtet nicht nur von ihresgleichen sondern darüberhinaus von einer unübersehbaren Menge von unbekannten Zuschauern, die sie selbst nicht erkennen konnten, deren böses Gelächter ihnen aber in den Ohren schallte, wenn sie zur Bonbonniere griffen oder den Federkiel in die Hand nahmen. Sie selbst verachteten sich bei diesen einfachsten, doch stets aus dem Dunklen verhöhnten Vorgängen am allermeisten und vermochten bald keinen Gruss und keinen Schriftzug mehr unverstört auszuführen. (TD, pages 62-63)

History, Lea tells us, has been silent about this paralysis of affect. She surmises that Goethe's appearance in Weimar ended the crisis.

> Man darf sich vorstellen, dass der junge bürgerliche Dichter gleichsam eine Übertragungsautorität darstellte und die kleine höfische Gesellschaft vom Trauma der bürgerlichen Bedrohungen entlastet hat [. . .]. (TD, page 64)

Goethe stands here for the establishment of a socio-literary tradition that became the dominant paradigm for ages to come. Strauss locates his own text, not at the beginning of a new paradigm, but rather on that post-paradigm precipice, from which the future has no distinguishable contours. He could fall into the abyss of panic, like the feudal aristocrats he describes, or he could struggle to make a walkable path into the unknown. "Theorie der Drohung" seeks to capture the Sinnesverwirrung of the 1970's that might otherwise be silenced by history. The searching principle of diachronic longing--with individual and collective implications--prevents capitulation to total confusion and subjective paralysis.

The dynamic constellation of characters in "Theorie der Drohung" articulates the thematic ambivalence of identity and the writing process and likewise structures the development of that theme. The struggle for articulation of one's inner self also finds structural manifestation in Strauss' symbols, time structures, and textual reflection. We have already discussed the ramifications of visible, physical presence as developed in Lea's person, the external perception of the narrator's repressed instincts in the context of their own history. The narrator must make a path to her, as he does literally when he ventures forth onto the as yet untrodden snow. Lea is also frequently associated with another natural phenomenon: fog. She appears early on as a "Sommernebel [. . .] von Frau" (TD, page 54). Later, when the narrator anxiously wonders whether Lea will return to him from her reunion with Don, he writes: "Es wurde Tag, oder zumindest wurde draussen der undurchdringliche Nebel sichtbar, und Lea war nicht zurückgekommen . . . ." (TD, page 92). Towards the very end of the text, Lea is described as being consumed by "Abermil- lionen von Schattenbakterien" (TD, page 99), an erosion of physical contours comparable, albeit even more menacing, to the effect of fog on physical objects.[39] The association of Lea with fog and shadow makes sense only from the vantage point of the narrator. She embodies after all the principle of remembering, the articulation of that which has been repressed. The crux of the matter is that as the narrator assumes Lea's appearance, it falls to him to struggle all the more to see her (to see himself) more clearly. He must reach out to her within himself. The ambivalence of this process--danger and hope--is given symbolic form in a mechanical image as well. The telephone--diachronic longing <u>in nuce</u>--in fact provides the narrator with the first perceptible sound of Lea's voice. Before he even receives the actual telephone call, his mood is one of excited anticipation and a sense of threat with regard to the telephone. This ambivalent response extends to everything around him, an environment in which every object harbors "einen telefonischen Reiz" (<u>TD</u>, page 44). The telephone image recurs in the narrator's account of his response to Alex Colville's painting "Departure," in which a woman stands in a telephone booth on the dock as a ship pulls out to sea. The narrator imagines the woman speaking on the telephone with her lover on the ship.

> Ich denke mir nämlich, die beiden haben beim Abschiednehmen kein Ende finden können und werden nun solange miteinander telefonieren, bis das Schiff nicht mehr zu sehen ist oder die Verbindung wegen allzu grosser Entfernung abreisst. (<u>TD</u>, page 97)

This allows him to see himself and Lea in the painting, which, he finds,

> verspricht das ersehnte Halt immitten einer Trennung, in einem unvergänglichen Augenblick zwischen Noch-Nicht-Verlassensein und endgültiger Abkehr . . . . (<u>TD</u>, page 98)

Again, ambivalence dominates the image. We shall encounter the telephone again in <u>Die Widmung</u>.

We have already seen, however, that Lea figures, not only as the external perception of the ego's repressed instinct, but also as the reinstatement of the memory of the past shared by the narrator and S.. The narrator forgets his past time with S. and also has difficulty measuring his present time with Lea.

> Es ist schon merkwürdig genug, dass ich den Zeitpunkt, zu dem ich schreibe, nicht zuverlässig bestimmen kann. Wann schreibe ich hier? Und wann geschieht oder geschah, worüber ich schreibe? Ich kann es nicht sagen, ich weiss es nicht. Sicher ist nur: Die Zeit mit Lea schuf ihre eigene Chronologie, und vielleicht habe ich darüber jeden Sinn für zeitliche Abstände verloren. (<u>TD</u>, page 55)

If Lea establishes her own time, she likewise establishes the chronology for S.-time; the narrator calls it her "Autorenschaft über meine Zeit mit S. [. . .]" (<u>TD</u>, page 67). Lea thus manifests the integration of past and present in a living, dynamic whole. When the narrator functions as ego, rationally organizing his present while ignoring his past, Lea reminds him of the past by giving it present form. As the roles reverse and the narrator actively seeks his past, Lea persists as troublesome present (the smell of her perfume), thus keeping the narrator from hypostasizing the past by excluding his present. This is the essence of the passage in which the narrator speaks of their opposing chronologies:

> Und es mag sein, dass in der Reibung dieser vollkommen gegensätzlichen Zeitgeschichten, ihrer Gegenwartserstarrung und meines voranschreitenden Erinnerns, jener tödlich gemischte Dunst entstand, in dem Lea bei lebendigem Leib verwitterte und zerfiel. (<u>TD</u>, page 100)

This ambivalent relationship between past and present and the struggle towards the living tension between the two is not, however, merely another element of structural ambivalence. It is an indictment of closed systems of understanding as we are wont to apply them to our lives. Psychoanalysis is one such system subject to indictment. Another, in this case, is the linear division of time establishing a chronology that kills experience once it is past and does not allow for any living structural link between past and present. The very categories of past and present presuppose a dichotomy between the two, a dichotomy which essentially denies the human subject that experiences both. The narrator's time with S.--S.-time--is filled with dialogue that is open to paradox but not void of meaning. S., trained in nutritional science, is first exposed to paradox and uncertainty in her conversations with the narrator, who describes her as having discovered "einen unentdeckten Kontinent ihres Bewusstseins" (<u>TD</u>, page 57). Reading literature avidly but no single piece in its entirety, she learns to weave "das Ungefähre, das Spekulative und Paradoxe" (<u>TD</u>, page 57) into new patterns that make sense but do not foreclose it. "An ihren immer geschickter forschenden Fragen merkte ich, dass sie alles, was sie erfuhr, in den verschiedenartigsten Zu- sammenhängen gut zu gebrauchen und auf verblüffende Weise neu zu kom- binieren verstand" (<u>TD</u>, page 58).

> Zahllose Theorieansätze fand sie wie im Schlaf, extravagante und vielversprechende, die beiläufigsten Bemerkungen organisierte sie zu Themen und Fragestellungen von übergeordneter Bedeutung, und ihre Fantasie war [. . .] überflutet von Plänen und Projekten [. . .].
> [. . .] Ihr einzigartiges Talent, [. . .], den gemeinsamen Augenblick der Wahrheit zu erwischen, in dem jene vom Lesen sich entfernende Lektüre das äusserste Fluidum des Textes streift, hätte am Ende vielleicht eine Theorie der Literatur hervorgebracht, derzufolge

> man Texte danach beurteilt, ob sie das souveräne Missverständnis, das inspirierte Versehen, den ungenauen Leser zulassen oder nicht. (<u>TD</u>, page 59)

S., as both descriptive id and repressed past, is thus not diametrically opposed to theory, but speaks instead for theory without fixed demarcations between elemental categories. This applies to both time and text. In fact, the self-reflective mode of Strauss' text literally enacts the struggle between past and present, between identity and ambivalence, in such a way as to preclude positing time past (i.e., no longer in any way present) or text external to reader or author (i.e., in no way present in the subjective agent). The ostensible linear chronology of "Marlenes Schwester" is, we have seen, undermined by the cyclical chronology of ambivalence. Strauss employs a similar technique in "Theorie der Drohung," where the six divisions of the text depict a linear progression of events. The text itself is, however, engaged in the struggle to articulate its own identity, in which the past is simultaneously present. The narrator, who likewise functions as author of the text, tells the story from the vantage point of the story's own future, i.e., Lea's disappearance and the narrator's departure for Copenhagen. Yet, even the terms "story" and "future" adhere to a chronology of linear progression. In fact, the text creates a constant present. The narrator-author inserts older textual segments from his past into the current text, thus rendering the dichotomy between past and present untenable. By telling the ostensible story from its presumed end, the text effectively seeks to establish its own memory--a memory vibrant in its own present, which is the text. The text thus becomes the locus for the diachronic struggle towards articulation of personal identity and history. Michael Rutschky notes that writing holds the lone promise of active experience in a decade (the 1970's) which he characterizes as "eine Zeit des Nebels."[40] Significantly, "Theorie der Drohung," which marks a bolder step away from the capitulation to ambivalence than is evident in "Marlenes Schwester," also unfolds the writing process as its own subject of discourse. The struggle for articulation of person in historical and social terms infused with the living dimension of the human subject and the particular challenge this poses to literature thus come more clearly into focus in "Theorie der Drohung." This sets the stage for Die Widmung, which--more clearly than any of the other texts considered here--articulates the challenge to West German literature in the 1970's.

Notes: Chapter II

[1] Although the story was first printed in <u>Neue Rundschau</u> in 1974, I shall cite the 1975 publication: Botho Strauss, "Marlenes Schwester," <u>Marlenes Schwester: Zwei Erzählungen</u> (Munich: Hanser, 1975). Future references to this piece will be abbreviated as <u>MS</u>; page references will appear parenthetically within the text.

[2] Gerhard vom Hofe and Peter Pfaff comment on the absence of a proper name for Marlene's sister: "Darin bleibt die Erzählung sozusagen ihrer heteronomistischen Ontologie der Subjektivität treu." See their essay on "Botho Strauss und die Poetik der Endzeit," in <u>Das Elend des Polyphem: Zum Thema der Subjektivität bei Thomas Bernhard, Peter Handke, Wolfgang Koeppen und Botho Strauss</u> (Königstein/Ts.: Athenäum, 1980), p. 113.

[3] Martin Roda Becher designates paradox as the form most characteristic for Strauss' work. See Becher, "Poesie der Unglücksfälle," <u>Merkur</u>, 32 (1979), Nr. 6, 627.

[4] Interestingly enough, the corporeality here is one that excludes sexuality, usually associated with the renewal of vital energies or life itself. See, for example, Sigmund Freud's comments on the difference between the erotic and death instincts in his letter to Albert Einstein of September, 1932, "Warum Krieg?", <u>Gesammelte Werke, chronologisch geordnet</u>, 3rd ed. (Frankfurt/Main: Fischer, 1968), XVI, 22. In an odd inversion, Marlene's disease could be seen as a manifestation of her erotic instinct: that which struggles to keep her alive.

[5] See Muschg's preface to Fritz Zorn, <u>Mars</u> (Frankfurt/Main: Fischer Taschenbuch, 1980), p. 22.

[6] See Claudia Kalasz, "Vereiste Spuren: Suche nach Erinnerung in Dichtungen von Botho Strauss," <u>Programmheft</u> [Theater der Stadt Heidelberg] (1978/79), Nr. 6, 39-40; and Michael Rutschky, <u>Erfahrungshunger: Ein Essay über die siebziger Jahre</u> (Cologne: Kiepenheuer & Witsch, 1980), p. 263.

[7] I take issue here with vom Hofe's and Pfaff's assumption that Marlene's sister does indeed die. See vom Hofe and Pfaff, "Botho Strauss und die Poetik der Endzeit," p. 114.

[8] Helmut Kreuzer, "Neue Subjektivität: Zur Literatur der siebziger Jahre in der Bundesrepublik Deutschland," <u>Die Gegenwartsliteratur</u>, ed. Manfed Durzak (Stuttgart: Reclam, 1981), p. 94.

[9] This name also figures in "Theorie der Drohung".

[10] Vom Hofe and Pfaff discuss the vampire metaphor in terms of dependence on a beloved other ("Botho Strauss und die Poetik der Endzeit," p. 114), but my contention is that the thematic and structural significance of the vampire metaphor is far greater than they would allow.

[11] Kalasz ("Vereiste Spuren," p. 35) discusses Strauss' characters as their own doubles by virtue of their inability to remember their past and hence establish or know their own biography. Christoph Türcke similarly characterizes Strauss' dramatic figures as their own doubles. See Türcke, "Auferstehung als schlechte Unendlichkeit: Zum theologischen Leitmotiv des Botho Strauss," Programmheft [Theater der Stadt Heidelberg] (1978/79), Nr. 6, 25. Citing Otto Rank's 1914 essay on doubles, Sigmund Freud sheds some light on the original function of the double, presumed to protect the ego from annihilation, the "immortal" soul probably being the body's first double. See Freud, "Das Unheimliche," Gesammelte Werke, chronologisch geordnet, 3rd ed. (Frankfurt/Main: Fischer, 1966), XII, 247. Marlene's promise of "immortality" to her sister is, however, anything but a consoling affirmation of her personal identity. On the contrary, it erases that identity, thereby outlining more clearly the contemporary dilemma, the negation of death equaling the negation of experience.

[12] Peter Beicken characterizes "Marlenes Schwester" in terms of "das Versteifen auf den Gefühlsanspruch gegenüber der pseudoaufklärerischen Verurteilung des Psychischen in der Politisierungsphase." Although the text should certainly be read against this broader context of the early 1970's, the emphasis on emotional intensity in "Marlenes Schwester" should not by any means be equated with a simplistic reversal of the political versus personal scheme. Beicken makes the same mistake with regard to "Theorie der Drohung," in which he also ascertains "Selbstbehauptung des Gefühls." See Peter Beicken, "'Neue Subjektivität': Zur Prosa der siebziger Jahre," Deutsche Literatur in der Bundesrepublik seit 1965, ed. Paul Michael Lützeler and Egon Schwarz (Königstein/Ts.: Athenäum, 1980), p. 175.

[13] Peter von Becker uses an interesting formulation to characterize Strauss' most recent dramatic production: Kalldewey, Farce. He calls it "eine Allegorie der liebestötenden Gesundheit, einer sterbenslangweiligen lebenslänglichen Vernünftigkeit." This could also double as a description of the principle that governs Marlene and the society of vampires. See Peter von Becker, "Die Minima Moralia: Notizen zu Botho Strauss 'Paare Passanten' und 'Kalldewey, Farce'," Merkur, 36 (February, 1982), Nr. 2, 1960.

[14] Sigmund Freud, "Triebe und Triebschicksale," Gesammelte Werke, chronologisch geordnet, 5th ed. (Frankfurt/Main: Fischer, 1969), X, 231. The English reference is Freud, "Instincts and Their Vicissitudes," Sigmund Freud: Collected Papers, trans. Joan Riviere (New York: Basic Books, 1959), IV, 81-82.

[15] Several reviewers as well as Hans Wolfschütz have alluded to Strauss' use of the Romantic motif of the lost shadow. Wolfschütz writes of "Marlenes Schwester" and "Theorie der Drohung": "Beide Erzählungen sind moderne Varianten der Geschichte vom verlorenen Schatten, beide spiegeln das Zerfallen individuellen Bewusstseins, und in beiden ist das auslösende Motiv dafür die Trennung von einem geliebten Menschen." See Hans Wolfschütz' entry on Botho Strauss in Kritisches Lexikon zur deutschsprachigen Gegenwartsliteratur, ed. Heinz Ludwig Arnold (Munich: edition text + kritik, 1978), II, no pagination. Although the literary allusion is often cited, no one as yet has undertaken a detailed study of Strauss' reception of this Romantic motif.

[16] Except in the aftermath of a nuclear blast, where the shadow has been burned onto matter while the object that cast it has been destroyed. Even here, however, the shadow is distinguishable from non-shadow, thus bearing witness to the previous existence of the original object.

[17] Kalasz, "Vereiste Spuren," p. 36.

[18] We are reminded of Adorno's comment that forgetting the past is a structural by-product of capitalist economy. See his essay, "Was bedeutet: Aufarbeitung der Vergangenheit?", Erziehung zur Mündigkeit: Vorträge und Gespräche mit Hellmut Becker 1959-1969, ed. Gerd Kadelbach, 5th ed. (Frankfurt/Main: Suhrkamp, 1977), pp. 10-28.

[19] Neither is Norbert Elias' Über den Prozess der Zivilisation: Soziogenetische und psychogenetische Untersuchungen, 5th ed. (Frankfurt/Main: Suhrkamp, 1978), which does in fact provide an historical account of some human behavioral affects from the vantage point of a theory of civilization.

[20] Yahweh's covenants with Abraham, Isaac, and Jacob are all sealed with the divine word and promise its fulfillment. The word binds, as for example when Jonathan says to David: "Für das Wort aber, das du und ich miteinander geredet haben: siehe, dafür steht der HERR zwischen mir und dir ewiglich." See I Samuel 20, 23, Die Bibel, 6th ed. (Stuttgart: Würtembergische Bibelanstalt, 1978), p. 306.

[21] Wolfschütz quite rightly points out Strauss' "Auflösung der linearen Fabel in Bruchstücke von Handlungszusammenhängen" but fails to note the structural relationship of these particles to each other. See Wolfschütz, "Botho Strauss," n.p. Günter Blöcker likewise comments on Strauss' "abgerissene Erzählgebärden, die zunächst den Eindruck der Diskontinuität erwecken," but Blöcker evades any structural analysis by claiming rather vaguely that these particles "nach und nach jedoch einen Gefühlszusammenhang vermitteln, dem der Leser sich anvertraut." See Blöcker, "Innenweltspiele: Botho Strauss als Erzähler," Merkur, 29 (July 1975), Nr. 7, 682.

[22]"Jenes Minimum an erzählerischer Autorität, das der Text selbst enthalten muss, um den Leser bei der Stange zu halten, hat Botho Strauss vorzeitig und durch unnötige Anbiederungsversuche beim Leser verschenkt." Thus, Lothar Baier moralistically reproaches Strauss without, however, acknowledging narrative authority as a socio-historical construct. See Baier, "Lektüre als Blindflug," Frankfurter Allgemeine Zeitung (May 10, 1975).

[23]Botho Strauss, "Theorie der Drohung," Marlenes Schwester: Zwei Erzählungen (Munich: Hanser, 1975), pp. 41-105. Further references to the text will be abbreviated as TD; page references will appear parenthetically within the text.

[24]Actually, the day is designated quite specifically as the day of the December solstice. This detail on the first page of the text is already laden with the ambivalence of both theory and threat. As a fixed category with which we measure the passage of seasons (time), it marks the beginning of winter. Yet, even this demarcation is qualified by the fact that this is true only for the Northern hemisphere; in the Southern hemisphere, the December solstice marks the beginning of winter's opposite, i.e., summer. The threat of winter, so to speak, is likewise qualified by the fact that the December solstice is set off chronologically by the autumnal and vernal equinoxes, those points in calendar time when day and night are of equal duration. True, the December solstice falls in the period when darkness outlasts light, but it promises to move forward chronologically to the vernal equinox, after which the opposite is true and light dominates. The prerequisite for the fulfillment of the promise of light is, of course, that the human race survive the winter. A seemingly minor detail thus captures the thrust of the entire text. "Theorie der Drohung" addresses a threat to the survival of Western society and the ambivalent capacity of literature either to challenge or succumb to it.

[25]Vom Hofe and Pfaff, "Botho Strauss und die Poetik der Endzeit," p. 121.

[26]Vom Hofe and Pfaff, "Botho Strauss und die Poetik der Endzeit," p. 123. The total identification of the narrator with Lea at the end of the text is a common assumption and a not altogether incomprehensible one, given that the narrator says, "Ich war Lea" (TD, page 105). As I read the text, however, the assumption is also highly problematical. The narrator's assertion that he has become Lea is immediately subject to qualification: "Oder zumindest: ich hatte mir alles, was von Lea übrig geblieben war, zueigen gemacht" (TD, p. 105). As I shall argue in the body of this study, a careful reading of this qualification in the context of the dynamic tension between Lea and the narrator as developed in the text yields a very different conclusion regarding the vital potential of literature.

27"Es," Lexikon der Psychologie, ed. Wilhelm Arnold et al. (Freiburg, Basel, Vienna: Herer, 1980), I, col. 526.

28Sigmund Freud, "Das Ich und das Es," Gesammelte Werke, chronologisch geordnet, 2nd ed. (London: Imago Publishing, 1947), XIII, 252-253.

29"Wir haben uns die Vorstellung von einer zusammenhängenden Organisation der seelischen Vorgänge in einer Person gebildet und heissen diese das I c h derselben." Freud, "Das Ich und das Es," p. 243.

30Freud, "Das Ich und das Es," p. 286.

31Freud, "Das Ich und das Es," p. 247, and Freud, "Das Unbewusste," Gesammelte Werke, chronologisch geordnet, 2nd ed. (London: Imago Publishing, 1949), X, 274-275, respectively.

32As will be discussed later, Lea's gradual physical disappearance cannot be read as the narrator losing his identity to her. Rather, by assuming her outward appearance, he regains his chance of integral identity. He no longer needs the perception external to himself and has in fact re-internalized the knowledge of his own past.

33At one point, the narrator notes that the true nature of his joint project with S. was "die unerschöpfliche Produktion von Gespräch, welches stets Gespräch über Noch-zu-Besprechendes war" (TD, p. 57).

34The implications of Lea's curse will be detailed later.

35Vom Hofe and Pfaff, "Botho Strauss und die Poetik der Endzeit," p. 122.

36Martin Roda Becher, "Nekromantische Märchen," NZ-Basel (September 13, 1975). Kalasz sees the plagiarism as another indication of the dichotomy between reality and concept, which precludes experience. See Kalasz, "Vereiste Spuren," p. 40.

37Vom Hofe and Pfaff, "Botho Strauss und die Poetik der Endzeit," p. 123.

38Vom Hofe and Pfaff, "Botho Strauss und die Poetik der Endzeit," p. 123, speak of "die Ohnmacht der Kunst."

39Schattenbakterien is in fact the quintessential diagnosis for what afflicts the moribund sister in "Marlenes Schwester": a disease that threatens her with loss of individual contours.

40Rutschky, Erfahrungshunger, p. 112.

## Chapter III
## DIE WIDMUNG:  CRISIS OF EXPERIENCE AND ARTICULATION

"Dieser Mann ist eine grosse Hoffnung unserer Literatur. Vielleicht wird von ihm der Roman seiner Generation kommen." The prose piece which prompted Marcel Reich-Ranicki to lavish such praise on Botho Strauss paints, ostensibly, a "Porträt eines Verliebten und Verlassenen."[1] <u>Die Widmung: Eine Erzählung</u> is indeed often touted, denounced, and sometimes even analyzed on the basis of its portrayal of the emotional crisis sparked by a lover's desertion, a contemporary crisis of epidemic proportions.[2] Helmut Kreuzer has characterized the book as "zeittypisch schon in der Figur des verlassenen Mannes, der sich an die glücklose Liebe und das Leiden an ihr fixiert."[3] The fact that the publishing company ordered the third printing of <u>Die Widmung</u> six weeks after its initial publication indicates something about the numbers of readers who felt that this book spoke to them.[4] The central character's desertion by his lover is undoubtedly the point of departure for Strauss' text as well as for the protagonist's taking pen to hand.

> Seit anderthalb Wochen arbeitet er nicht mehr. Er hat weder gekündigt noch sich krankschreiben lassen. Dabei hätte er allen Anspruch auf ein Attest. Verlassenwerden ist schliesslich ein härteres Übel als ein Blinddarmentzündung. (<u>W</u>, page 9)

Yet, <u>Die Widmung</u> is anything but a narrative account of a love relationship gone bad. The reader neither learns anything about the actual relationship between Richard Schroubek and Hannah Beyl nor witnesses the initial separation. Schroubek himself remains totally in the dark as to why the person most important to him has abandoned him. "Warum ist sie gegangen? Was habe ich ihr getan? Es bereitet mir fast theologische Qualen, dass ich es nicht wissen <u>kann</u>. . . ." (<u>W</u>, page 115).[5] It is not a specific relationship qua love affair that is at issue here, but rather the fundamental experience of being deserted, feeling abandoned, and the need for qualitatively new forms of articulation appropriate to such experience. The title of the 1977 text differs from those of the two earlier pieces in that it contains only one substantive reference. Semantically, however, <u>Widmung</u> implies a reaching out to something beyond itself. Schroubek's journal is, clearly, dedicated to Hannah, as the second section of the text attests ("Für H.," pages 19-122). Yet, the first section of Strauss' text also comprises its own dedication, entitled, appropriately enough, "Die Widmung." This cannot be confused with Schroubek's textual dedication to Hannah. Strauss in fact dedicates his account of Schroubek's dedication to us, the readers, thus articulating the diachronic longing of the text.[6] Just as Schroubek longs for his lost lover, the text longs to be read. In short, the title already raises the issue of the viability of literature in the 1970's. We have already seen the problematic of language as developed in "Theorie der Drohung" reflecting on the quest for personal identity. <u>Die Widmung</u> radicalizes related themes by shifting structural focus.

> Die Ich-Forschung ist [. . . ] immer Sache eines anderen. Jedenfalls verhält es sich seit einem halben Jahrhundert so. Seitdem kennt die Geistesgeschichte der Paarfiguren ein neues Gespann: den einen, der unentwegt redet, und den anderen, der schweigt und versteht. (<u>W</u>, page 41)

Reflecting on psychoanalytical theory--Freud's famous essay on the ego and the id was published in 1923--this passage from <u>Die Widmung</u> can also be read as an allusion to Strauss' prose oeuvre, i.e., his own (literary) history of pair figures. On the one hand, Hannah and Schroubek can be seen as a pair, but this constellation differs markedly from the pair figures in either "Marlenes Schwester" or "Theorie der Drohung." Hannah does not threaten Schroubek's existence, nor does he assume hers.[7] The ambivalence characteristic of the two earlier texts yields here to a new emphasis on <u>Ausdrucksnot</u> as a personal, social, and literary phenomenon.

<u>Die Widmung</u> begins with a passage quite comparable to the beginnings of both earlier texts in its depiction of a general atmospheric malaise and the oppressive amorphousness of unarticulated specificity.

> Ganz Europa leidet gegenwärtig unter dieser Hitze. Dreissig Grad im Schatten, Mitte Juni, leichte Quellbewölkung, jeden Tag das gleiche. Es soll ein Jahrhundertsommer werden. Morgens um sieben fährt der erste Sprühwagen unter seinem Fenster vorbei. Er wacht im selben Trübsinn auf, der ihn am Abend eingeschläfert hat. (<u>W</u>, page 7)

The generally oppressive condition here is heightened by the extreme heat, which afflicts the entire continent. Suffering itself connotes a low voice of articulation from within the caverns of non-articulated being. "Es fehlt überall am Normalen, das ihm jetzt guttäte" (<u>W</u>, page 7). This apparent need for a generalized (non-specific) state of moderation is qualified later in the text when separation--that traumatically extreme emotional state which is the locus of the protagonist's suffering--is designated as that which is in fact general and normal.

> Jeder, der einer Trennung oder Zerstörung ausgesetzt ist, erfährt dies als das Negative und als das Besondere, während ihm das Zusammenbleiben als das Positive und das Allgemeine erscheint. In Wahrheit liegen die Verhältnisse jedoch umgekehrt, und das Negative, das Scheitern, die Trennung, der Irrtum machen das Allgemeine aus, wofür allein schon Zahlen und Tatsachen sprechen. So ermittelt schliesslich die äusserste Subjektivität des Scheiterns den einzig verlässlichen Erfahrungswert für das Wort 'normal', das ja im übrigen ziemlich unnahbar ist. (W, pages 25-26)

This identification of extreme subjectivity with normalcy raises the question as to the very specificity of experience. Indeed, Die Widmung manifests the quest for the articulation of this specificity against the background of generality, understood both as the experiential oppression of non-articulated being and as the positive sense of human community.[8] Schroubek has, at times, gladly found comfort in the non-articulation of specificity voiced in the language of general identity.

> [. . .] überall wo es Kunden gibt, ensteht dieses Gerede über Gott und die Welt und des Menschen Schicksal vom Wunderkind zum Unglückswurm. Es kommt immer wieder vor, dass er sich darin geborgen oder zumindest ganz gut aufgehoben fühlt, zumal wenn er selbst nicht mitreden muss. Er liebt das Geschwätz, weil es Überfluss ist. Wieviele unsinnige Wiederholungen gebrauchen die Leute, wieviele Widersprüche und Namen Dritter und doch, ohne sich zuzuhören, erzielen sie fast immer die schönsten Übereinstimmungen. Solange niemand schreit oder befiehlt, solange niemand in wirkliche Ausdrucksnot gerät. (W, page 9)

This last sentence, however, characterizes precisely Schroubek's situation. His crisis of articulation, a potentially fatal one,[9] is linked quite clearly to his separation from Hannah, a brutal abandonment that remains incomprehensible to him. It is a situation that reveals the very depth of that fundamental of all human fears. "[Die Trennung] rührt unmittelbar an den Ursprung aller Angst und weckt ihn auf. Sie greift mit einem Griff so tief, wie überhaupt Leben in uns reicht" (W, page 27). Schroubek rejects the popular, psychoanalytical notion that separation represents a death in life, to be overcome by continued participation in the active life (W, pages 36-37). Schroubek quits his job at the bookstore and arranges his business affairs such that he will not, for any reason, have to leave his apartment, where he devotes himself to the sole task of keeping a journal to be presented to Hannah upon their reunion. "Ich überbrücke eine gefährliche Unterbrechung unseres Gesprächs" (W, page 37). The crisis of articulation is not a stagnant one: "Mein Verlassensein von H. nimmt zu" (W, page 21). The crisis becomes progressively more acute, and Schroubek's journal entries comprise a desperate attempt to stay the crisis of abandonment through the articulation of his present experience in Hannah's absence.

The crisis of articulation confronted by Schroubek extends, moreover, beyond his emotional trauma of the present. It likewise characterizes his relationship to his own past experiences on several different levels. Void of the contours that would allow him a sense of his own specificity, his childhood memories flow into his tormented present, rendering the two virtually indistinguishable.

> Jetzt, kurz nach dem Zusammenbruch der Lust, sind dieselben Schmerzen wieder da, die er schon als Kind empfand. Es ist ihm, als sei er überhaupt nicht vom Fleck gekommen. Vielleicht lebt er ohne Vergangenheitssinn wie Schlemihl ohne seinen Schatten. Nach einunddreissig Jahren, denkt er, äusserlich gesehen, ein halbes Leben ohne Biografie. [. . .] Dreissig Jahre ausgewogene Gegenwart, in der er gross wurde und klein blieb [. . .]. (W, page 15)

Here, the eternal present exerts the oppression of unarticulated (unappropriated) experience. "Schon wieder heute. Der wievielte Teil eines welchen Ganzen?" (W, page 32) begins the second section of Schroubek's journal. Yet, the present is not only oppressive, and the memory of the past is not only emancipatory. There is, on the other hand, the memory of continuity, which deadens the living dimension of past experience.

> Dem Gedächtnis der Dauer erscheint alles ebenbürtig präsent. Anstelle der Differenz, anstelle eines Zeitmasses, das zwischen Hoffnung und Widerspruch, Erinnerung und Fortschritt unterscheiden kann, vermehrt sich eine seltsam gedrängte, sammlerische, nervöse Synchronität. (W, page 16)

The authoritative capacity of memory tends to dominate the present by silencing it, as the following passage conveys:

> Die dröhnende Lautsprecherstimme von der Erinnerungstribüne antwortet dem undeutlichen, erregten Zwischenrufer aus der Gegenwartsmenge mit grosser Gelassenheit. 'Ruhig, mein kleiner Schreihals, ruhig! Bedenke, am Ende wirst du nichts gesagt haben, gar nichts. Denn ich allein werde dir immer Mund und Stimme gewesen sein.' (W, page 24)

Memory of the past can likewise silence both the present of now and the lived present of the past by structuring it according to preconceived categories of experience. The imagined "Verhör über einen gewissen Zwischenfall in den Kindheitstagen" (W, pages 92-95) has an unnamed authority questioning an unnamed subject about the possible sources and manifestations of his disease, knowledge of which the subject denies. The subject's response to the goal-oriented questions are vague and unsatisfactory to the interrogators: he does not know, he cannot remember. The critical allusion to psychoanalysis is clear and becomes even clearer when Schroubek rejects the analyst as potential partner in the quest for personal articulation.

> Ich liege ihm gewissermassen nur Modell, insofern er aus meinem Gegurgel das abstrakte Werk seiner Menschenkenntnis formt, von dem ich selber recht wenig zu Gesicht bekomme. (W, page 98)

Schroubek responds with indifference to psychology's eagerness to explain his experience by citing, for example, an Oedipal complex.

> Unterdessen will ich mich weiterhin einer Art der Analyse zuwenden, deren Worte an der Realität des Unbewussten mitwirken und diese eher zu vermehren suchen, statt sie der alternden Idee einer Entwicklung zu unterwerfen. (W, page 41)[10]

This notion of multiplying levels of reality as opposed to reducing them not only reflects a critique of psychoanalytical models but also raises the issue of the telos of literature. The passage on a childhood interrogation is followed immediately by a commentary on Dante's accidiosi:

> [. . .] sie haben die Fähigkeit verloren, eine deutliche Sprache zu sprechen. Aus ihrem Mund quillt ein unverständliches Gurgeln, sie blubbern im Schlamm. Nur der Dichter versteht sie und kann ihr Kauderwelsch übersetzen. (W, pages 95-96)

In the textual context of Die Widmung, this passage challenges literature to mediate the living dimension in which past and present coincide as equals, in fact, as inseparable albeit not unarticulated components of experience. The present is neither void of past nor its mere end-product. Similarly, the past cannot be reduced to neatly closed systems, for it too had its own present, manifest in the human subject that lived it.

By the same token, the crisis of articulation with regard to Schroubek's past addresses the shortcomings of yet another system of categorizing human experience, i.e., politics. Schroubek's political knowledge of National Socialism is filtered, first and foremost, through his physical and emotional perceptions of his father, who despised the Nazis but did not fight them. "Durch ihn hat er im Affekt erfahren, was politisch ist, lange bevor er mitreden kann" (W, pages 10-11). The communicative as well as cognitive powers of affect are silenced by traditional political categories, just as Schroubek's political enlightenment taught him to rise above--but in appearance only--the rowdy influence of sexual drives on political discourse.

> Das Qualvollste, das Unauslöschliche daran scheint ihm heute der tiefe Wirrwarr zu sein, der in den späteren Jungensjahren entstand, als sich politischer Eifer und sexuelle Triebmanöver miteinander vermengten. Nichts mehr hielt seinen Begriff, alles wurde im Affekt gesagt, und die verborgenen Motive liehen den vorgeschützten ihre subversive Kraft. (W, page 11)

Even now, Schroubek occasionally wonders about the personal historical context of a political statement.

> Die Erregung lenkt ihn ab und die Frage: was steckt dahinter? wo nimmt der Redner seinen Eifer her? beschäftigt sein Interesse stärker, als es für das Verständnis von Programmen und Argumenten nützlich sein kann. (W, page 12)

This underscoring of affect does two things. First, it negates the stark truth value of streamlined, generalized and generalizable, categories that claim to comprehend human experience but in truth explain it into non-existence. "Man muss den ganzen Menschen kennen, um zu verstehen, was er im einzelnen meint" (<u>W</u>, page 100). Second, it establishes a connection between sexuality and language, between desire and memory. "Niemals habe ich eine grössere Freiheit und Sicherheit in der Sprache gefunden als im Dialog, der unter Einfluss eines körperlichen Verlangens geführt wurde. Begehren und Gedächtnis reizten einander, das eine exaltierte im Schutz des anderen" (<u>W</u>, page 28). The disruption of this integral connection results in the loss of articulation ("die Stimme"). Pondering the loss of this connection, which he has in common with the cleaning woman, Mrs. N., Schroubek finds neither one of them has a sense of integral physical identity, albeit for different reasons. The cleaning woman has alienated her body through utilization--"parallel als Instrument für Arbeit und Sexualität; infolgedessen körperliches Selbstgefühl gleich null" (<u>W</u>, pages 68-69)--while Schroubek ascertains virtually no use for his body at all: "physisches Schweigen" (<u>W</u>, page 69). The cleaning woman has had no enlightenment; Schroubek suffers from too much (<u>W</u>, page 68). The crisis of articulation manifest in Schroubek's sexual silence thus reaches back to his childhood memories of his father--his introduction to politics and German history and the implied crisis of <u>their</u> articulation--as well as out to the woman who is absent, as both sexual and conversational partner.[11]

A third level of past experience that gets lost in the crisis of articulation is the relationship with Hannah itself, the experience of her desertion.  Once again, psychoanalysis is faulted for killing lived experience by squeezing it into preconceived categories.

> Man willigt irgendwie in die Erkenntnisse von damals ein, findet sie endlich bestätigt durch eigene Anfälligkeiten und Leidensspuren--ohne je den Verdacht aufzugeben, dass das zu früh und erfahrungslos Gewusste selbst zu den Erregern der gegenwärtigen Krankheit gehört. (W, page 88)

Schroubek bemoans the psychoanalytical eradication of Hannah herself as well. "Ausgerechnet das, was mich am tiefsten trifft, verschwindet in ein Schema von Betroffenheit, in dem vor lauter Papa und Mama der eigentliche Leidensgegenstand, meine einzige Freundin kaum noch fühlbar ist" (W, pages 101-102).  Memory is, however, a Janus figure. To be sure, Schroubek needs his "Urlaub zum Erinnern" (W, page 37), but he himself is aware of the danger implicit in memory as a system of categorizing--externalizing--the past.  "In Erinnerung bleibt man sich immer als Gehender, die Erinnerung macht alles zur Passage--aber wie war das Warten und Versäumen, wie das Nicht-mehr-weiter-Wissen? Die Erinnerung schweigt davon" (W, page 40).  More precisely, memory can tie the loose ends of human experience by using the hangman's knot to stop vital circulation.  For this reason, Schroubek avoids narrated memories, which would effectively execute the object of his desire, Hannah.  "Er erzählte ja nicht, er hoffte!" (W, page 106).  Remembering must be vibrant if it is to contribute to the struggle for articulation.  When Schroubek writes: "Vielleicht könnte ich den Sommer überstehen, wenn ich ihr zurückgebliebenes Eau de Cologne regelmässig benutze. Der Duft würde mir die schlimmste Gegenwart vom Leib halten" (W, page 32), he refers of course to the acute awareness of Hannah's absence. The reference to the textual interplay between present and past goes beyond this: "die schlimmste Gegenwart" is the one void of any past, for it denies the subjective integrity of experience.[12] It is noteworthy that Schroubek's most immediate confrontation with his past experience with Hannah comes in the mediated form of Fritz, whose desertion by Hannah echoes Schroubek's own and allows for the common designation of Fritz as Schroubek's double. Yet, they are doubles only to the extent that they are clones of thousands of other men whose lovers have abandoned them; the double identity between Fritz and Schroubek is, at best, non-identity. Schroubek must reject this bond with Fritz--"Ich bin kein Leidensgenosse" (W, page 110)-- since it squelches his own specificity. Fritz is characterized at different times as both evidencing "Ausdrucksverstopfung" (W, page 109) and dampening "Erinnerungswut" (W, page 49). Fritz thus embodies the crisis of articulation and the absence of integrated memory. What distinguishes Schroubek from Fritz is the former's writing.[13] The crisis of personal articulation thus emerges--not surprisingly so in a text by Botho Strauss--at the same time as a crisis of language.

"[. . .] die 'averbale Kommunikation' erscheint der nostalgischen Linken nun als höchste Form der Kommunikation, und just in einer Zeit, da sie eine neue Sprache bräuchte, feiert sie Orgien der Sprachlosigkeit."[14] Michael Schneider's lament bespeaks, not a shift in paradigms, but a loss of paradigmatic faith characterizing the mid- and late 1970's. The domination of the political and/or psychoanalytical concept over experience is at the heart of <u>Die Widmung</u>. A variety of images attest to the dilemma of language alienated from experience.[15] Schroubek's hairdresser tells of his dire thirst for milk in Manhattan. "Keine Milch, Whisky überall, aber kein Tropfen Milch, kriegen Sie nicht, so einen Teppich hatte ich auf der Zunge. . . " (W, page 8). The world of this man's most fundamental needs is at odds with the environmental system which does not acknowledge the legitimacy of those needs. This is a type of crisis of articulation, one which manifests itself at the juncture between articulated need (milk) and systemic negation (whisky). A piece of dredging equipment lying on the ground reminds Schroubek of a dead man whose dentures lie next to him; the means of articulation have been expropriated from the human subject and its living sphere of activity. "Sinnüberladene leere Schaufel--das Ding ist nur noch ein unscheinbares Anhängsel am übermächtigen Symbol" (W, pages 33-34). Perhaps the most poignant situational image of the crisis of articulation perpetrated by conceptual systems alienated from experiential specificity is the account of the Mongoloid child who tries to tell his mother, sitting next to him and absorbed in her knitting, what he actually sees in the zoo: a pigeon has landed on the giraffe's head. He manages to say "Giraffe," but this fixed category hardly conveys the child's particular vision. The child's physical strain is intense but finally gives way to defeat when the mother, who fails to look up from her knitting, responds with an affirmation of a standard definition, which is grossly inappropriate to the child's experience and effectively silences his attempts to articulate anything at all. "Der überschüssige Sinn, den die generalisierende Bestimmung produziert--sie trifft zu and zugleich daneben--bringt das Kind zum Schweigen."[16] Both the child and his mother are, in effect, <u>Sprachbehinderte</u>. This crisis is not one of individual but of social proportions.

> So ergeht es uns nicht anders als jenem abessinischen Eingeborenen, der einen wichtigen Mythos nicht mehr wusste und sich deshalb nicht erklären konnte, weshalb er zu verschiedenartigen Anlässen ein Stück Butter auf dem Kopf trug. 'Unsere Vorfahren kannten den Sinn der Dinge, aber wir haben ihn vergessen.'
> Wir kennen den Sinn der unzähligen Überbleibsel, in denen wir uns ausdrücken, noch sehr viel weniger. Das allermeiste ist uns Butter auf dem Kopf. (<u>W</u>, pages 84-85)[17]

The emphatic alienation from one's experience underscores the dilemma of contemporary language. Some type of articulation is, on the one hand, necessary and desirable; yet, the language most commonly applied to experience effectively negates it--qua experience--by positing its truth content outside the human agent. Schroubek's own response to this is ambivalent. A grammatically correct German sentence offers him solace in the face of his own unarticulated chaos, just as the body parts of the passengers on a crowded bus keep him standing without any effort on his part (<u>W</u>, pages 9-10). "Jeder Satz, gemacht und ihm entfremdet, wurde als Ding unter Dingen begrüsst [. . .]" (<u>W</u>, page 105). The designation of Schroubek's sentences as objects just like any others illuminates his catastrophic encounters with things in his apartment. The damage done by the honey he spills on his carpet is nothing compared with the effects of his frantic attempts to clean it up (<u>W</u>, pages 71-73). The comical desperation in his efforts to fix the flushing system on his toilet is likewise revealing. A stuck chain causes the toilet to overflow. Schroubek's first reaction is to close the door on the problem and ignore it, but fearing an encounter with the building custodian, he decides to do the repair work himself. Resorting to a pair of scissors in place of hammer and pliers, he climbs onto the plastic cover of the toilet, only to find it cannot support his weight.

> Richard rutschte ab, schlug mit dem Gesicht gegen die Wand, die Brille sprang herunter, und die aus den Fingern gekippte Schere fiel mit der Spitze auf seinen Oberarm und dann zu Boden. Er richtete sich auf und stieg aus der Kloschüssel. Er wimmerte vor Schrecken. Das Wasser strömte unvermindert von der Höhe und über den rechten Arm rann ein dünner Streifen Blut. (W, page 74)

This scene frequently causes comment on Strauss' "slapstick" humor, but its textual significance lies in the connection between words and things as alienated artifacts. Tellingly, Schroubek designates his toilet adventure as his last "Stummfilm" (W, page 75). The crisis of language precludes the appropriation of experience. The lovelorn Polish girl who commits suicide by consuming a variety of objects in her environment--"vier Löffel, drei Messer, neunzehn Münzen, zwanzig Nägel, sieben Fernsterriegel, ein Messingkreuz, einhundert und eine Nadel, einen Stein, drei Glasscherben und zwei Perlen ihres Rosenkranzes" (W, page 39)--literally dies because her environment (the objects of her experience) cannot be thus appropriated. The street prostitute, on the other hand, challenges the standard function of a traffic light by appropriating it for her own use. "Dabei bediente sie sich des Stop-Zeichens als einer Art Reklamesignal für ihren Körper und setzte den öffentlichen Zweck der Ampel ausser kraft" (W, page 35). Since this is done only for business purposes, however, the prostitute merely replaces one alienated function of the traffic light with another. The crisis of the true appropriation of experience is extreme, and the language serving that appropriation is just as ineffective as the windshield wipers on the automobiles caught in an unbelievable hail storm (W, page 122). Another situational image conveying the severity of the crisis of experience and articulation is the tale of the painter-prisoner who commits suicide after twenty-two years of prison life. Instead of painting historical costumes, he yearns to paint landscapes but can no longer imagine them and refuses to paint them from prints.

> Dabei war er, wie ich glaube, bis an jene tödliche Grenze der Nachahmung gelangt, die den Meisterkopisten plötzlich vor seinem Machwerk zurückschrecken lässt. Er aber wollte kein Kopist sein und sah voller Verzweiflung, dass er, gerade wenn er sein Äusserstes gab, doch immer nur das äusserst Ähnliche zustande brachte. Er hatte sich ans Ende seiner künstlerischen Bewegungsfreiheit gemalt. Eine zweite Zelle von erstickender Enge umgab ihn, aus der keine Fluchtwege nach innen mehr möglich waren. (W, page 30)

It might be argued, as vom Hofe and Pfaffe do, that this passage refers to the virtual impossibility of art in our time,[18] but to do so would be to underestimate the broader implications for experience beyond the artistic one. The prisoner is not actually prevented from expressing that which he desires to express--i.e., painting landscapes --while he is denied the appropriate tools to do so. Paint and brush are available, to be sure, but he is forcefully refused access to the actual experience of that which he longs to express. The crisis of alienated experience and articulation has rather dire consequences: in this case, death.

Copied landscapes, like the plagiarized texts in "Theorie der Drohung," deny the subjective agent of experience and hence preclude experience itself as anything but alienated self-experience, external to the subject. Another word that connotes the same categorical negation of experience is repetition. The photographer's assistant is so inept with objects that he is characterized as handicapped; his wife calls him a "'Vernichtungstrampel'" (W, page 75). He chronically--repeatedly --destroys everything he touches. Yet, he is astonished anew every time the same thing happens to him.

> Da erkannte Richard, worin die Lebenstechnik dieses Behinderten bestand: er hielt das Element und den Begriff der Wiederholung aus seinen Erfahrungen heraus; er beugte sich nicht ihrer Macht. (W, page 79)

The photographer's assistant thus preserves the living dimension of his experience by refusing to categorize it or acknowledge it as repeated (and hence alienated) experience. The question of repetition is raised again in one last rebus, in fact, the one with which Die Widmung closes. A "Wunschkonzert" on television brings a popular singer from days of yore back for a repeat, live performance. He does not sing but tries to lip synchronize the words to his own record.

> Der aus der Vergessenheit herbeigezerrte Künstler besass weder die Übung noch, in diesen Minuten, das Gedächtnis, sein Lied einwandfrei lippensynchron vorzutäuschen. Einmal wagte die Kamera eine Grossaufnahme, sprang aber sofort erschrocken zurück. Denn während die Erinnerung noch in grossen Tönen sang, war der Mund des alten Mannes plötzlich zugefallen und zuckte textvergessen und murmelte Flüche. (W, page 145)

This image has been subject to various interpretations. Vom Hofe and Pfaff stress the singer as artist and his failure to reproduce his song as the end of art; Beicken reads the passage as a "Vergänglichkeitsallegorie." Michels grants Beicken's point but extends the significance of the passage to emphasize the singer's inability to remember (i.e., repeat) his song. The scratches on the record, Michels argues, attest to the fact that the older generation's easy forgetfulness of its own past is no longer tenable.[19] These aspects can, however, be subsumed under the crisis of experience and articulation. It is not by any means tragic that the singer cannot synchronize his own text. Indeed, it would be worse if he could, since that would effect a repetition of time as well as of experience. What is crucial in the image of this "Wunschkonzert" is precisely the disjuncture between present and past. The singer fails <u>because</u> he tries to repeat the past, which he thus honors as dead memory. What is needed, the text tells us, is a diachronic relationship between past and present with its locus in the human subject. This relationship, in turn, must find articulation through a new medium.

"Nur noch das Schreiben schützt Richard vor dem Verlust jeglicher Geschichtsverbindlichkeit: Schroubek schreibt ja weiter und in seiner Schrift läuft er Hannah 'auf der Asymptote nach'."[20] Schroubek's own writing is seen, and quite rightly so, as that instance through which he seeks access to his own history, to his lost lover: in short, to himself. The writing process is certainly much more than a mere substitute for Hannah's presence.[21] Most of the critics who have treated <u>Die Widmung</u> posit a more complex relationship inherent in writing as a means to articulate the self.[22] Based on absence, however, either of Hannah or any integral identity between concept and experience, writing becomes at best a negative articulation of self.

"Das Schreiben stiftet den Zusammenhang als Verlust."[23] What this critical position fails to take into account are the structural ambiguities within the text itself with regard to Schroubek's writing. As a sole voice, Michels introduces these ambiguities into the discussion on Die Widmung when he points out Schroubek's double aversion: on the one hand, to the textual petrification of his name (his self) and, on the other hand, to the petrification of self in an unarticulated, eternal present.[24] The ambivalence of the writing process becomes quite clear when we compare two passages pertaining to the textual articulation of Schroubek's own name.

> Das erste Wort, das er deutlich schreiben kann, ohne Lücken zwischen den Buchstaben, ist Richard, der eigene Name. Als es fertig ist, bringt er es den Eltern und sie legen es in die Mappe ein, in der schon sein erster Zahn, seine ersten Haare, seine ersten Fingernägel aufbewahrt werden. Sie legen seine Schrift zu den ausgeschiedenen und leblosen Dingen seines Körpers, die sie für ihn sammeln wollen. (W, page 18)

> Was ist aus dem Kind geworden, das vor dem ersten Wort, das es selber schrieb, die Flucht ergriff, von seinem Erstgeschriebenen mit Entsetzen abliess und sich nicht bereit fand, es fortzuführen? Meine Güte, ein Buchhändler ist dann aus ihm geworden. [. . .] Bis ihn ein Liebesunglück aus seinem Beruf und dem Umlauf der Bücher herausschleuderte und so weit zurück schickte, dass er sich zuletzt vor seinem erstgeschriebenem Wort wiederfand und nun, gierig und mühsam, alles versuchte, daran anzuknüpfen, es endlich fortzusetzen. (W, pages 119-120)

Here we have essentially two approaches to the writing process. The first relegates the written word to the status of a finished product: alienated from the writing subject. Like the externalized memory of the old singer (the record), the word becomes a dead thing. The second approach seeks to reinstate the writing process as a living connection between unarticulated self and diachronic text "[. . .]

infolgedessen bildet das Schreiben (das ich immerhin brauche, damit irgend etwas nach aussen kommt und ich nicht ganz durch mich verschluckt werde . . .) die aufbegehrende Mitte all dessen, was verstopft, geteilt und eingeschnürt ist" (W, page 27). Schroubek's journal entries thus become the meeting ground between past and present, between interior and exterior. It is the locus of the self trying to articulate and thus appropriate experience. The association between Schroubek's text and his dialogue with Hannah is made quite clear. Bridging "eine gefährliche Unterbrechung unseres Gespräches" (W, page 37), "das gewissenhafte und entsetzliche Protokoll ihrer Abwesenheit [. . .] sollte die Lücke zwischen dem Abschied und der Wiederkehr ausfüllen, so dass sich später das Ganze eines niemals abgerissenen Gesprächs wiederherstellen liess" (W, page 106). Yet, the living dimension manifest in Hannah's person is absent from the text except as the object of Schroubek's desire, and it is not a given that he will be able to reinstate a vital relationship to his experience. He is of course himself the key to this task. "Richards Material war sein eigener Zustand [. . .]" (W, page 106). He can only come closer to Hannah, to his experience of her abandonment, through himself. At the same time, there are indications that Schroubek is aware of the problematic nature of his attempts to speak in the first person. "Ich habe mich jemandem anvertraut, der sich selbst verleugnet" (W, page 21). This first incidence of Schroubek speaking the voice of the first person in fact addresses his self-denial. The first-person voice of the journal entries denies itself. We may well ask, how does the assertion of the self effect its opposite? When Schroubek painfully admits that he has no idea why Hannah has left him, he concludes: "Ich selber bin der ganze Grund und krieg ihn nicht zu fassen" (W, page 115).[25] This statement is particularly revealing in light of a comparable passage in "Theorie der Drohung," in which the narrator writes: "[. . .] ich war aller meiner Rätsel Lösung./ Aber diesmal nicht, diesmal kam es ganz anders" (TD, page 86). In the earlier text, the solution to the narrator's puzzle was, in large part, located in Lea, the externalized perception of his repressed present and past. "Theorie der Drohung" followed the gradual re-internalization of that perception, thus voicing the hopeful challenge to the text. The fact that Hannah figures in such radical and complete externalization from the protagonist attests to the increased severity of the crisis of articulation. Hannah voices neither past nor present; she is characterized primarily by silence. The words she does speak at the final encounter are mundane and vapid; her response to Schroubek's question as to why she called consists of "'Schon erledigt [. . .] Inzwischen ist es okay'" (W, page 138). She neither tells him why she left nor does she read his journal entries, which after all are dedicated to her. This radical externalization renders Hannah's fate comparable to that of the singer's memory, Schroubek's first tooth, and his first written word: his own name. The "I" of the journal entries runs the risk of perpetrating the same alienation on itself. "Ich habe mir einen kleinen Satz erfunden, in den ich ab und zu hineinschlüpfe, wenn ich mir nichts mehr vorstellen kann" (W, page 29). This is a dangerous escape route, for it precludes the possibility of Schroubek's reunion with Hannah. "Nur wenn ich nicht in der ersten

Person schreibe, sehe ich sie, in fünf, sechs Monaten, wieder nebeneinander sitzen, Hannah und mich [. . .]" (W, page 118). This may seem illogical at first, since we have already ascertained that Schroubek's self is the key to his experience. The first person that forecloses the articulation of that experience is in effect the first person that appears as alienated, dead text. Even the sentence just cited evidences the ambivalent possibilities of writing in the first person, inasmuch as it rejects the first person but speaks it at the same time. Schroubek is conscious of this ambivalence. "Er konnte es einfach nicht mehr beurteilen, ob sein verschärftes Notieren ihn eher tiefer verletzte, als er es ohne dies war, oder, im Gegenteil, ihn immer wirksamer kurierte" (W, page 58). Is it "lange Überanstrengung" or "zähe Vernachlässigung seiner selbst" (W, page 142)? Both are possible. Schroubek's last known entry into his journal--"'Ich bin noch nicht ganz am Ziel . . .'" (W, page 144)--is subject to immediate erasure, "denn so liess sich nicht an das Voranstehende anknüpfen" (W, page 144). The positing of a goal outside oneself precludes the diachronic articulation of the text.[26] The telephone symbolism throughout the text is thus quite apt. Schroubek's final (written) message to Hannah reads: "'Bittet dringend um Anruf'" (W, page 144). His initial euphoria on the occasion of Hannah's first telephone call --"Die Verbindung ist wiederhergestellt, die Sperre gebrochen!" (W, page 61)--proves false, not least of all be- cause Fritz receives the call and not Schroubek. What is needed to break the crisis of identity and language is the initiation of the living, diachronic connection.

The narrative voice of Die Widmung itself speaks the ambivalent voice of hope and despair with regard to the crisis of articulation. The text at large is not identical with Schroubek's journal entries, which comprise the middle section ("Für H.") between "Die Widmung" and "Berlin ohne Ende." With an eye to the preceding discussion of the importance of the voice of the self, it is striking that the first and last sections avoid any use of the unmediated "I", but are narrated in the third person. The middle section consists of eleven subdivisions which vacillate between and sometimes mix the first and third persons. Michels reads the retreat into the third-person narrative voice as an anchor in a sea of ambiguity.

> Die Angst davor, das eigene Selbst als konturenlos, als diskontinuierlich und treibend zu erfahren, ohne dass letztlich gefürchtet werden müsste, es könnte gänzlich zerfallen, lässt das Erzähler-Ich nach dem Modell der Besitzergreifung gerade die Schrift zum Medium der Selbstvergewisserung machen: in der Selbstdistanz der dritten Person wird eine Bindung behauptet, die der Schrift die Aufgabe einer nicht mehr bestimmten, vergangenen Metaphysik zutraut, das Vergängliche, Zerfliessende halten zu können.[27]

This so-called security is deceptive: it rests solely on the text as alienated externalization of the self. The clue to the narrative schizophrenia in Die Widmung lies instead in the notion of "Biograf": "das Leben hat, nach der Niederwerfung des Subjekts, damit begonnen, seinen Rest selber zu schreiben" (W, pages 24-25). Schroubek writes: "Seit Wochen verfolgt mich ein winziges, aber überdeutliches Biograf, zu dem ich verzweifelt das zugehörige Subjekt suche" (W, page 40). A life's story (history) from which the subject has been deleted is the identifying mark of the dead text. Die Widmung's narrator reflects on the modus of the text.

> Nun sein in die offenen Hände vergrabenes Gesicht . . . In wessen Hände? Wer hält plötzlich seinen Schädel wie eine aufgeschnittene Melone? Tut es weh oder ist es Geborgenheit, sich von einem Fremden beschrieben zu fühlen, einem getreuen Biografen der leeren Stunden, von jemandem, der bis zuletzt den Überblick bewahrt? (W, page 44)

By itself, this passage might imply just that security to which Michels refers. Its textual context, however, has the opposite effect. The narrative Überblick is analogous to psychoanalytical and leftist political theories that deny the human subject any status as a living being whose experience extends beyond the realm of existing categories. The fact that Die Widmung closes with a section articulated in the third person merely underscores the urgency of the crisis of language that allows only for alienated subjectivity. Schroubek does not necessarily abandon writing altogether. He merely concludes: it cannot be done this way. The implication is, clearly, there must be another avenue open to the appropriation of self and experience. Schroubek recalls his travels back and forth between West and East Berlin: "Die Trennung einmal ausgeschritten, nicht ohne eine gewisse schizophile Genugtuung, als Sammler des Geteilten" (W, page 40). And yet, Berlin, the divided city, is "ohne Ende." Spatially this is absurd, since the boundaries of Berlin are perhaps more clearly delineated than any other city's. Like the human body that houses the subject, however, it is without finite demarcations in terms of historical time and subjective experience. There is no end to Schroubek's dilemma, but neither does the text close a lid on the subject struggling to overcome that crisis.

<u>Die Widmung</u> is popularly denounced for its alleged homage to the retreat into the private sphere, not least of all because of the manner in which the protagonist retreats into his apartment to cultivate his emotional wounds. This renders particularly interesting the passage explicitly addressing the retreat into the private sphere on the occasion of Dante's <u>accidiosi</u>.

> Was aber heisst 'privat' für den accidioso, den Niedergeschlagenen? Er greift sich in den Mund, bricht vorne die Zähne heraus, zerrt an seiner Zunge, schraubt sie herum, bis sie abreisst, fasst noch tiefer in seinen Rachen, packt sich den Kehlkopf von innen her, zerdrückt die Knorpel und Bänder und gurgelt in diesem blutigen Schlamm. Nun, man wird sagen, er habe sich 'ins Private' zurückgezogen, während er doch gerade diese Zuflucht sich nimmt, ja sogar das letzte Gehäuse des Eignen, den Körper unbewohnbar macht. (<u>W</u>, pages 98-99)

Schroubek in effect renders his apartment--where his self resides--"unbewohnbar." Enclosing himself like an embryo in an artifical womb, he fails initially to realize the implications of the missing umbilical cord, in this case, the telephone connection to the outside world. The final urgent request for a telephone call from Hannah indicates a transition from Schroubek's abortive embryonic existence towards the perceived need for the missing link. We have seen that the crisis of articulation and experience rests, in part, on the externalization of the self, which then appears as the product of experience instead of its subject. This position is not qualified but expanded by the recognition that the self cannot survive, indeed, does not even exist as a monad, complete unto itself. The diachronic longing between self as the subject of experience and that which comprises experience is everywhere evident in Die Widmung, most notably with regard to writing. Schroubek's journal entries only manifest one level of the composite reflection on the writing process as articulated diachronic longing. Even on this level, there are many avenues of diachronic outreach stemming from the writing self. Through his writings, Schroubek reaches out to others (Hannah), to his own emotions of the present, as well as to the experience of his past. This entails reaching out to his childhood, which establishes links not only to his personal history (biography as opposed to Biograf), but also to German social and political history.[28] We must not forget, however, that Schroubek is not the only one who writes. He is an avid reader of literature written by other people, and Strauss himself writes the text we read. Die Widmung is not merely _about_ diachronic longing; the text itself voices that longing.

This brings us to the potential social function of literature or, more precisely, the reading of literature, since Die Widmung posits the literary text only as the juncture of the writing and reading processes (Schroubek writes in the hopes that Hannah will read; he reads what other authors have written; Strauss writes, presumably, in the hopes that his text will be read; we, in turn, read what someone else has written). Schroubek's readings of Busch, Novalis, Amiel, Turgenev, Kleist, Dante, and Goethe occasion a variety of significant comments on the written word as genre. It is contrasted with other artistic media, such as theater or film, precisely on the basis of its inherent quality of diachronic longing.

> Während die sogenannten darstellenden Künste, Theater
> oder Film, im Umgang mit dem Text, sein Geheimnis als
> Rest niemals akzeptieren können, sondern ihn auffüllen
> mit vielen fragwürdigen Mittlerschaften, bis ein kom-
> plettes rauschendes Präsens hergestellt ist. Voll-
> füllte Erscheinung, Gesichter, Körper, Stimmen, Schau-
> spieler--die uns mit ihren fernsehdurchspülten Köpfen,
> mit ihren Autofahrerbeinen vormachen wollen, wie Cäsar
> ging! In Anwesenheit dieser Menschen kann man sich
> nicht erinnern, sie löschen die Schrift, das diachrone
> Verlangen. (W, page 83)29

The blockage of diachronic longing is effected here by a medium in which physical presence and temporal present obscure the historical texture of cultural experience. This negation of historical difference can be related to the principal of resurrection in Die Widmung.30 This principle is first raised, so to speak, in the context of Schroubek's father's daily nap. This death-like state is canceled every day when the father rises to have his afternoon coffee, causing Schroubek to rejoice in his resurrection from the dead. The association with resurrection is further made to Wilhelm Busch's character-- "die scheintote Madam Sauerbrot" (W, page 17)--as well as to the postwar experience of people returning home: "die Ära der Spätheimkehrer, die Vermissten-Religion, die gewaltigen Wiedersehen auf westdeutschen Bahnhöfen, wie er sie in den Wochenschauen der ersten Kinobesuche miterlebt, das sind echte Verwandlungen der Sauerbrot" (W, page 17). The common bond in Schroubek's experience of his father, literature and social history is the solace which the child finds in the "Wiederrufbarkeit des Todes, die mögliche Umkehr aus letzter Abwesenheit" (W, page 17). This last phrase makes a clear connection to Schroubek's adult experience of Hannah's departure. Let us proceed cautiously. The principle of resurrection, like the principles of repetition and copying we have encountered elsewhere in the text, stays death and separation. But what dangers does this entail? The aged Z., deserted by his wife after a long life together, copies her handwritten letters to the point of such perfection that he can no longer distinguish between her originals and his copies. He has in effect lost the object of his desire (W, page 22), the specificity of his experience. Resurrection stills the child's fear of death, but it too negates historical specificity. Not coincidentally, the description of Schroubek's reaction to his father's resurrection is followed by this sentence: "Die Sensation der Auferstehung hat dann Geschichte gemacht in ihm" (W, page 17). Resurrection as an historical principle becomes "Gedächtnis der Dauer" (W, page 16), negating difference while emphasizing sameness. This sameness in turn yields to the crisis of articulation, since it fails to acknowledge the specific textures of historical experience. Yet, these textures are present, as Schroubek's comments on words such as "Entsagung," "Ehre," and "Scham" indicate (W, pages 80-84). These words are rooted in other times. The person of today's world understands their meaning, at best, in quotation marks.

> Etwas verwirrt dich dabei, du spürst ganz deutlich eine kulturelle Erfahrung, die du selber nicht gemacht haben kannst. Doch kaum ist das Wort geäussert, da, merkst du, sinkt es auch schon wieder, unhaltbar schwer, zurück in die Geschichte. Es war wohl doch nur ein Zitat. Ein Paar Gänsefüsschen, das dich gekitzelt hat; das Wort selber hat dich nicht berührt. (W, page 84)

The cultural, historical alienation of the word need not, however, render its content dead experience, severed from the present. Literature has the capacity to mediate the cultural experience of the past.

His reading of Kleist's <u>Marquise von O . . .</u>, for example, leads Schroubek to the following conclusions: "Es gibt Emotionen, die existieren nunmehr durch das Buch," and "Einen [. . .] abrupten Zuwachs von Gedächtnis kann letztlich nur das Buch ermöglichen" (<u>W</u>, page 82. The literary text as cultural memory of historical experience does not function as dead artifact merely documenting the past. Rather, the principle of diachronic longing links the contemporary reader to a social past which is--regardless whether the reader is conscious of the fact--part of that individual's own past, since each individual is at the same time an ontological being. The reading process thus offers a diachronic fullness of cultural experience.

This positive aspect of literature also entails a critical one. Schroubek has the following to say about Turgenev's <u>Fathers and Sons</u>:

> Wir haben vielleicht, in einem solchen Buch, uns selbst auf einer Höhe der Empfindungen kennengelernt, auf der wir irgendwie weiterbeschäftigt werden wollen, nun ausserhalb des Buchs. Wir haben zwar auf imaginärem Wege (des Romans) die vergessene Leidenschaft wieder aufgefunden, aber das, was sie in uns auslöst, ihr Affekt, ist keineswegs imaginär, er ist ganz wirklich, wie Tränen oder Zittern eben wirklich sind; ein Gefühl, das gebraucht werden will, es verlangt nach persönlicher Erfahrung. Aber in unserer alltäglichen Gegenwart entspricht ihm nichts. Dort ist alles auf magere Gemütskost abgestellt. Das wirkliche Leben bietet keine Gelegenheiten, an denen man sich satt erleben könnte. So hockt sie in uns, nach dem Buch, die startbereite Leidenschaft, doch niemand ruft sie ab. Und auf die Dauer schmerzt dies Hocken in der angespannten Krümmung. Wir empfinden mehr als wir verausgaben dürfen. Das Mehr an Wirklichkeit, das sich der Triebleser erwarb, muss er bei sich behalten. (<u>W</u>, pages 81-82)

The designation of the reader as "Triebleser"--compare this with writing as a function of primary instinct in "Theorie der Drohung"-- makes it clear that basic emotional and cultural needs are not being met by contemporary reality. The diachronic longing of literature reaches from that barren present to the treasure of past cultural experience.[31] Prototypical for the barren present with no diachronic sense of past time and social, cultural connections is the medium of television, which figures consistently in <u>Die Widmung</u>. Both Beicken and Michels mention Schroubek's ambivalent relationship to television as well as this medium's opposition to literature.[32] The disparate relationship between the two media is not, however, as complete as it might seem. Initially, Schroubek does not watch much television. "Ich habe im TV schon zuviel verschwinden sehen, als dass mein Herz noch an Bildern hinge" (<u>W</u>, page 39). As his crisis deepens, he watches more and more television until he stops writing and the television is on constantly (<u>W</u>, page 125). This seems quite odd, given that the trait most commonly associated with television is precisely that which characterizes his crisis of articulation: the eternal present void of diachronic contours. Television is a repulsive stream of amorphous time (<u>W</u>, page 69); when Schroubek stops writing, he watches "Heute" and "Tagesschau" over and over again (<u>W</u>, page 104). Yet, he has no experiential sense of current events. "Er verlor das Interesse an den Fragen der Zeit. Vorgänge des öffentlichen Lebens erreichten ihn nur durch TV und erreichten ihn also nicht" (<u>W</u>, page 103). Schroubek is not totally blinded to events affecting society at large. He does <u>see</u> such things through television, particularly in terms of climactic catastrophes (extreme heat, drought, forest fires, hail storm) but he is unable to experience them in a living context.

The television images are unconnected particles of reality. Why, then, does Schroubek find any comfort at all in television?

> Es gab ihm einen Rest von Geborgenheit, einer unter zwanzig Millionen vergessenden Zuschauern zu sein, die wie er im selben Ausstrahlungskäfig, in derselben Isolation denselben Geschehnissen untätig beiwohnten. (W, page 104)

This is not merely Schroubek's masochistic perversion, as might seem to be the case. What we have here is the acknowledgment of a community of viewers denied their subjectivity in the crisis of experience. This is to be sure a negative community of television zombies.[33] At the same time, however, it posits a social community. The crisis of articulation and experience is neither individual nor strictly literary but in fact social. This social component is the common bond between literature and television, the latter being a specifically modern technological form of non-communication. It is the contemporary lack of connectedness, the retarded articulation of diachronic longing, which Schroubek laments when he writes:

> 'Alles scheint geheime Filiation zu sein', höre ich eben noch, im Ausschalten, einen Literaten Goethe zitieren im Radio . . .
> Wenn das wahr wäre! (W, page 102)

It is significant that Schroubek ultimately sits down at his own desk to write and turns on the television at the same time. Neither the blind worship of the literary past, nor the unmitigated denunciation of the television medium characterizes Die Widmung. Rather, the textual interplay between literature and television underscores the diachronic longing between past and present, as well as between the individual and the social--a relationship which extends from the human subject back into cultural history and out toward the contemporary community of subjects alienated from each other, their experience, and their common past. <u>Die Widmung</u> thus poses a literary challenge in a social context while at the same time acknowledging that the crisis at hand cannot be resolved by literature alone.

The opposition to the conceptual domination of lived experience infuses all aspects of <u>Die Widmung</u>, not the least of all its stylistic components. To begin with, the narrative structure of the text refuses to be subsumed under an identifiable plot that could be retold. As Michels puts it: "Das Geschehen wäre dann als Vergangenes veranschaulicht, nicht als Gegenwärtiges."[34] An identifiable plot that could convey the full flavor of the text is foreclosed, first, by the fact that Schroubek seals himself in his apartment, his "experiences" consisting essentially of writing journal entries, watching television, and thinking about Hannah, his childhood, and literature. He constantly refers to the world outside his apartment, although he does not interact with it in a direct way. "Die in den Momentbericht eingestreuten Vergleiche, charakterisierenden Bemerkungen und Reflexionen zeigen, dass sich hier ein Erzähler-Subjekt nicht mehr im Kontinuum einer zusammenhängenden Geschichte erzählt."[35] This <u>can</u> be interpreted as a critical statement regarding the inability to attain or experience identity in contemporary social reality, as when Michels notes the following in his response to Reich-Ranicki's critique of Strauss' discontinuous narrative style:

> Aber gerade die sogenannten Digressionen, die Abschweifungen, Exkurse oder aphoristischen Zwischenbemerkungen stellen auch die in dialektische Bilder entäusserten

> Selbstverständigungsversuche eines erzählenden Subjekts
> dar, dem es unmöglich geworden ist, ein Leben in einer
> einheitlichen erfahrbaren Wirklichkeit zu leben.[36]

This position, however, places the subjective voice (Schroubek) at the center of experiential chaos, further positing that the "Prinzip des Zusammenhangs des Zusammenhanglosen" motivates the act of writing in order to provide the self with contours.[37] Yet, we have already seen that the narrative voice itself is problematic and cannot justifiably be identified as an integral one in the midst of external chaos. The narrative "I" walks the tightrope between externalized (alienated) self and integral writing subject. Furthermore, the emphasis on a suffering but nonetheless identifiable subject obscures perception of the hope that speaks from disharmony. If the subject is seen as lost in the midst of narrative confusion, then the obvious connotation is indeed a negative one. If this confusion is seen in light of the objection to the annullment of experience through <u>a priori</u> conceptual categorization, then the non-identity of plot <u>and</u> narrative voice cannot be seen solely as negative indices of alienation. Instead, they insist on open spaces, a prerequisite for a qualitatively new vision of subjective experience. Michels is perhaps blinded by his consistently hermeneutic interpretation of <u>Die Widmung</u>. In most instances, he shows great insight, but he sees only "das Misslingen von Kommunikation" without questioning the notion of communication and understanding itself. A more extreme example of fitting the text's disjunctures into a cohesive (categorical) interpretive system can be found in the essay by vom Hofe and Pfaff, who, we recall, consider Strauss' work against the background of the aesthetic tradition of ontological subjectivity since Romanticism. They conclude that "[Straussens romantische Ironie] mit der Ontologie eines Identitätssystems korreliert, das wie dasjenige Hegels den Geist mit absoluter Macht ausstattete."[38] The insistence on existing interpretive categories explains why even those critics who look at <u>Die Widmung</u>'s aesthetic structures with a critical eye see only the death of identity, which leads them in turn down the path to aesthetic bliss <u>ex negativo</u>: literature as the place of worship that houses subjectivity married to its own demise.

The negative aspects of non-identity and non-experience are certainly present in the crisis of articulation, the stuff from which <u>Die Widmung</u> is made, but the domination of lived experience is not total. There are open spaces even besides those implicit in the narrative structure of the text. The question as to how one articulates the crisis of articulation finds partial response in Strauss' particular use of the rebus. There are two essential components to the rebus: the image and the riddle. Particularly on the first count, Strauss' use of rebus must be understood in opposition to Freud's use of the same term. We have already noted Strauss' explicit rejection of psychoanalysis as a closed system for interpreting human behavior.[39] Strauss likewise rejects Freud's approach to visual images for the same reason. Freud himself uses the term "Bilderrätsel (Rebus)" in his treatise on dream analysis.[40] Yet, Freudian analysis provides extensive lists of visual symbols and their appropriate meanings, which can in turn be applied to all dreams for purposes of interpretation. Schroubek expresses his dissatisfaction with this methodology on the occasion of his mother's telephone call from Athens. She has remarried and taken a new name, which leads Schroubek to wonder what his own name is:

> So entsteht ein vergnügliches Rebus, das selbst der Amateur-Analytiker leicht auflösen kann. Jedermann wird schnell herausfinden, was mir der Verlust von H. 'in Wahrheit' bedeutet. Aber was ist das für eine trübsinnige Wahrheit? Dass das Unbewusste keinen neuen Schmerz mehr anerkennt. (<u>W</u>, page 101)

Schroubek does not wish to be

> [. . .] schnell ergriffen von alten primären Symbolen: Blindheit, Meer, Haus, Schrift, Pferd. Bei gleichzeitig aggressivem Überdruss an kleineren, 'sozialeren' Symbolen: Spiegel, Geld, Schuhe, Blume, Teig, Uhr--und was dergleichen Plunder uns täglich in seine niedrige Ordnung ruft. (<u>W</u>, page 114)

The allusion to Freud's register of symbols could not be clearer. The Freudian rebus externalizes symbol from dreamer in order to transcribe the latter into a system of behavioral categories. The specificity of individual experience is irrelevant, or silenced by the weighty apparatus of general conceptual patterns. Strauss incorporates rebuses into the text in an altogether different vein. One need only recall the images of the hairdresser looking for milk in Manhattan, the Mongoloid child trying to articulate his vision of the giraffe to his mother, the prisoner refusing to paint landscapes from prints, or the prostitute reappropriating the traffic light--just to name a few-- to note that these are not composites of individual (externalized) symbols but situational images. We are reminded of Schroubek's statement: "Man muss den ganzen Menschen kennen, um zu verstehen, was er im einzelnen meint" (<u>W</u>, page 100). For Strauss, the image <u>is</u> the experiential situation. The quality of riddle in the image does not lend itself to easy decoding along the lines of Freudian symbol analysis but instead persists as riddle in the midst of a situation in which there are no clear guidelines to define or categorize experience. Again, this bears witness both to the crisis of identity as well as to possibilities for circumventing that crisis. Particularly as contrasted with the conception of realism associated with the adolescent magazine Der Späher, the quality of riddle in Strauss' rebuses evidences more possibility than protest. As youths, Schroubek and his peers were encouraged to read Der Späher and participate in its program to foster a sense of reality in young people otherwise seduced by pulp literature. Schroubek describes the project as follows:

> Es war eine Art Bestimmungsbroschüre für die tägliche reale Umwelt. Je nach Beobachtungsgebiet waren typische und seltene Gegenstände aufgezeichnet, die es in der Wirklichkeit zu finden galt, und die, je nach Rarität, mit unterschiedlichen Gewinnpunkten bewertet wurden. (W, page 86)

Schroubek indeed won a great many medals, but the more he played the game, the more he cheated. The cessation in publication of Der Späher did not particularly bother him.

> Ich hatte nach etwa fünfzehn Heften genug von der Wirklichkeit gesehen und wollte wieder zurück in den freien Dschungel. Heute ertappe ich mich gelegentlich dabei, dass ich das Angebot des Sehenswerten ebenso sammlerisch und raritätsbewusst durchmustere, wie ich es als Späher gelernt habe. Zum anderen kann ich kaum das Wort 'Realismus' aussprechen oder 'realistische Methode', ohne dabei als erstes schreckhaft an die Wahrnehmungspflichten zu denken, die mit diesen unsinnigen und unsinnlichen Heftchen verbunden waren.
>
> Das Reale erspähen blieb unbefriedigend. (W, page 87)

The programmatic categorization of objects according to value points and Schroubek's subsequent rejection of that "reality" have much in common with the Freudian register of symbols in keeping with psychoanalytical categories. This is all the more fitting, given that the passage just cited is immediately followed by a description of the excitement Schroubek felt at sixteen discovering Freud and what he thought was a means to unmask reality ("das Reale demaskieren," <u>W</u>, page 87). He found instead the access to his own reality, his experience, blocked by precisely that which was supposed to open that access route. The allusion at the end of the passage to literary realism--one manifestation of which can be found in <u>AutorenEdition</u> literature dealing with the student movement--clearly indicts that approach to literary style on the same charges that psychoanalysis and <u>Späher</u>realism face. Literary texts that posit reality external to the subject and capable of conceptual, generally applicable categorization deny the possibility for lived experience or even any living dimension of the literary text.

Strauss thus insists on the situational image and the riddle for their refusal to bow to facile categorization that effectively negates the subjective agent of human experience and hence experience itself. At the same time, the rebus does not float without any meaning whatsoever on the surface of <u>Die Widmung</u>. The situational image-riddle is itself situated in the body of the text, thus relating diachronically to Schroubek's dilemma.[41] The porous nature of the textual relationship among the individual components is certainly evidence of the crisis of articulation, but even more importantly, it speaks the insistent voice of hopeful, hitherto unchartered possibility. The particular composition of Strauss' rebuses, however, reveals an aesthetic paradox that precludes the full exploration of that possibility. The crisis of articulation is in fact stated quite articulately in these rebuses. Yet, this is the only thing they are capable of articulating. They form perfect bubbles, enveloped but not penetrated by the rest of the text. The interplay between rebus and the rest of the text is a mediated one. This by no means conflicts with the statement of crisis, but it does not allow for its resolution. The figures who populate the rebuses are void of social and historical specificity.[42] Their situations demonstrate a point, but "the point" prevails where a subjective agent of full diachronic dimensions--personal, temporal, social, historical--is absent. This is where the riddle threatens to lose its extension to subjective specificity in a social context and thus threatens to lose its element of hopeful promise as well. The aesthetic option is either to develop the promise by extending the principle of diachronic longing or to relinquish it by allowing the crisis of articulation to dominate the text. For this reason, Die Widmung marks a significant watershed in Strauss' prose. An analysis of Rumor will reveal which path Strauss ultimately chooses.

Notes: Chapter III

[1]Marcel Reich-Ranicki, "Gleicht die Liebe einem Monolog?", Frankfurter Allgemeine Zeitung (September 10, 1977); also in Entgegnung: Zur deutschen Literatur der siebziger Jahre (Stuttgart: Deutsche Verlags-Anstalt, 1979), pp. 330-334.

[2]Botho Strauss, Die Widmung: Eine Erzählung (Munich: Hanser, 1977). Further references to this work will appear parenthetically as W within the text. For a sampling of critical texts in which the crisis of abandonment or separation figures strongly in the discussion of Die Widmung, see Volker Hage, "Das Ende der Beziehungen: Über den Zustand der Liebe in neueren Romanen und Erzählungen: Eine Bestandsaufnahme," Aufbrüche, Abschiede: Studien zur deutschen Literatur seit 1968, ed. Michael Zeller (Stuttgart: Ernst Klett, 1979), pp. 14-25; Klaus R. Scherpe and Hans-Ullrich Treichel, "Vom Überdruss leben: Sensibilität und Intellektualität als Ereignis bei Handke, Born und Strauss," Monatshefte, 73 (Summer 1981), Nr. 2, 188; Michael Schneider, "Botho Strauss, das bürgerliche Feuilleton und der Kultus der Zerfalls: Zur Diagnose eines neuen Lebensgefühls," Den Kopf verkehrt aufgesetzt, oder Die melancholische Linke: Aspekte des Kulturzerfalls in den siebziger Jahren (Darmstadt, Neuwied: Luchterhand, 1981), pp. 236-241; Edgar Wilhelm, "Das Ende der Verhältnisse-- Trennungsproblematik in der gegenwärtigen Literatur," TAZ [Tageszeitung] (July 3, 1980); and Hans Wolfschütz, "Botho Strauss," Kritisches Lexikon zur deutschsprachigen Gegenwartsliteratur, ed. Heinz Ludwig Arnold (Munich: edition text + kritik, 1978), II, no pagination.

[3]Helmut Kreuzer, "Neue Subjektivität: Zur Literatur der siebziger Jahre in der Bundesrepublik Deutschland," Deutsche Gegenwartsliteratur, ed. Manfred Durzak (Stuttgart: Reclam, 1981), p. 90. Klaus Hartung designates separation as "das zentrale Thema der linken Kultur," noting the added component of loneliness in the political context. See Hartung, "Die Repression wird zum Milieu: Die Beredsamkeit linker Literatur," Literaturmagazin, 11 (1979), 60. Hartung does not discuss Die Widmung in this essay.

[4]"Der Roman von Botho Strauss: Qualität bahnt sich immer ihren Weg," Buchreport (November 4, 1977), Nr. 44.

[5]The same perplexed question is also posed earlier in the text (p. 44): "Warum ist sie weggegangen? Er war der Antwort um keinen Schritt nähergekommen."

[6]Paul Konrad Kurz identifies three addressees for Schroubek's dedication (Hannah, the literature Schroubek reads, and the ego he seeks to know) but overlooks the structural function of the text's own dedication. See Kurz, "Botho Strauss: Die Widmung," Über moderne Literatur: Zur Literatur der späten siebziger Jahre (Frankfurt/Main: Josef Knecht, 1979), VI, 78. The English translation of the text thus

detracts somewhat from the structural integrity of Strauss' text. See Devotion: A Novel, trans. Sophie Wilkins (New York: Farrar-Straus-Giroux, 1979).

⁷While it might seem that Schroubek cannot live without Hannah, her absence does not keep him from being. (Hannah's emphatic absence itself represents a marked divergence from the pair figures of the earlier texts.) Schroubek's difficulties asserting his personal identity (speaking the "I" of his own subject) stem rather from problems of language. These will be elaborated within the body of this chapter.

⁸The notion of human community will be given more detailed attention later.

⁹One entry in Schroubek's journal brings the association between Ausdrucksnot and Atemnot home: "Ausgestossen, in Atemnot, aus einem kurzen, würgenden Schlaf. Die panische Gewissheit: das Herz schlägt nicht mehr, es steht! Jetzt, deine letzte Chance, aufwachen, die Lage begreifen, dein stilles Herz selber massieren! Ich sagte: es ist ganz unmöglich, diesen Zustand länger zu ertragen" (W, pp. 27-28).

¹⁰This passage only echoes Strauss' early admiration for Michel Foucault's approach to knowledge and history: "Das archäologische Vergleichen geschehe nicht im Bewusstsein des Vereinheitlichens, sondern des Vervielfältigens." See Botho Strauss, "Versuch, ästhetische und politische Ereignisse zusammenzudenken," Theater heute, 11 (1970), Nr. 10, 61.

Peter Beicken, Gerd Michels, and Michael Schneider all discuss Strauss' denunciation of applied psychological categories. Beicken, citing Strauss' "Negation bisheriger Erklärungsmodelle," also makes the connection between the treatment of psychoanalysis and the treatment of leftist political theories as exemplified in the West German student movement. See Peter Beicken, "'Neue Subjektivität: Zur Prosa der siebziger Jahre," Deutsche Literatur in der Bundesrepublik seit 1965, ed. Paul Michael Lützeler and Egon Schwarz (Königstein/Ts.: Athenäum, 1980), p. 176; Gerd Michels, "Skeptische Melancholie: Zu Botho Strauss' 'Die Widmung'," Textanalyse und Textverstehen (Heidelberg: Quelle & Meyer, 1981), p. 164; and Michael Schneider, "Botho Strauss, das bürgerliche Feuilleton [. . .]," p. 238.

Adorno's critique of psychology is likewise evident in Die Widmung: "Wenn alle Psychologie seit der des Protagoras den Menschen erhöhte durch den Gedanken, er sei das Mass aller Dinge, so hat sie damit von Anbeginn zugleich ihn zum Objekt gemacht, zum Material der Analyse, und ihn selber, einmal unter die Dinge eingereiht, deren Nichtigkeit überantwortet." Likening psychoanalytical procedures to the general division of labor in capitalist society, Adorno claims: "Psychotechnik ist keine blosse Verfallsform der Psychologie, sondern ihrem Prinzip immanent." See Theodor W. Adorno, "Ich ist Es," Minima Moralia: Reflexionen aus dem beschädigten Leben, Gesammelte Schriften (Frankfurt/Main: Suhrkamp, 1980), IV, 69.

Strauss also shares a common bond with the French critics of the Oedipal orientation of Freudian psychoanalysis. Deleuze and Guattari write: "[. . .] statt an der wirklichen Befreiung mitzuwirken, ist die Psychoanalyse Teil jenes allgemeinen bürgerlichen Werkes der Repression, das darin besteht, die europäische Menschheit unter dem Joch von Papa-Mama zu belassen und nie mit diesem Problem zu brechen." Strauss breaks with this critique of "General Freud," however, in that he looks for new, non-finite ways of grasping connections (Zusammenhänge) rather than proclaiming schizophrenia and forgetting as the cure to psychoanalysis. See Gilles Deleuze and Félix Guattari, Anti-Ödipus: Kapitalismus und Schizophrenie I, trans. Bernd Schwibs (Frankfurt/Main: Suhrkamp, 1974), esp. pp. 63 and 87, and Rhizom, ed. Dagmar Berger et al. (Berlin: Merve, 1977), esp. pp. 27 and 40.

[11]The simplistic assertion that sexuality hardly figures at all in Die Widmung takes the absence of "sex scenes" at face value and fails to acknowledge the textual integrity of the work. Reich-Ranicki, for example, makes this mistake in "Gleicht die Liebe einem Monolog?", Entgegung, p. 332.

[12]Note the similar textual function assumed by the fragrance of a woman's perfume in both Die Widmung and "Theorie der Drohung."

[13]Michels comes close to pointing this out. Michels, "Skeptische Melancholie," p. 157.

[14]Michael Schneider, "Von der alten Radikalität zur neuen Sensibilität," Kursbuch, 49 (October 1979), 184-185.

[15]The images here are, more appropriately, examples of rebus (image riddle), the structural implications of which will be discussed later.

[16]Michels, "Skeptische Melancholie," p. 152. Vom Hofe and Pfaff, considering the pigeon as symbolic for the Holy Ghost and the promise of salvation, read this episode in terms of the "verlorene metaphysische Bedeutsamkeit der heilsgeschichtlichen Überbleibsel [. . .]." See Gerhard vom Hofe and Peter Pfaff, "Botho Strauss und die Poetik der Endzeit," Das Elend des Polyphem: Zum Thema der Subjektivität bei Thomas Bernhard, Peter Handke, Wolfgang Koeppen und Botho Strauss (Königstein/Ts.: Athenäum, 1980), p. 110.

[17]Benjamin Henrichs is quite right when he points out the collective nature of Schroubek's affliction but misses the point when he defines the illness as a loss of emotional capacity. The collective ailment is, more appropriately, the moribund capacity to articulate emotions and experience. See Henrich's review of Die Widmung, "Ein Liebesunglück," Die Zeit (September 2, 1977).

[18]Vom Hofe and Pfaff, "Botho Strauss und die Poetik der Endzeit," pp. 127-128.

[19] Beicken, "'Neue Subjektivität'," p. 176 and vom Hofe and Pfaff, "Botho Strauss und die Poetik der Endzeit," p. 128. Although Michels does not actually use the word, the reference here would seem to be to the older generation's history of National Socialism, thus indirectly raising the issue of Vergangenheitsbewältigung. See Michels, "Skeptische Melancholie," pp. 165-166.

[20] Michels, "Skeptische Melancholie," p. 166.

[21] Michael Schneider falsely claims that Schroubek writes as a substitute for his lost lover "--ein eigentlich gespenstischer Vorgang, der von Strauss nirgendwo problematisiert wird." Michael Schneider, "Botho Strauss, das bürgerliche Feuilleton [. . .]," p. 240.

[22] See, for example, Michels, "Skeptische Melancholie," pp. 158-159, and vom Hofe and Pfaff, "Botho Strauss und die Poetik der Endzeit," p. 124.

[23] Beicken, "'Neue Subjektivität'," p. 176. See also Claudia Kalasz, "Vereiste Spuren: Suche nach Erinnerung in Dichtungen von Botho Strauss," Programmheft [Theater der Stadt Heidelberg] (1978/79), Schweppenhäuser, "Tauchen im Schlamm: Zur 'Widmung' von Botho Strauss," Programmheft [Theater der Stadt Heidelberg] (1978/79), Nr. 6, 10, 13, 16-17; and vom Hofe and Pfaff, "Botho Strauss und die Poetik der Endzeit," p. 124.

[24] Michels, "Skeptische Melancholie," p. 156.

[25] A similar passage can be found on p. 44. The association made between Schroubek's loss of Hannah, his journal writing, and mourning yields an interesting constellation in light of the following statement by Freud: "Bei der Trauer ist die Welt arm und leer geworden, bei der Melancholie ist es das Ich selbst." Taking issue with Freudian theory, Schroubek rejects the notion that Hannah has died or that his separation from her represents a death in life. The combination of Schroubek's persistent efforts to relate to external reality (Hannah) and the highly problematic status of his "I" thus conflates the Freudian categories of mourning and melancholy, another example of Strauss' critical approach to Freud. For the pertinent passages in Die Widmung, see pp. 34, 36-37, and 89. See also Freud's essay, "Trauer und Melancholie," Gesammelte Werke, chronologisch geordnet (London: Imago Publishing, 1949), X, 427-446; esp. pp. 431 and 445.

[26] Hannah herself is referred to as a goal (W, p. 89).

[27] Michels, "Skeptische Melancholie," p. 155.

[28] The experience of National Socialism is not analyzed, but it does figure here explicitly for the first time in Strauss' prose work. An allegorical piece from 1963 might conceivably be read against the background of National Socialism. See Botho Strauss, Schützenehre: Erzählung (Düsseldorf: Eremiten-Presse, 1975).

²⁹In light of Strauss' activity as playwright and theatrical director, it would be particularly interesting to do a detailed study on his approach to the function of the theatrical medium as compared with that of the literary text discussed here.

³⁰Christoph Türcke has written on "Auferstehung als schlechte Unendlichkeit: Zum theologischen Leitmotiv des Botho strauss," in the Programmheft ]Theater der Stadt Heidelberg] (1978/79), Nr. 6, 18-29. Türcke analyzes the theological ramifications of "zur Allgegenwart erstarrte Bewegung" in a fascinating essay but grants Strauss' work at best a negative capacity to counter the end of history. My contention is that Die Widmung at least articulates different possibilities for looking at history but by no means presumes its end as an accomplished fact.

³¹Michels' comments on Schroubek's reading habits stress the interplay between fiction and reality but skirt the issue of diachronic longing as projected back onto past cultural experience (Michels, "Skeptische Melancholie," p. 161). Roland Koch of the University of Siegen finds that Schroubek reads literature as a surrogate for life (Koch, unpublished manuscript on "Botho Strauss: Die Widmung, Zur Darstellung einer leidenden Persönlichkeit in Krisensituationen," 1980, p. 12). This is not entirely true, since Schroubek's readings enhance his sense of emotional life without making him feel any less of a void in the reality of his present.

³²Beicken, "'Neue Subjektivität'," pp. 176-177, and Michels, "Skeptische Melancholie," p. 162. Türcke, "Auferstehung als schlechte Unendlichkeit," p. 28, talks about television in terms of the "Sendeschluss der Menschheit." Koch, "Botho Strauss: Die Widmung," p. 18, notes that Schroubek's television habits locate him in the present, whereas he is otherwise characterized by his foible for the nineteenth century.

³³This bond of victimization reminds us of Fredric Jameson's comments on the collectivity of the "we-object," a term borrowed from Sartre's Being and Nothingness. See Jameson, Marxism and Form: Twentieth-Century Dialectical Theories of Literature (Princeton: Princeton University Press, 1971), pp. 249-250.

³⁴Michels, "Skeptische Melancholie," p. 147. See also p. 158.

³⁵Michels, "Skeptische Melancholie, p. 152.

³⁶Michels, "Skeptische Melancholie," p. 147. Beicken, "'Neue Subjektivität'," p. 175, likewise comments on the "Fehlen des Zusammenhangs, der Identität."

³⁷Michels, "Skeptische Melancholie," pp. 148 and 155. See also the related comment on p. 156: "Es bildet sich kein geschlossener Kreis, der biographisch oder psychoanalytisch entschlüsselt würde. Da

es immer der Erzähler ist, der im Mittelpunkt aller 'Ereignisse' steht, führt er in diesen selbstgeschaffenen Inszenierungen Bewegungen aus, die nur noch eine zerfallende Kontinuität in Raum und Zeit besitzen."

[38]Vom Hofe and Pfaff, "Botho Strauss und die Poetik der Endzeit," p. 126.

[39]Michels, "Skeptische Melancholie," p. 164, and Beicken, "'Neue Subjektivität'," p. 176, both point this out as well.

[40]Sigmund Freud, "Die Traumdeutung," Gesammelte Werke, chronologisch geordnet, 4th ed. (Frankfurt/Main: Fischer, 1968), II/III, 284.

[41]Michels comments on the narrator and the giraffe incident: "er relativiert damit die Figuren, indem er sie auf ein endliches Verhältnis zu sich selbst reduziert." Michels, "Skeptische Melancholie," p. 153.

[42]Hans Wolfschütz, for example, points out that the social status of Strauss' figures in general remains only vaguely defined. Wolfschütz, however, concludes from this only that this allows the figures to retreat into an artificially private existence. See Wolfschütz, "Botho Strauss," no pagination.

CHAPTER IV

RUMOR: POLARIZATION


I. <u>RUMOR</u>

While the pair constellations in "Marlenes Schwester" and "Theorie der Drohung" are marked by an ambivalence that is primarily menacing but also hopeful, and while <u>Die Widmung</u> bespeaks a crisis of articulation and the hope of diachronic longing, the paradox governing the pair figures in <u>Rumor</u> has petrified into a double bind from which even a faint glimer of hope has vanished.¹ Sitting on the precipice between the 1970's and the 1980's, <u>Rumor</u> allows for individual components of pivotal pair figures that are much more clearly distinguishable from one another than in any of Strauss' earlier prose pieces. Bekker, the protagonist, is certainly discernible as an individual. At the same time, he can survive as such neither with nor without the following triad: 1) Zachler, head of the Institute for News, where Bekker has worked sporadically for much of his adult life; 2) Grit, Bekker's adult daughter, with whom he has a reunion after ten years' absence; and 3) Bekker's stepfather, commonly referred to as the officer, whose memory repeatedly haunts Bekker. The tension spanning these poles is neither fluid nor dynamic; although they make constant reference to each other, the poles remain rigidly fixed in their respective elements. The diachronic longing, which we have come to know as a principle of hope in Strauss' earlier work, does indeed find a voice in Rumor, but it has become a voice of power, hatred, and humiliation, not love. "'Nur Hass verbindet. Hass, Hass, immer vornean, immer der erste sein'" (R, page 57). Other aspects of diachronic longing, particularly those involving history and social community, are even more persistent in Rumor than they are in Die Widmung or "Theorie der Drohung." It is indeed ironic that of the four texts considered here, the one which is most open diachronically is also the one which pronounces that principle of hope dead upon arrival. The title itself, a term with medieval German and Latin roots, consists of a single word connoting dull but persistent noise, disorder, restlessness. It is Bekker's calling to hear this rumor.[2] "Ich werd mal langsam weiterstreifen, die Stadt hinunter, Grit, weil da im Grund ein Rumor ist, der noch gehört werden will . . ." (R, page 42). The word Rumor figures in some form or another eight times within the text. It marks disjuncture and panic, as in "Risse, Rumor, Gewalt und Unrast" (R, page 52) or "[d]ie Unordnung, die immer noch unterdrückte Rede des Ganzen, ein Rumor bloss, aber überall stärker hervordringend" (R, page 147). The association here with oppressed speech also finds its way into Bekker's apocalyptic vision of "Rumor, Narr und Frau . . ." (R, pages 65 and 66), in which he plays the fool and his daughter is woman. Besides the menacing clamor in the distance, rumor also characterizes Bekker's speech as a drunken fool. The designation of Bekker as "rumorende[r] Nachtwächter" (R, page 197) alludes in fact to an additional, positive aspect of rumor. The vague noise in the distance sounds the alarm to danger, while Bekker challenges the menace by making his own noise. This obviously requires elaboration, but for the time being, it may suffice to note that this latter element actually allows for a diachronic facet in which the element of rumor makes reference to something outside itself. One of Duden's definitions for the verb form (<u>rumoren</u>) reads as follows: "seinem Unwillen Luft machen, gegen etwas aufbegehren."[3] The title of the text thus seems to partake of an ambivalence we have found to be characteristic of Strauss: rumor signifies both attack and counter-attack at the same time. Whereas indistinct murmurs haunt the characters of his earlier works, however, that threat is given much clearer focus in <u>Rumor</u>. Just what it is that spurs Bekker to combat remains to be seen.

Like Strauss' other prose works, <u>Rumor</u> cannot be reduced to a straightforward, chronological progression of plot, something which has caused numerous critics to lament the author's annoying failure--sometimes seen as inability--to create a coherent narrative.[4] Yet, <u>Rumor</u> evidences a more clearly discernible plot progression than any of the works previously discussed. It begins with Bekker's return to Zachler's Institute, where he encounters his daughter, whom he has not seen for ten years. He spends the night of the monthly company party drinking and talking to Grit, who subsequently invites him to share her apartment with her for the interim, inasmuch as she has just curtailed her relationship with Joseph, her placid lover. Father and daughter plan and execute a vacation to the Mondsee, scene of joint vacations dating back to Grit's childhood. The woman's illness puts a painful end to the holiday and entails debilitating surgery, from which Bekker helps her recuperate by attending to household chores. As Grit regains her strength, she finds herself suffocated by her father's increasingly lethargic and slovenly presence; finally, she forces him to move into a hotel. The first line of the text--"Bekker ist tatsächlich zurückgekommen" (R, page 7)--can thus be read as his return to the Institute as well as to Grit, but his return is a tenuous one, particularly with regard to the Institute. Bekker does not confront his former employer directly, nor does he actually return to work for the Institute again. Rather, he encircles Zachler and the Institute obsessively like a fortress he feels compelled to smash without ever initiating a frontal attack. It is the call to challenge his arch enemy that gives Bekker's life meaning and vitality.

> Langsam und zögernd beginnt der Vater davon zu sprechen, wie sehr er Zachler vermisse; wie unverzichtbar ihm seine Feindesstellung gegen diesen Mann sei. Diesen ewig Besseren, gegen den er immer aufbegehrt, der ihn aber auch zur höchsten Anspannung seiner Kräfte herausgefordert habe. Nun finde er sich gänzlich isoliert und abgesperrt von diesem Menschen, den er fast seinen Todfeind nennen möchte, und einen solchen gebe man niemals auf, bevor nicht der Kampf wirklich bis zum Ende ausgetragen worden sei. Doch fürchte er, dass seine Kräfte nachlassen, sein Kampfgeist erlahmen werde, da er ja nicht an ihn herankäme. '[. . .] Man findet im Leben nur einmal einen solchen Gegner, um den es sich lohnt, auf der Höhe seiner Kräfte,--und seines Ansehens!--zu bleiben, und wahrscheinlich ist das eine noch seltenere Kostbarkeit als die sogenannte grosse Liebe.' (R, pages 54-55)

Bekker does not know how to reach Zachler to call him forth to battle but is nonetheless driven by the need to do so.[5] He has the distinction of being the only employee who has ever tried to leave the Institute more than once. "Meines Wissens bin ich der einzige, der es mehr als ein Mal versucht hat" (R, page 23). Everyone else who ever tried to escape the oppression of the Institute did so only once and returned to the fold with a broken will and a reliable, unquestioning loyalty to the Institute. The employees are constantly reminded of how difficult life outside the Institute would be.

> So wurden und werden auf allen Stufen und Etagen die Leute bei Zachler in Abhängigkeit bewahrt. Sie werden künstlich mittelmässig und scheiternd gehalten, damit sie sich, bei fortdauernd niedrigem Gehalt, ängstlich an die Betriebsfamilie, an Zachler und die Sektorenvorstände anklammern. Natürlich gab es auch ausser mir hin und wieder jemanden, der aus eigenen Stücken die Firma verliess und draussen was Besseres suchte. Und natürlich musste ihm das danebengehen, weil die Firma ja lange genug eine Zuchstätte seiner Komplexe und Schwächen war. Aber dann, was für ein Fest des Vorstands, was für eine kraftvolle Bekundung der Familie!., wenn ein Unglücklicher leise wieder vorsprach und um Rückeinstellung ersuchte. [. . .] Meistens konnte sich der Vorstand für alle Zukunft auf ihn verlassen. (R, pages 22-23)

There is another exception to this pattern of degradation and dependence besides Bekker. Reference is made once to an employee who hanged himself. "Ein Ortlepp, der wüsste schon wohin. Der wusste es immer. Der einzige Zachler-Feind, der einzige den Chef nicht nachäffende Geist im Institut" (R, page 154). Bekker sees the preservation of dignity in this suicide. By contrast, he frustrates Grit by not knowing where he wants to go (on vacation). There is in fact only one objective to his travels and travails.

> Im übrigen gibt es für Bekker nur ein wahres Reiseziel: die Chefetage in der Behrendstrasse, Büro Numero Eins, wo sogar übers Wochenende, wenn niemand da ist, dezent das Deckenlicht brennt, wo ein gewisser Zachler eines Tages zu Tode erschrocken hinter seinem Schreibtisch aufspringen wird, nachdem Bekker die Tür aufgerissen hat und hereingestürzt ist und wie kein zweiter vor ihm steht . . . . (R, pages 62-63)

Bekker, a man in his early forties, indeed has a long history with Zachler and the Institute, one which spans the last twelve years.[6] We are given two accounts of this history, one by Bekker himself, and the other by Bruno Stöss, a fellow employee, who likewise began working for the Institute in 1968 and periodically assumes the persona of narrator. Both accounts depict Bekker, having abandoned his studies toward a degree in law, as an unskilled worker called upon to do a wide variety of tasks. Bekker stresses the degradation, while Stöss gives us the additional information that Bekker's striking creativity initially made him "de[n] engste[n] Vertraute[n] des Chefs" (R, page 11). Only later, with the onslaught of increasing specialization--a trend in which Bekker did not participate--did he become insignificant in the company. Instead of assuming leadership for a particular sector or project, he repeatedly tried to leave the Institute and find work at the university. We are not told why Bekker had such limited success with university employment, but we learn from Bekker that something compels him to return again and again to the Institute. One passage in which he makes this clear also tells us something about his reasons for joining the Institute in the first place.

> Ich stehe noch einmal, ein letztes Mal gewiss, vor dem Eingang des Instituts, zu dem ich als junger Mann aus der bedrückendsten Herkunft wie zu einem Tempel der Seligen geflohen bin, von dem ich mir endlich freie Entfaltung, gute und richtige Lehre, Lebenssinn erhoffte und wo ich doch, unter Zachlers Herrschaft, in die allerschrecklichste Strafanstalt geriet, in die ein auf Selbständigkeit hoffender Mensch nur geraten kann. Vier Mal, im ganzen vier Mal in meinem Leben habe ich versucht, diesem magischen Gefängnis zu entfliehen und anderswo Arbeit und Auskommen zu finden. Immer wieder hat es mich auf eine ekelerregende, aber unwiderstehliche Weise zurückgezogen, immer wieder bin ich, und jedes Mal unglücklicher, zurückgekehrt. (R, pages 21-22)

For Bekker, born in the 1930's, the "bedrückendste Herkunft" is one of National Socialism, war, post-war restoration, and West Germany's economic miracle. It is surely no coincidence that 1968--the year most commonly cited as the height of the student protest movement--marks the time at which Bekker hopes to find personal and social majority (Mündigkeit) under the auspices of the Institute.[7] What first appeared as a temple, however, is unveiled as a prison. To understand this duality, we must look more closely at the two outstanding characteristics of the Institute and its functions. The first entails the Institute's approach to knowledge. We have already noted the emphasis on specialization. The following passage further delineates the Institute's tasks as it sees them:

> Das Institut vertreibt know how in praktisch allen wichtigen Bereichen der modernen tätigen Gesellschaft. Hier arbeiten wir alle unter einem Dach: der Betriebswirt, der Verwaltungsjurist, der Informatiker, der Urbanist, aber auch der Fachmann für Touristik, der Psychologe, der Sozialpädagoge. Jeder kontrolliert in seinem Fach den Stand der neuesten Entwicklungen, analysiert Nachrichten, fertigt Hintergrundberichte an, die als sogenannte newsletter von unseren Kunden in Wirtschaft und Lehre und den politischen Verbänden bezogen werden. (R, page 10)

The Institute in effect manages "gebrauchsfertiges Wissen" (R, page 10), contrasted with the creative intelligence associated with university scholarship. The Institute manages information regarding all aspects of human life, functioning as a human relations engineer whose sense of synthesis is mechanical at best but certainly not experiential. Not despite, but rather because of the Institute's high degree of specialized expertise, it is denounced as a "Scheisshaus des Geistes und eine Zuchstätte des Idiotismus" (R, page 11). There is an integral relationship between the Institute's approach to the social organization of knowledge and the second complex characteristic of the

Institute. Its approach to knowledge negates experiential wholeness; knowledge is not a passageway to majority, but a product like any other, to be managed, monitored, and distributed. Bekker repeatedly rants against the Institute's cultivation of strong leaders and spineless, mindless followers. The Ichschwachen outnumber the Ichstarken, who gain daily in strength (R, page 14).

> Hörigkeit und blindes Verfallensein an die ichstarken Naturen, Nachäffung des Vorgesetzten, die Sucht, die Wut, sich Bindung zu verschaffen um jedweden Preis, und sei es um den der Selbstaufgabe, diese Krankheit greift jetzt bei uns in erschreckendem Masse um sich. (R, pages 12-13)

This is an essential principle of operation in Zachler's firm, but it likewise extends beyond company life.

> Aber auch ausserhalb der Firma, unter Freunden und Bekannten, ist es nicht viel anders: jeder sucht in seiner näheren Nachbarschaft nach seinem Führer, seinem Guru, seinem Atemgeber, sei es nun der Chef oder ein Dr. med. oder ein Aikidomeister. In allen Winkeln erhebt sich irgendein Menschenbefehler, ein Ausstrahler, ein kleiner Schamane. (R, page 13)

The eagerness with which even "gebildete, besterzogene Menschen genauso wie grobe Klötze oder Ahnungslose" (R, page 13) relinquish their capacity for independent thought and self-determination distinguishes Bekker from his fellow employees at the Institute. Yet, Bekker is not a leader, either. He refuses that role. Admiring his colleague's "lodernde Intelligenz," Bruno Stöss thinks:

> Unter all dem Winke-Winke von uns anderen ist Bekker wahrhaftig eine schneidende Gebärde. Wenn er je Macht besässe (und sie besitzen wollte!), er könnte mehr Leute an sich ziehen und stärker binden als selbst Zachler, der inzwischen allein durch seine Stellung verführt und glänzt, im Wesen aber kaum noch Feuer hat. (R, pages 8-9)

Zachler's power reinforces itself. Void of real brilliance or passionate spirit, he is, however, "de[r] immer stärker werdende [...] Chef" (R, page 7).[8]

The Institute's initial allure as "Tempel der Seligen" is twofold. Given the historical context of post-war Germany, the rapid development of economic and technological progress promised the birth of new life and the capability to make it good. The narrower context of 1968 alludes to the exciting hope of changing society through the active critical participation of politically enlightened citizens. Yet, the promise and the hope proved illusory. The price exacted by the post-war organization of West German society is hidden under the abundant splendor of material goods and specialized "know how." This is what Bekker means when he describes Zachler as "the world's dirtiest pig, [...] de[n] skrupellose[n] Konkurrent[en] mit der betrügerischen Preisstaffel" (R, page 203). The compartmentalization of knowledge practiced by the Institute also involves the negation of history.

> Ich sage dir: ein, zwei Generationen noch, und es werden vollkommen erinnerungsfreie Menschen durch ihr Schicksal schweben. Die werden einfach alles vergessen haben. Nach uns werden sie alles vergessen. Nach uns werden sie alles vergessen, was einmal war . . . Dummer Zauber Geschichte. War da was? . . . Die Leute im Institut sagen, man muss sich die Sache schon jetzt mehr als eine Art weitflächiges Relais denken. Nicht mehr die Wurzel, die tiefe, die Herkunft, sondern das Relais, unzählige Schaltungen auf einer Ebene gleichzeitig, brummedibrumm, Verknüpfungen und enorme Speicherbestände, ein Chip, winziges Steuerteilchen, elektronische Riesenhirne, kann man gut und gern auf fünftausend Handarbeiter verzichten, daumenkuppengross, ein Chip; nicht die Wurzeler, nicht die Tiefe, aber die kleinen flachen wüsten Relais . . . (R, page 39)

Peter Schütze quite rightly notes Bekker's perception of the horror emanating from the disappearance of historical consciousness; for this reason alone, he cannot be dismissed as a spokesman for <u>Neue Innerlichkeit</u>.[9] It is a sense of history that permeates the city streets Bekker roams and from which he draws his strength.

> [. . .] wie entstieg diesem Gehen umgeben von Mauern, Geschichte und Gestank doch ein pochendes Bewusstsein und eine Willenskraft, welche sich schliesslich in ein unbezwingbares Verlangen nach einer nie gekannten körperlichen Ausschweifung steigerten, einem Kampfesorgasmus, aus dem es kein Erwachen mehr geben dürfte. Jeder Schritt wurde plötzlich ein bebender auf Zachler zu . . . Wohin mit soviel Energie? (<u>R</u>, pages 72-73)

The passage is followed by a discussion on anarchists and terrorists between Bekker and a "Hühnchen von Nachtfunkredakteur" named Ludwig. Bekker's opinions are mixed. He respects the terrorists' absolute "Krieg gegen Jetzt."

> Es ist richtig, wenn manche es an der Zeit finden, das Böse und das unwiderruflich Böse zu tun. Wann, wenn nicht vorm Absoluten der Übeltat, würden wir fähig, unsere Gemeinschaft tiefer zu erkennen, zu bezweifeln? Es gibt Stunden des massiven Eisgeistes, in denen Hass die einzige Wärme ist und nur Sprengung Atem schafft. (<u>R</u>, page 74)

At the same time, he sees the danger that this perfectly calculated evil could make its perpetrators "zu heimlichen Geistesbrüdern eben jener Macht und Staatsmaschine, die sie stören wollen" (<u>R</u>, pages 74-75). Then again, the omnipotent state finds its first real worthy opponent in "[dieser] kleinen, stammelnden Elite von Hassern, die ihm ein paar blutige Gespenster in den Schlaf getrieben haben" (<u>R</u>, page 75).[10] What Bekker cannot decide is whether the battle between state and anarchy is the last of the old battles or the first of the new

> gegen die unabsehbare, frontlose Gleichförmigkeit und Ebene der Politik und des ziellos wimmelnden Lebens. Ist es ein Akt der Fäulnis oder ist es ein Akt der Geburt? Ununterscheidbar die Richtungen: vor/zurück blind/sehend, links/rechts. [. . .] Sicher ist nur: die alten Entscheidungen gelten nicht mehr. [. . .] wir sind wieder im Busch. (R, pages 75-76)

The loss of credible paradigms thus echoes in Rumor as well. Bekker confesses: "Bin ein Patriot, weiss aber nicht, an wen soll ich mich wenden. Aber wo ist zu meiner Treue der Herr?" (R, page 78). Bekker is a restless warrior without a clearly defined cause in a positive sense. His cause is to resist Zachler's domination, but he does not know how to seek direct confrontation with his arch enemy or even to what extent Zachler influences events in his life, for example, when Zachler manipulates Bekker's release from charges of violating immigration laws (R, page 213). It is unclear whether Zachler feels anything but indifference towards Bekker, who after all poses no real threat to the Institute. "Es kostete ihn wenig Mühe, den verrannten Krieger, der zur Schlacht nicht zurückfindet, wieder frei zu bekommen" (R, page 212).

What we have then in the Institute is the institutionalization of the following things: compartmentalized know how, thorough degradation and submission to power, and the annihilation of history. This truncation of experience precludes the diachronic extension from the individual into contemporary society as well as into social history. In short, this is the abrogation of the subject as either social or historical agent. Tellingly, this is the crux of Bekker's encounter with Bongie, his old science teacher and former Nazi. Bongie's flight from Nazi ideology had crystalized in his biological theory that every development in the human organism results from "Tippfehlern der genetischen Übertragung" (R, page 143); the human being is not the center of anything but just another piece of biological data. Bekker finds his teacher's old lectures relevant today: ". . . da müssen sich die Denker heute doch fragen: wo bist du nur geblieben, teures Subjekt der Weltgeschichte, heiliges Ich?" (R, page 144). In the midst of "lauter Gesetzesherrschaft und fremde[r] Ordnungen," Bekker asks:

> Wo sollte da noch für ein Ich Platz sein? So kommt es, dass selbst dem Philosophen das menschliche Subjekt vom erhabensten zum langweiligsten Gegenstand seiner Betrachtungen geworden ist. Der Mensch? sagt er, Schwamm drüber. Das Menschenkind, die ewige Nummer Eins der Weltgeschichte? Schwamm drüber. Dies Wesen beginnt nun endlich, das Spiel der Regeln zu durchschauen, dem es sein Erscheinen in der Geschichte verdankt. Inzwischen weiss es immerhin so viel, dass dieses selbe Spiel der Regeln es auch wieder aus der Geschichte heraustragen wird. (R, page 145)

Things take over the world; a grill and a piece of chewing gum assume speech (R, pages 145 and 146). The annihilation of the human subject is in fact what provokes Bekker's wrath against the Institute. Bekker, who is capable of speaking as I, albeit neither consistently nor as one willing to lead where others will follow, knows there is no place for him in the Institute. Yet, his actions show that he also knows there is no place for him outside it, for the Institute is everywhere. This is why he must return again and again to Zachler's firm--"die unentrinnbare Arbeitsstätte" (R, page 224). When Michael Schneider concludes that Bekker internalizes Zachler's system by capitulating to it,[11] he posits his own belief in the individual intact outside the system and capable of resisting it. This oversimplifies matters. Bekker does not surrender to the system out of weak will, nor does he internalize it. Rather, by acknowledging its permeation into every aspect of contemporary life, he declares the battle unavoidable; there is no place to hide or escape intact. This does not, however, mean that he is capable of defeating Zachler in man-to-man combat, as it were. We have already noted that Bekker ultimately does not know how to reach Zachler. The enemy is insidiously intangible. The Institute in fact does not stand for any particular organization but for the pervasive institutionalization of experience in the Federal Republic of Germany, a phenomenon which effectively negates experience itself. The state is implicated, as are all other social institutions, but the crux of the matter is the process of institutionalization per se, the very organization of contemporary society. Experience is reduced to data, and human beings renounce their potential as subjective agents by identifying with the system that at best acknowledges them as statistics. <u>Rumor</u> thus voices a far more comprehensive social critique than any of the three earlier works discussed here.[12]

In a related diachronic extension back into German history, Bekker is haunted by the Third Reich, most clearly present in the figure of his deceased stepfather. An officer in the Nazi army, he was dishonorably discharged for insubordination,

> ein gefällter, zerrissener Kämpfer, rachsüchtig und selbstherrlich, und nur mir, seinem geliebten Schützling, zärtlich zugetan und ihn mit dem geballten Rest seiner Lebenskräfte erfüllend, die da waren: Hass, Verachtung, Vernichtungsdrang und Wille zum Tod . . . (<u>R</u>, page 21)

The textual relationship between Bekker and his stepfather is a complex one. On the one hand, Bekker is created in the officer's image. Both are characterized as raging warriors with a frustrated will to destroy an evil system; both are cursed with the degradation of that frustration; and both take to drink. Bekker seeks, imagines discourse with the officer, who can neither help nor counsel him in death (R, page 59). Bekker's nocturnal radio broadcast begins

> [. . .] mit einer zarten Anrufung des alten Offiziers, er nutzt den grenzlosen Äther des Rundfunks, um sich zunächst mit der Seele eines Toten in Verbindung zu setzen. Alles was ihm einfällt, dreht sich um den Offizier, dessen Gut und Böse, dessen Sprache und Unsinn ihn verfolge bis auf den heutigen Tag, so dass er oft schon glaube, zeitlebens nichts als das leise, strebende Wiederholen einer entbehrten Rede von sich zu geben. (R, pages 195-196)

The older generation's experience with National Socialism thus persists as absence in Bekker's mind. He cannot ignore that past because it haunts him, but neither can he come to grips with it directly, since neither his stepfather nor National Socialism is part of his present experience in unmediated form: another double bind situation. Bekker can come to terms with his stepfather's experience only by grappling with his own evil system. The Institute is to Bekker what National Socialism was to the officer. Immediately before he describes his history with Zachler, Bekker discusses his stepfather, saying of him:

> So erhebt sich wieder dieser Schatten mächtig über meinem Rücken und es ist, als ob das frühe Böse jetzt erst richtig wirke und mache, dass sich der enge Umlauf meiner Lebensschritte immer enger zuschliesst und bald vielleicht in einem tollen Wirbel um die eigene Achse endet. (R, page 21)

The point is made again later: "Jetzt also, auf der Kippe zu Zachler zurück, steigt mir im Rücken das Majorsmonster wieder auf, der greuliche Erzieher" (R, page 23). Although the officer provides a locus of identity for Bekker, the substance of that identity--defeated warrior--calls upon Bekker to challenge, not repeat it. This renders the officer "der greuliche Erzieher" and puts him in the same company with Zachler. "Wenn [Zachler, das Weltschwein] den Mund aufmacht, dann öffnet sich der Sarg der deutschen Wehrmacht!" (R, page 197). Bekker's battle thus extends simultaneously into the present and into the past (his biography and German history). These fronts are in effect fused in Bekker's struggle to assert himself as subjective agent in history.

The memory of Bekker's stepfather is not the only instance in which a diachronic link is established between National Socialism and contemporary West Germany. The motif of the concentration camps (die Lager) runs throughout Rumor. Bekker recalls a conversation in a New York bar with an American who could not bear to hear Bekker speaking German and only agreed to stay when Bekker switched to English: "der Grund sind natürlich die Lager, die deutschen" (R, page 31). Bekker exchanges one horror story after another with the American, feels shame and yet pride to be German--

> und zwar, weil man hier etwas dafür tun musste, weil es eben eine gewisse Mühe verlangte und man sein Willkommen nicht gratis kassierte. Ich empfand auch, ich weiss nicht weshalb, plötzlich einen heftigen Stich Heimweh und Liebe zu meinem/zu einem zweifellos imaginären Land. (R, page 33)

This closing qualification makes it clear that Bekker is not proud of what it has actually meant to be German, but what it could mean. The

German language itself bears both the stigma of the camps as well as resistance to their total victory.

> Dass das Deutsch in diesem einzigartigen Vernichtungswerk nicht untergegangen war, dass es einem Hitler nicht gelungen war, auch das Deutsch noch mitzuverheizen [. . .], dies ganze Deutschsein trotz Hitler erfreute mich im Innersten, während ich oben auf englisch lallte und stotterte, und ich schämte mich auch nicht, dass wir ausgerechnet über das Lager lallten und stotterten, fand es am Ende gar des Unaussprechlichen würdig, dass wir in einem schweren, scherzlosen Rausch immer dasselbe zum selben Thema sagten, why? (R, page 33)

We should not overlook the obvious here. The very fact that Rumor is written in German manifests the diachronic tension between the text and German history. The repeated use of the word Lager to characterize contemporary situations, particularly with regard to the relationship between the sexes, likewise spans the bridge between present and past:

> Hier, in diesem zugepflochten Haus findest du ein ganz gewöhnliches KZ, eines unter Millionen. Ein Mann misshandelt seine Frau. (R, page 25)
>
> Stille Folter und Vernichtungszimmer. Eine Blutgrube das Bett. Das Lager in jedem. (R, page 28)
>
> Der Unmensch aus bedrängter Leidenschaft, das Lager intim, nicht lebenswertes Leben der Liebeskranken und der Ausgeliebten. (R, page 44)

Power, humiliation, abuse, and capitulation characterize not only the concentration camps and contemporary relationships, but the Institute as well. The description of discipline in the internment camp in the stadium[13] is reminiscent of the systematic degradation in the Institute (compare R, page 23).

> Sie haben dem Gehenkten die Zunge hervorgezogen und mit einer dicken Stecknadel durchstochen. Daran hängt, auf

> kleinem Zettel geschrieben, jeweils die Losung des
> Tages, und jeder Gefangenenobmann muss frühmorgens ganz
> nah an die Zunge herantreten, um die nichtssagenden
> Weisheiten zu lesen, welche die Diktatur in ihrer
> winzigen, zierlichen Handschrift abgefasst hat [. . .].
> (R, pages 29-30)

What Bekker sees around him is in fact a hell on earth, and Strauss weaves a tapestry of that image.

> Hier ist es, Tartarien. Mehr kommt nicht. Von himmel-
> weit unter der Erde, wo sie die Alten dachten, ist un-
> sere Unterwelt emporgetaucht bis ans Tageslicht, für
> jedermann begehbare Hölle . . . . (R, page 25)

Every time Bekker wanders through the city or even on its outskirts, his direction is characterized by "hinunter" (R, pages 25, 36, 42, 131, 148) until finally: "Bekker geht nun Nacht für Nacht wieder die Stadt hinunter" (R, page 194). Bekker need not descend into hell like Dante, since hell has become ubiquitous, but he does see things that others fail to perceive. He is characterized as both "Seher" (R, page 98) and "Voyeur" (R, page 117). The notion of the underworld also links the three generations: the officer ("In einem Lichtschacht ohne Licht ist jemand," page 37), Bekker, and Grit ("[. . .] er ist für einen Augenblick versucht, sie rücksichtslos von den Schläuchen zu reissen und aus diesem fürchterlichsten Eck der Unterwelt davonzutragen auf seinen Armen," page 130).

The image of hell on earth is further elaborated by the notion of paradise lost. Reality is a "Gartengefängnis" (R, page 215), and God is a prison guard who has vacated his post (R, page 30). He is either ignorant of the human fate (R, page 30), or annihilates the human race in disgust (R, page 66). Bekker's encounter with the group of Pakistani illegally seeking employment in the Federal Republic is, significantly, cloaked in terms of paradise and salvation. The Pakistani are described thus:

> Ein kleiner Trupp Verschleppter und Ausgesetzter, denen man jetzt häufiger in der Stadt begegnet. Sie haben sich in ihrer Heimat als Arbeitskräfte für Deutschland an einen Menschenhändler verkauft und müssen nun erleben, dass sie im gelobten Land weder gebraucht noch auch nur geduldet werden, weder Anstellung noch Aufenthaltsgenehmigung bekommen. (R, page 198)

Under normal circumstances, one is not supposed to sell one's soul to gain entry to the promised land; yet, this inverted admission to paradise is a fate the Pakistani actually share with Zachler's employees, who have sold their soul to the company store, as it were. Bekker's radio monologue includes an account of foreign workers that classifies them as crusaders from the South.

> [. . .] er [. . .] berichtet von den Grossen Kreuzzügen aus dem Süden, mit denen Millionen von Hungerleidern aus aller Welt in unser glaubensschwaches und unterbevölkertes Land eindringen, um ihre Not zu lindern und uns Greise zu bevormunden. (R, page 197)

Elsewhere, the Pakistani are described as pilgrims, "Gänger [. . .] aus dem Fernen Osten" (R, page 199). These crusades in reverse are foiled by reality; the Federal Republic is neither the promised land nor garden paradise. Moreover, Bekker sees himself as the pilgrims' savior; he can offer them jobs and papers. "Er lacht einmal heftig in die Luft, beglückt über das Leichte des Menschenretters, das ihn da anwandelt" (R, page 199). Recalling his radio monologue, he uses a revealing phrase: "Sass stundenlang allein unterm Kreuz des Mikros" (R, page 216). By rescuing the Pakistani from their plight, he senses he can save himself as well.

> Besessen und rücksichtslos, als ginge es geradewegs um
> das eigene Überleben an diesem Abend, wirbt Bekker um
> das Vertrauen dieser Männer, möchte sich eindrängeln,
> förmlich hineinkuscheln in diese Fremde, in die blau-
> schwarze Kuhle dieser ihm zugewandten, hörenden Schar.
> (R, page 201)

Bekker sniffs "[. . .] am Fremden [. . .] wie der Ekstatiker [. . .]" (R, pages 205-206). Given Bekker's complacent self-image as saviour with respect to the Pakistani, we may well ask why he ultimately reports their illegal presence to the police, causing their arrest and probable deportation. He seems to act in a trance.

> Gegen Morgen wird er durch einen bitteren Traum, eine
> innerste Vertreibung aus dem Schlaf gestossen. Ohne
> recht zu wissen, wie ihm geschieht und was er zu tun
> gedenkt, rafft er sich auf und kriecht auf allen vieren
> aus dem Zimmer. (R, page 206)

This is indeed the way of the prophets. The designation of Bekker's action as both "Liebe und Liebesverrat" (R, page 210) makes sense only if one looks beyond the immediate level of betrayal. The failure to betray the Pakistani would result in their taking root in the promised land, which is in fact not a paradise but a garden prison, a "Markt ohne Seelen" (R, page 218). The only act of salvation left to Bekker is to protect them from their false hope, the further pursuit of which would require that they, too, sell their souls to the company store.

We have seen Bekker assume the persona of frustrated warrior-crusader and questionable savior. He also figures significantly as father in the text. The polarization characteristic of the relationship between father and daughter does not exclude all interaction between the two or even the alternating exchange of weakness and strength. Yet, this ambivalence does not allow for any fruitful approximation; it resolves instead into a polarized stalemate. Grit's disease--its source, its manifestation, and Grit's response to it--embodies that stalemate. Comparable to the illness that plagues Marlene's sister, Grit's affliction is an "Aufstand der Schmerzen" (R, page 121); like Marlene's sister, Grit never fully recovers nor wholly succumbs to her disease, but is faced with its constant threat, even after her operation (R, page 189). Whereas the ailing sister's physical state is an inverted manifestation of health, Grit's condition attests to her identity as passive victim. She does not share Bekker's drive to combat and resistance. Void of any diachronic extension, her struggle has retreated to the last lonely stronghold of her person. She is her own passive battlefield. What is this struggle, then, that consumes her? We must not forget that she is the third link in the generational chain. The suitcase Grit takes to the hospital belonged, significantly, to the officer. Grit is confronted with her father's drinking bouts, just as Bekker experienced his stepfather's drunken binges. Family history repeats itself. The manifestations of Grit's disease, emanating from her spinal marrow--"Zentrum der Ängste" (R, page 189)--in fact date back to her childhood. (We are reminded of Freud's designation of the ego as the "eigentliche Angststätte.") And yet, neither parent ever noticed her deformed foot. Grit reproaches her father: "'Habt ihr mich eigentlich mal richtig angeguckt? [. . .] Also weisst du, man sieht sich sein Kind doch an, ob auch alles in Ordnung ist an ihm. Eltern wissen doch besser als das Kind, was gerade ist, was krumm'" (R, page 118). Blinding themselves to their child's deformity, the parents in effect bequeathed a diseased legacy to the next generation: the failure to come to grips with their own past. Aborted <u>Vergangenheitsbewältigung</u> manifests itself in Grit's disease, thus implicating more than a mere family history. The three generations in <u>Rumor</u> are infused with and reflect German national history.

The repeated designation of Bekker as <u>Vater</u> underscores his ineptness at this role. When Grit is at her weakest--on vacation at the Mondsee and after her operation--Bekker assumes a posture of help and strength, which prompts Grit to wonder if Bekker could not be, after all, "[. . .] ein ganz unbetrunkener Mann [. . .], auf den man sich vielleicht doch verlassen könnte, wenn es einmal ernst wird und Gefahr droht" (<u>R</u>, page 116). As soon as Grit begins to recover from her operation, albeit not from her fundamental disease, Bekker degenerates mentally and physically into a slovenly creature who evokes "Ekel und Erbleichen" (<u>R</u>, page 226) in his daughter. His very presence in her apartment consumes her oppressively; she cannot seem to rid herself of the decrepit, disgusting man who fathered her and, indeed, she consistently encourages him to return to the fold of the Institute, as if that would solve his problem or hers. It would seem then that Bekker calls Grit forth to battle; she must fight his domination of her life if she is to survive. Although Grit is not generally characterized as a warrior, she does exhibit hints of resistance and self-defense. She initially rejects Joseph, her lover, because he is too peaceful and passive. "Er war in allem gelind und weich, gab nie Widerstand, wenn ihm was nicht passte" (<u>R</u>, page 51). Describing what she wants, she says: "'Ich suche jemanden mit Kräften, die ich noch gar nicht kenne.

Jemanden, der mal eine ganz andere Sprache spricht'" (R, page 53). It is significant in this context that Grit is a professional foreign language secretary and travel agent. If we recall Bekker's comments on the German language on the occasion of the bar conversation about concentration camps, it becomes clear that Grit's mode of resistance is to flee the real battlefield; she has neither the strength nor the drive to face the real challenge. It is only after excruciating and debilitating pain that Grit, "ohnmächtig einverstanden," (R, page 121), agrees to an operation. Otherwise, she had decided

> [. . .] die Krankheit wieder sein zu lassen, was sie immer war, und mit ihren Beschwerden, an die sie sich halbwegs gewöhnt hatte, weiterzuleben wie bisher. (R, pages 114-115)

Likewise, she fails to take up Bekker's challenge. At first she isolates him--displaces the battlefield--by banning him to the far corner of her apartment. Ultimately she removes him forcibly and moves him into a hotel. She cannot abide his condition, feels contaminated by it. "Facing" the problem by removing it from her sight, she cannot even do this with complete conviction and rage. She feels regret and pity for her father, who does not physically resist his displacement (R, pages 230-231). Grit's "Raserei von Befreiungswut" (R, page 229) is really a false liberation. The fact that her father's heavy breathing continues to haunt her through the telephone after his departure attests to this. Other incidences of father-child relationships in the text are also described in terms of power, degradation, and lack of real confrontation. The son of the Nazi science teacher wreaks vengeance on him by becoming a real estate broker and evicting his father from his own home. The businessman who comes late to a company meeting in a restaurant uses his one-armed child to elicit pity from his superiors but reaps revulsion instead. Grit's failure to challenge her father effectively is paradigmatic for an entire generation.

> Niemals geheissen, sich aufzulehnen, geboren zu akzeptieren und zurechtzukommen, fehlen ihrem Wesen, wie bei so vielen ihrer Altersgenossen, die Schwingungen des Kampfes und der Unduldsamkeit. Es scheint ja, die Zeit habe aus unseren Kindern das Gegenteil von Vatermördern gemacht. (R, page 101)[14]

Grit has booked Oedipus on an indefinite holiday excursion, a clear allusion to the persistent generational failure to confront modern German history. The diachronic extension into the past is only one aspect of the challenge Bekker embodies for Grit. Another involves Bekker's personification of the contemporary fate of the subjective agent of history, "teures Subjekt der Weltgeschichte, heiliges Ich" (R, page 144). Enduring a fate reminiscent of Gregor Samsa's metamorphosis, Bekker is "Schabe" (R, page 221) and "Vieh" (R, page 222), banished to isolation within his daughter's apartment. "'Warum isolierst du mich so?! Warum Denn? Ich halte es nicht länger aus'" (R, page 221). Bongie's scientific theory that the human being is merely the product of one genetic code equal to any other in nature seems to find proof in Bekker's fate. The father descends deeper and deeper into the animal realm. With increasing frequency, he forgets to flush the toilet, leaving his excrement for Grit to find.

> Dass er sich immer mehr gehenlässt, sich wahrhaftig in eine unwürdige Kreatur verwandelt, erregt nicht bloss ihren Abscheu; es bestürzt sie vielmehr, dass sich dieser gehütete Gestank ja auf irgendeine Weise an sie oder gegen sie richtet, eine verschlüsselte Botschaft, ein schon aus dem Tierischen wirkendes Signal, das der

>     verstummte Mann aus furchtbarer Entfernung ihr sendet.
>     Denn alles, was er anstellt in seinem trägen Brüten,
>     scheint nur um ihretwillen getan und scheint mit ihr
>     doch sprechen zu wollen. (R, pages 226-227)

The message to Grit in effect sounds the alarm to the danger of subjective agency denied. By stifling the alarm, Grit denies herself any possibility for counteracting the danger; she and her generation become accomplice to their own subordination.

Michael Schneider says of Bekker's relationship to his daughter: "Obwohl das eigene Kind ihm fremd ist (und bleibt), verkörpert es für ihn ein Stück Heimat und Nestwärme in der allgemeinen Kommunikationswüste" and "in Grit liebt er den verlängerten (und scheinbar noch heilen) Teil seines eigenen Selbst."[15] This is misleading, inasmuch as it overlooks the conflicts in their relationship and underestimates the polarization of the two figures. It is striking that a man driven to seek combat with his arch enemy actually spends so much time and energy with his daughter. This apparent contradiction does not seem quite so puzzling if we recall the role that hatred plays as the driving force in Bekker's life. His daughter, on the other hand, offers the faint promise of love and, as the younger generation, hope for the future. Bekker says of her: "mein Kind, das von damals, ich liebe es endlich jetzt" (R, page 65). "Er ist süchtig nach Harmonie mit dem Kind" (R, page 101). And yet, this promise of a "Liebesja" (R, page 219) proves illusory. Grit, afraid of contamination by her father's premature old age and senility, cries, "'Das ist keine Liebe! [. . .] das ist wirklich keine Liebe!'" (R, page 229). Bekker himself acknowledges the impossibility of genuine fatherhood and love.

> Wie sollte er nach so vielen Jahren in innerster Wüstenei, Hass, Roheit und Rücksichtslosigkeit noch der Liebe und Sorge fähig sein? Und selbst der natürlichste Blick, diesen Menschen als sein Kind zu erkennen, war ihm ja abhanden gekommen. Er verspürt einen schneidenden Mangel, nicht wirklich Vater zu sein, in jeder Regung, jedem Verhalten, gelassen, streng und lieb, tief ver- bunden und vernünftig--es nicht auf selbstverständliche Weise und ganz zu sein, so als gäbe es Den Vater als eine absolute, vollkommen naturfeste Gestalt. (R, page 168-169)

Bekker's relationship to his daughter is described in anything but "natural" terms. On the contrary, he sees her as a woman, for whom he feels sexual desire. This has, first of all, positive connotations. Woman, as the third element in Bekker's apocalyptic vision of "Rumor, Narr und Frau . . ." (R, pages 65 and 66), is a partner in seeing the danger of the subject's demise. Bekker muses on women in general:

> So sind sie längst zu Schwestern der Tatbestände geworden, trüber Rückstand ausgeglückter Mühe, und ein Versprechen zu Besserem werden sie niemals mehr sein . . . Und doch bleibt nur ein Ort, wenn du den gesamten Horizont abgehofft hast, ein Ort auf der Welt aller Sehnsucht wert, kein Haus in der Heide, kein noch so guter Garten und nicht die Freiheit, sondern allein das Ganz Andere Gesicht. (R, page 95)

Perhaps that face will prove to be Grit's.

> (Ist das vielleicht der Eingang, wie? Vielleicht dort der erste Durchschein des untersten Höllenkreises, zu dem ich hinunter muss? Man weiss ja heute nicht mehr, wo eigentlich der Eingang verborgen ist . . .) (R, page 104)

Bekker imagines Grit's touch freeing him from his "Säulenstarre" and opening up his "ungesonderte Masse der Wünsche und Begierden" (R, page 109). Grit herself plays "die flüsternde Verführerin" (R, page 107) to her father, albeit for the benefit of the foreigner who is dining in the same restaurant. And yet, the promise of sexual love between man and woman is empty. The following passage describes the scene in which father kisses daughter:

> Die Einkehr in den offenen Mund unter dem offenen Auge --so hohl, so weich, so gastfrei und doch nichts weiter, als trete er in ein anderes leeres Zimmer. Er schleicht auf der Zungenspitze einmal vor und wieder zurück, es rührt sich nichts. Das war der Kuss. (R, page 64)

Grit exhibits only a very faint sexual desire after her recuperation from surgery, but the object of that desire is Joseph, her placid lover. Toward Bekker, her disease serves to eradicate (his) sexual desire. When Grit undresses from the waist down to reveal her visible physical afflictions, the atmosphere is clinical: "der delirierende Phallus geköpft und seiner ruchlosen Hirngespinste beraubt" (R, page 117), but it is not until after the operation that Bekker's dream of a female "Riesentorso am Firmament" (R, page 117) is shattered. Her pubic hair is "jetzt ein Ort, der allein dem Schmerz, der Lähmung, der geschlechtslosen Krankheit zugehört [. . .]" (R, page 181).[16] While still in the hospital, she requires his embrace to help her urinate in the bed pan.

> Sie halten sich umarmt genau wie Liebende. Und doch sind es Griffe der Nothilfe, und das bedeutungsvolle Warten gilt einem kleinen Pipi und lenkt sie ganz voneinander ab. (R, page 177)

Grit becomes

> [d]ie eine Keine. Es bleibt mir nichts--nichts als bescheiden in meinem Eck zu hocken und auf ihr Wohl zu masturbieren. (R, page 110)

In fact, Bekker is ultimately reduced to masturbating in Grit's presence, "hastig wie sonst kaum noch eine Handbewegung an ihm ist" (R, page 227). Grit assumes the role of stern mother who forbids such indiscretion. <u>Rumor</u> is replete with tales of the battle between the sexes, but Grit does not even engage in this battle. It is telling that the strange woman seeking Bekker's help in the pizzeria spurs him to a diatribe against women with regard to the battle between the sexes. When he discovers this woman is pregnant, he changes his tune.

> Was für ein Irrtum, welch gemeines Verkennen! Alles was ich an diesem Wesen beurteilt habe, war falsch. Sie ist schwanger, sie trägt ein Kind, sie hat Hoffnung. (<u>R</u>, page 166)

When Grit reveals her fear and dream that she has been raped and impregnated by the male nurse in the hospital, Bekker raises the possibility that it could just as easily have been he who raped her. She claims not to understand but then forbids him to sleep in the room next to hers; her bedroom remains locked to him (<u>R</u>, pages 193-194). The pregnancy she imagines then results in mutant births and miscarriages.

> [. . .] die Angst, die einen Namen sucht, erschafft dann stets dasselbe Greuelbild einer Schwangerschaft, in der die Frucht des Bösen in vielen winzigen Missgeburten ausgetragen wird. (<u>R</u>, pages 189-190)

Grit's womanhood thus fails to fit into any of the traditional categories with which woman has been idolized as the key to some higher dimension of hope, knowledge, creativity, and survival. She is neither the mother of hope, nor the partner in sexual union, nor a worthy opponent in the battle between the sexes. Moreover, even the social defiance implicit in incestuous love is denied realization. Bekker ponders the sex act with his child: "Höchste Weihe der Liebe ohne Zweck und die Feier ihrer gesellschaftswidrigen Natur, Blutschande" (<u>R</u>, page 110). Yet, it never comes to this. <u>Rumor</u> in effect stands Oedipus on his head. The child (Grit) fails to kill the father (Bekker) who oppresses her, and the man-child (Bekker) fails to mate his mother (in Grit). Bekker, lonely warrior that he is, breaks the social tabu against incest just as he breaks the silence (tabu) against German history. Neither one of these challenges to the status quo is fully executed; Bekker is indeed "de[r] verrannte [. . .] Krieger" (R, page 212).

Given the self-reflective nature of Strauss' earlier texts, one would be inclined to expect Rumor to problematize its own language. This is indeed the case. Language as topic and as medium of this text attests likewise to a polarization of possibilities. Bekker's conversation with Bongie--significantly the same one in which he asks what has happened to the precious subject of history--also includes a diatribe against a false sense of order and meaning established through language.

> Der Ordnungen haben wir schliesslich viel zu viele gesammelt und wild aufeinander getürmt und ein bestürzend Übermass an Sinn in die Welt gesetzt. Zuviel der Logiken, Beweise, Erfahrungen, Vernünfte, als dass das Ganze nicht doch auf die krauseste und ursprünglichste Unordnung hinausliefe. Die Unordnung, die immer noch unterdrückte Rede des Ganzen, ein Rumor bloss, aber überall stärker hervordringend. (R, pages 146-147)

In a similar passage, the real order of things is likened to the speech of a child, "das abends zu lange aufbleiben durfte" (R, page 66): rumor. Language--and Strauss makes it clear he means the German language--is an institution. Like Zachler's Institute, it operates on the basis of power and alienation of the human subject.

> Das Deutsch der Mitwelt: nur entfernt, auf quälende Weise halb nur verständlich. So fällt der ganze Körper mit den Verhältnissen auseinander, fallen Seele und Dinge rumpelnd auseinander. (R, page 148)

In an extensive monologue in Grit's presence, Bekker urges tree and human being to greet each other again; the tree could die mourning the death of its human companion (R, pages 214 and 216). The eradication of the subject in language is reflected in the increasing popularity of the English word "center": "So heisst jetzt alles Center, Center, je weniger Mitte die Stadt noch zu bieten hat" (R, page 153). The element of aggressive domination in German emerges clearly from the description of the encounter between a German couple and a Danish couple, who met on vacation and come together again on the German's home turf. The Danes irritate the Germans with their awkward inability to express themselves, and the Germans, "[. . .] jetzt bei Heimvorteil, [. . .] reden ausschliesslich über sich selber und bauen lauter Standpunkte wie eine Festung um sich auf" (R, page 156). Bekker acknowledges elsewhere: "Nur wer deutsch spricht, kann mir etwas tun" (R, page 161).

Grit's language is characteristic for her passive submission to a fate that threatens her existence. Her response to Bekker's visions is either silence or lack of understanding or both. "'Wie?' fragt Grit, 'versteh nix'" (R, page 66). When she does speak, her sentences are conspicuously normal, perfectly understandable, colloquial. "'Was machst du?' fragt Grit mit sich fallenlassendem Begreifen. 'Wie soll das weitergehen?' Und: 'Wann gehst du endlich wieder zurück ins Institut?'" (R, page 213). A comparison is drawn between Grit's post-operative inability to urinate and the barrenness of language.

> Der Leib ist Gestein, verschlossen der Leib, verschlossen die Sprache. [. . .] Aber unter unserer stockend trockenen Rede muss ein Grosser Fluss sein . . . (R, page 178)

Bekker tries to wend his way to this river of life, and he seeks it through language despite the following lament:

> Die Deutschs der Menschen sind so . . . ich weiss nicht . . . so zu. Es rasselt, und abgehackt. Sprachballungsräume. Bloss raus hier! Raus aus der Sprache. . . !
> (R, page 78)

Rejecting the language of domination and submission, he opts for increasingly disorderly speech patterns of his own. Bekker's deconstruction of coherent, communicative German is not to be equated with foreigners' speech habits in German. The Hungarian doctor's German fails to inspire credibility, and the Korean nurses' German is "zerstückelt" (R, pages 120 and 126), as is that of the Danes. The difference is that these people are speaking a foreign language. Bekker must appropriate his own native tongue in order to articulate his place in German history.

Aside from Bekker's epithets as warrior and father, there are numerous others reflecting his incapacity for speech: "der Stammler," "der aufgebäumte Redner," "der gründliche Schweiger," and "der verstummte Mann." His bouts of silence and confused, incoherent speech frequently coincide with his numerous drunken binges. His speech in the bar in New York is "radebrechend" and "lallend" (R, page 32); his nightly visitations upon the city's bars make him a well-known figure, "[. . .] gennant Der Stammler und sich selbst so anzeigend, bevor er seine ungehobelten Monologe herausschleudert" (R, page 194). And yet, he need not be drunk to speak incoherently.

> Manchmal redet er unklar und zusammenhanglos auch, wenn
> er gar nicht betrunken ist. Dann schleicht, was er
> sagt, dicht an der Grenze zu Dämmer und Idiotie. Das
> Seltsame ist nur: in solchen Augenblicken meint man
> einen Verfall seiner gewohnten ebenso wie zugleich
> einen Aufstieg bisher noch unbekannter Kräfte seines
> Geistes wahrzunehmen. (R, page 56)

This ambivalence as to the significance of his incoherence is analogous to his ambivalent status as raging warrior and prematurely broken old man. Grit is puzzled by her father, "der an einem Tag einen fürchterlichen Redeschwall ausschüttet, um dann an den folgenden den Mund gar nicht mehr aufzumachen" (R, pages 96-97). Bekker has two particularly notable monologues: his nocturnal radio broadcast culminates in "ein lautes, undefinierbares vaterländisches Geheul" (R, page 197), and his lengthy monologue in Grit's presence surely seems totally incomprehensible to her (R, pages 214-217). If we replace words such as "incoherent" and "incomprehensible," however, with "visionary," then Bekker's ramblings assume another dimension.

> Die Augen können es gerade noch deutlich sagen: Sieh
> her, was Unbegreifliches mit mir passiert!, während der
> Mund es schon nicht mehr deutlich zu sagen vermag. Er
> redet daneben, stammelt, mischt Dummheit und ältere
> Weisheiten, die heute keiner mehr versteht. (R, page
> 92)

Is it decrepit senility or visionary wisdom that prompts Bekker's monologues? Not only his monologues, but also the images that haunt his brain can indeed be described as visionary. When asked if he recalls earlier vacations at the Mondsee, this is what his inner eye sees.

> Vor seine Augen [. . .] steigen plötzlich Bilder von
> Verheerung und er entsinnt sich kaum. Aus ihrem runden
> Imbisswagen am nördlichsten Vorsprung der Stadt treten
> Vater und Tochter in silbergrauen Schutzanzügen heraus
> in den ewigen Sandsturm.

> Aber sie torkeln und taumeln doch nur auf der Stelle, versuchen schwerfällig zu hüpfen, Hand in Hand. Unter ihren Füssen ein berstendes Scharren, als schöben ganze Erdschilde sich übereinander.
> Als da sind: Rumor, Narr und Frau . . . (R, page 65)

The fool is in fact the third element of Bekker's apocalyptic vision, and Bekker's visions are those of the fool, whose visionary status is, not coincidentally, much more ambivalent than that of the prophet.[17] Traditionally, the fool is either a sinner--particularly with regard to women--who does not know God or else a speaker of unabashed truth.[18] He is insane, or he is inspired. Sebastian Brant's Das Narren Schyff is a compendium of folly and demise. "Äussere Indizien für das unmittelbar bevorstehende Weltende sieht Brant im allgemeinen Sittenverfall, im Versinken der Welt in Sünde und Narrheit und im damit verbundenen 'abgang des gloube' [. . .]."[19] All of these elements--sin (incest), truth (vision), lack of paradigmatic faith, and fear of the apocalypse--are present in Rumor. Bekker plays the fool in all its variations. Drunk, he talks for money (R, page 194). "Visionen machte ihm das Gesicht Eines Menschen" (R, page 195). The radio journalist invites him to play "den Mitternachtsnarren [. . .], live" (R, page 195). The broadcast is conceived as a "Sendung," one in which "möglichst alles auf leichte Weise drunter und drüber gehen und der Hörer nicht unterscheiden soll, was Ernst ist oder Parodie [. . .]" (R, page 195). Bekker's status as a fool also provides a link to his Nazi science teacher (R, page 137) and, more importantly, to the officer. An early recollection of his stepfather could also stand for Bekker at the end of Rumor.

> All die Jahre über habe ich nicht mehr an ihn gedacht, diesen häuslichen Narren mit dem Gesicht eines Silen, den zeternden Staatsfeind im Ruhestand, Rache an seinem elenden Kommandeur sich täglich frisch mit der Frühstücksmilch aufkochend; aber dann brach ihm doch auf halber Strecke der Kopf zusammen. Betrogen um den Feind, den Kampf, das Töten, kreiselte er unlebendig dahin, gab nur noch ein schläfriges Wiederkäuen des alten Hasses, der grossen Verurteilungen von sich, die einst die ganze Hitze seiner Person gewesen waren. (R, page 24)

Bekker drinks like his stepfather, has a nose "wie die eines Silen" (R, page 224), and for a while performs domestic chores for Grit. More significantly, he too has failed to find the battlefield where he could confront his arch enemy. The fool who sees what others do not voices "ein leises, andauerndes Murmeln [. . .], etwas, das dürr und gerümpelt klingt, wie wenn Vergessenes, Entfallenes selbst spräche . . ." (R, page 214). Yet, the strain of articulating his apocalyptic vision drains Bekker of more and more strength.

> Plötzlich verstummt er. Inmitten der Beschwerde hat sich sein Mut mit einem Mal erschöpft. Im ersten Augenblick Aufbäumung, im selben schon wieder Unterwerfung-- [. . .] (R, page 222)

Bekker speaks less and less until finally: "Der Alte schweigt die meiste Zeit" (R, page 225). Rumor closes with the heavy breathing that haunts Grit on the telephone, a wordless vision that sounds, at best, a weak alarm. The ambivalence of Bekker's condition persists throughout the text--"Züge der Kraft und solche des Verfalls beherrschen nebeneinander dasselbe Gesicht [. . .]" (R, page 223)--but it is clear that the element of demise has gained the upper hand. Even the visionary gibberish of the fool, Bekker's resistance to the language of domination and alienation, yields to a voiceless rumor, the paralysis of hope.

One reviewer wrote of <u>Rumor</u>: "Ambivalenz bis ins kleinste Detail."[20] We know ambivalence to play a key role in Strauss' prose work. Yet <u>Rumor</u>, while drawing on this ambivalence, relegates the individual components of any diachronic connection to polarization. This precludes the fulfillment of diachronic extensions; the poles do not integrate or approximate each other in any fruitful way. This is true of the constellation of characters in <u>Rumor</u>--Bekker and Zachler's Institute, Bekker and his stepfather, and Bekker and his daughter. Each of these constellations in turn has broader ramifications beyond Bekker's personal struggle. Through the Institute, the officer, and Grit, Bekker is linked to society, history, and the future, respectively, but the link is an iron rod that keeps Bekker at bay. At the same time, the warrior-fool who takes up the cause of subjective agent in history is welded to that rod. This polarization and petrification are reflected in the frequent associations made between old age and rigidity. "Fürchte mich bloss vor noch mehr Alter. Und dass ich starrsinnig werde" (<u>R</u>, page 110). Bekker clearly shows increasing signs of old age and senility; constant references are made to his physical and mental demise. The word for this process appears in Bekker's last great monologue. "Nichts schöner als alt werden in junger Demokratie. Schmatzig, stramme Hose überm Arsch! und Marasmus" (<u>R</u>, page 215). Playing on Musil's notion of "Marasmus der Demokratie," Strauss thus associates Bekker's demise with society's decay.[21] This is the diachronic reflection of the text on its extratextual conditions threatening the human subject with total disintegration.

It has already been noted that Grit, as woman, harbors no hope, either in love or in sex. This relegates Bekker to the rigid isolation of the visionary. He imagines his child's touch has freed him from his "Säulenstarre" (R, page 109), while his last monologue includes a reference to Simon Stylites, founder of the pillar-saints (R, page 215). Simon Stylites spent forty-three years--approximately Bekker's age--on a pillar, from which he preached to the people, whose touch could not reach him.[22] Associating pillar with television tower, Bekker allows us to make the association between his nocturnal radio broadcast, and the visionary's sermons. The erection of the pillar phallus knows no diachronic release; there is no "Kampfesorgasmus" (R, page 73). Bekker does not want this isolation, as he does not want to be separated from Grit, who after all embodies the future. Yet, he is subject to isolation and displacement. Even his language degenerates to the point of voiceless rumor. Bekker's condition has been called "Verfall als Protest."[23] While the element of protest is not totally absent, it runs counter to the thrust of Rumor to credit Bekker's physical and mental deterioration with too much effective opposition to domination. His resistance is severely weakened. He has in fact become the moribund warrior, much like the Maori warrior to whom he likened the officer.

> Der Maori nämlich, ein fröhlicher und mutiger Krieger, ein Mensch mit höchst entwickelten Moralbegriffen, voll subtiler Bedenklichkeit und von ausserordentlicher physischer Widerstandskraft--ihn konnte eine einzige Demütigung fällen und in ausweglose Apathie versenken. Die reine Apathie breitete sich vom Gemüt über alle Körperorgane aus, die Muskelbewegungen schliefen ein und er starb binnen weniger Tage den Vagustod . . .
> (R, page 58)

Bekker is not quite dead yet, but there is certainly little reason to hope his premature aging process will reverse.

And what of literature itself? Does it still tender the hopeful promise of diachronic longing voiced in <u>Die Widmung</u>? Bekker's self-designation as "Sänger" (<u>R</u>, page 198) alludes to his capacity as visionary fool. Significantly, he is not a poet. Indeed, of all the prose texts considered here, the writing and reading of literature are of least significance in <u>Rumor</u>. Grit does read a novel, which she discusses briefly with her father. She is puzzled by the protagonist's designation as M., but concludes complacently that M. must be the author, Malomy. Bekker problematizes this assumption.

> 'Wäre es so, dann könnte Malomy ja einfach Ich sagen. Aber selbst wenn der Ich sagte, wäre es deshalb noch keineswegs sicher, dass er, Malomy, der Autor, auch der Held des Romans ist. So ist es bei vielen Romanen.'
> (<u>R</u>, page 103)

This is much too complicated for Grit: "Was für ein unnötiges Rätsel!" (<u>R</u>, page 104). Strauss sets a sly trap here for the glib interpreter of his works all too eager to equate a character in <u>Rumor</u> with Botho Strauss because their initials are the same and their names so similar in sound.[24] Bruno Stöss does indeed speak for literature in <u>Rumor</u>, not because he has the same initials as <u>Rumor</u>'s author, but because of his function within the text. Stöss is nowhere characterized as anyone professionally or otherwise affiliated with literature, but he is the narrator for the entire first section and significant portions of the remaining two sections of the text. Stöss differs from the narrators in Strauss' earlier prose works in that he knows and interacts with Bekker on the level of plot. This interaction is not extensive but highly significant, since it marks the relationship between the "I" of literature with the "I" of history--another instance of the text's own diachronic extension to extratextual reality. Neither warrior, leader, nor savior, Stöss is another employee at the Institute. The fact that he also began working for Zachler in 1968 is surely an allusion to the radical call to literature either to be an integral, political part of society or not to be at all. One way or another, Stöss has remained within the Institute, while Bekker has waged his struggle to assert his subjective agency. Stöss understands Bekker's hatred for Zachler (R, page 10) and chronicles it, but he himself does not challenge the Institute. People do not take him terribly seriously.

> Mich Normbruder [. . .] lassen sie hübsch beiseite stehen. [. . .] Wenn ich spreche, denken die Leute gern an etwas anderes . . . (R, page 14)

The principle of literature is itself institutionalized, subordinate to the principles organizing society at large. The real struggle for subjective agency is not in Stöss' hands, but in Bekker's. And he is fighting a losing battle.

Both Stöss and Bekker speak in the first person at different points throughout the text. The first section of Rumor (pages 7-19) is narrated entirely by Stöss, who describes the scene at the company party, provides us with background information on Bekker, and identifies his connection with events in the book. The second section (pages 21-67) consists of two sub-sections. Bekker's voice speaks the first (pages 21-50), recognizable as the conversation (monologue) which, we know from Stöss, he had with Grit through the night of the company party. The second section (pages 51-67), entailing Grit's and Bekker's interaction as they try to plan a joint vacation, is again narrated by Stöss. His narration is, however, interspersed with Bekker's visions, the last one of which (in this section) is apocalyptic (R, page 65). The third section spans the rest of the text (R, pages 69-231) and covers the vacation at the Mondsee, Grit's disease and operation, and Bekker's degeneration. Bekker's visionary voice predominates with increasing persistence. Even when Stöss reasserts his narrative voice, it is so infused with insight into and familiarity with Bekker's vision that it is extremely difficult, if not impossible, to distinguish the specificity of Stöss' voice. It is as though Bekker, who speaks for himself, also speaks through Stöss; Stöss does not speak through Bekker. Stöss' yielding of authority to Bekker is only apparently challenged when Bekker, under arrest for violation of immigration laws, asks Grit to contact Bruno Stöss for assistance.

> Er bittet sie, sich mit Bruno Stöss, dem ehemaligen und einzigen Vertrauten im Institut, in Verbindung zu setzen, denn wie er sich erinnern könne, habe der ihm früher einmal in einer anderen Sache einen ausgezeichneten Anwalt beschafft. (R, pages 210-211)

Interestingly enough, Stöss chooses not to contact a lawyer, but to contact Zahler instead, thinking this may be the last opportunity to reconcile Bekker and Zachler with each other (R, page 211). Zachler does indeed use his influence to effect Bekker's release, but it is never clear whether he does so because he desires Bekker's return to the Institute or whether Bekker is too beaten a warrior to be of any significance. Bekker remains oblivious to Zachler's role in his release. This incident says a great deal about the principle of literature. If we read the fact that Stöss once obtained a good lawyer for Bekker as an oblique allusion to the analysis of subjectivity in literature articulated in Adorno's aesthetic theory, then the fact that Stöss contacts Zachler instead of a lawyer speaks for the conviction that only with the extratextual reinstatement of subjective agency in societal organization can there be any hope for survival or revitalization of the human subject. The principle of literature thus acknowledges its own capacity as mere mediator, at best, in an extreme situation verging on final disaster. Since reconciliation does not ensue, the implication is that literature has failed. It is not that it is too weak to fulfill its responsibilities, but that it faces odds beyond its real control. At this critical juncture in the text, something very revealing happens to Stöss' voice: it disappears.

> Grit hatte getan, worum sie gebeten worden war, doch Bruno Stöss im Institut hatte nach eigenem Gutdünken einen anderen Weg eingeschlagen, keinen Rechtsanwalt beauftragt, da er zu wissen glaubte, wie man den Vorfall auf weniger aufwendige Weise erledigen könne. (R, page 211)

The narrative person appears here in the third person. We may well wonder who is minding the store. What we have here is a double abdication. Bekker is reduced to a voiceless rumor, and Stöss vacates the text where we might otherwise expect him to assert his voice more clearly. When neither the literary subject of the text nor the social subject of history can assert its agency, then there is indeed little hope for salvation from Bekker's apocalyptic vision.

If "Marlenes Schwester," "Theorie der Drohung," and <u>Die Widmung</u> voice a progressive struggle for subjective identity in the face of consumptive ambivalence and a crisis of experience and articulation, Rumor concludes the series--and the decade--in a testimony to the polarization of possibilities.[25] Is this a conscious decision informed by cultural pessimism on Strauss' part, or is it aesthetic paradox? Surely there are elements of both in Botho Strauss' prose project of the 1970's. No writer is free from the historicity of subjective and literary possibilities, and no writer fails to make some decisions about which of those possibilities to pursue. Botho Strauss is subject to both denunciation and admiration for his intelligent cultural pessimism. That element is stubbornly present in Rumor, although much less so in the earlier works. And yet, even in the face of this cultural pessimism, there are aesthetic questions which the responsible scholar must not ignore. One of the aesthetic paradoxes of Die Widmung is the relative scarcity of diachronic extensions. The crisis of longing finds a voice, but there is no voice for the actual extension, particularly social and historical extensions. By contrast, Rumor abounds with just such extensions. They are frustrated, to be sure, but extensions nonetheless: backwards into history, forwards into the future, and outwards into society. Even the directional adverbs here are misleading, since all extensions convene in Bekker as the warrior-subject. In an interview with Volker Hage, Botho Strauss has the following to say about Rumor: "'Rumor', sagt er und meint mehr das Wort als das Buch, 'ist etwas, das man verspürt, wenn mann aufmerksam lebt, und nicht, wenn man auf seinen Nabel schaut.'"[26] If Rumor reflects a conscious attempt on the author's part to stress the individual less and socio-historical phenomena affecting the individual more, we have an informed decision with aesthetic implications. Richard Schroubek's persona is certainly in conflict, and the text of Die Widmung is its battlefield. Social, historical, and literary phenomena are not absent from the text, but the focus of Die Widmung is still the text struggling to say "I". Rumor displaces the battlefield outside the text. Bekker embodies the contemporary plight of the human subject per se. Opening the text up to more general categories and topics such as ontological subjectivity, society, and history entails the risk of falling prey to these categories at the expense of the human subject struggling to attain its agency. It is a curious trap, since the subject can hardly assert its agency outside history or society. Rumor's rigid polarization and denial of hope in effect leave no room for subjective agency; without the element of hope and struggle, general categories can reign unchecked. Bekker's visions, for example, are neither syntactically nor semantically but textually far more cohesive than the rebuses in Die Widmung; they are ontological visions focused in the ontological subject's eye. Lest there be any misunderstanding, the function of general categories in Rumor is not by any means comparable to that in the literature of the student movement discussed in the first chapter of this study, where the subjective agent never sees the light of day in the first place. The ambivalence that structures "Marlenes Schwester" and "Theorie der Drohung" and also figures, albeit less significantly, in Die Widmung, is menacing, and yet it also houses hope. As long as things are fluid, there is always the possibility, however remote, for subjective survival. By stopping the flow of ambivalence in Rumor, Strauss also silences hope. The fact that the act of writing is of least significance in Rumor only supports the conclusion that this text marks the end of a prose project spanning the 1970's.

## II. EXCURSION ON PAARE, PASSANTEN

Indeed, Strauss' most recent prose piece represents a marked deviation from the format of the four texts examined here. Although the scope of the present study prohibits a detailed analysis of Paare, Passanten, largely essayistic in style with occasional impressionistic excursions, it is nonetheless of interest to note the recurrence of certain familiar themes. First and foremost, Strauss deplores the loss of history as a threat to survival.

> Die Leidenschaft, das Leben selbst braucht Rückgriffe (mehr noch als Antizipationen) und sammelt Kräfte aus Reichen, die vergangen sind, aus geschichtlichem Gedächtnis. Doch woher nehmen . . .? Dazugehörig sein in der Fläche der Vernetzung ist an die Stelle der zerschnittenen Wurzeln getreten; das Diachrone, der Vertikalaufbau hängt in der Luft.[27]

The history of National Socialism haunts German life into the present in a paradoxical stalemate. Neither fully appropriated nor wholly erased, it is lost and present at the same time. It resists Bewältigung and also, Strauss surmises, introduces "eine 'geschichtslose', statische Epoche" (PP, pages 172 and 183). Contemporary society is organized like a computer that reduces all dimensions of history to a single arbitrary plane from which the human subject eventually disappears.

> Indem wir die Maschinen der integrierten Schaltkreise erfanden und bauten, die Computer, Datenbänke, Super-

> speicher--wurden wir nicht insgeheim von der Idee geleitet, dass die entscheidende kulturelle Leistung unseres Zeitalters darin bestehen müsse, Summe zu ziehen, eine unermessliche Sammlung, ein Meta-Archiv, ein Riesengedächtnis des menschlichen Wissens zu schaffen, um uns selbst gleichzeitig von diesem zu verabschieden, unsere subjektive Teilhabe daran zu verlieren? (PP, page 193)[28]

As one person and as representative for the species, the individual faces another threat, unthinkable in its magnitude. Ultimate nuclear catastrophe lurks on the horizon, presiding like a "Hirn über der Erde" (PP, pages 166 and 170) over everything the individual does, feels, thinks. And yet, Strauss conjectures: "Es gibt keine reale Angst vor einem kollektiven Schicksal" (PP, page 164). Fear itself has become part of the "Fertigteil-Sprache, in der man inzwischen gelernt hat, über die Seele zu sprechen" (PP, page 163). Strauss does not believe in the individual (PP, page 189) but relies nonetheless on his/her existence--rather than on any social movement per se--to find the key to survival and a better life (PP, pages 169-170). "Im Rücken abgeschlossen, bist du nach vorn ein open end-Geschöpf" (PP, page 176). This admittedly vague notion of "the individual" bears the telltale signs of the ambivalence so characteristic of Strauss' work.

On the other hand, Paare, Passanten delineates the function of literature much more sharply.

> Man schreibt einzig im Auftrag der Literatur. Man schreibt unter Aufsicht alles bisher Geschriebenen. Man schreibt aber doch auch, um sich nach und nach eine geistige Heimat zu schaffen, wo man eine natürliche nicht mehr besitzt. (PP, page 103)

The social function of literature is, as Strauss sees it, radically curtailed. Authors are no less handicapped than any other professional group, and there is no new literature capable of resisting its fate as a commodity slated for consumption (PP, page 105). Strauss is merciless in his conclusions regarding the state of the art.

> Das Buch zur Metapher für das universale Archiv unserer Kultur zu erheben, wäre heute ein ebenso harmloser wie obsoleter Privatspass. [. . .] Wo die Schrift selbst aus dem Zentrum der Kultur verschwindet, wird der Aussenseiter unter den Schriftstellern, der Exzentriker, zur trolligen Figur--der Radikale, der in die Wurzeln greift auf einem im ganzen abrutschenden Kontinent. (PP, page 106)

Strauss thus strips himself of any illusions as to the ultimate significance of his own literary endeavors. The struggle for survival and a better life is posited, unequivocally, outside the literary text. What this imports for Strauss' future development as a writer is an intriguing question that remains to be answered. The "we" that predominates in Paare, Passanten could indicate an increasingly essayistic style crafted to accommodate the voice of the cultural commentator. Or, giving the author credit for being an "open end-Geschöpf" himself, one might look for a radically new approach to fiction and the literary subject. In either case, the prose penned by Botho Strauss in the 1980's will surely charter a different course from that which he pursued in the preceding decade. The broader issue of the current decade's challenge to literature in general is taken up in the concluding chapter of this study.

Notes: Chapter IV

[1] Botho Strauss, Rumor (Munich: Hanser, 1980). Further references to this work will appear as R parenthetically within the text.

[2] I use the English term in the archaic sense of clamor or low, indistinct noise. The German Rumor can also mean report or gossip; the verb rumoren implies a noisy groping or rummaging action.

[3] Duden (Mannheim/Vienna/Zürich: Dudenverlag, 1980), V, 2195.

[4] See for example Armin Ayren, "Zerfallsprozesse in Einzelbildern," Badische Zeitung (May 14/15, 1980); Reinhard Baumgart, "King Lear, 42, Beruf: Seher," Der Spiegel, 34 (February 25, 1980), 211; Paul Konrad Kurz, "Zerfall einer Person--Der neue Roman von Botho Strauss," Die Presse (June 7/8, 1980); Barbara Meili, "Zuviel gewollt, nichts erreicht," Zürcher Oberländer (June 14, 1980); Rolf Seeliger, "Hier rumort es zwischen den Zeilen," Tageszeitung (February 27, 1980); Günter Zehm, "Wie Bekker auf den Schnuller kommt," Die Welt (March 15, 1980). While noting the relative insigificance of plot, Dieter Bachmann does not denounce the lack of epic continuity in his review, "Der Lärm, in dem man lebt und untergeht," Tages-Anzeiger (April 16, 1980).

[5] See for example Rumor, p. 56.

[6] Anton Krättli falsely claims that Bekker has "zu wenig Geschichte." Strauss actually provides his protagonist with quite a bit of history: a stepfather who served in the Nazi army, childhood school experiences, marriage, fatherhood, and work. See Krättli's review, "Von Grund auf unversöhnlich," Rargauer Tagblatt (May 14, 1980), also printed as "Ein Zigeuner am Rand des Universums," Schweitzer Monatshefte, 5 (1980), 432.

[7] The German word Mündigkeit implies a coming of age that surpasses mere legal majority. The fully mature individual capable of independent thought and action is mündig.

[8] The historical connotation of Führer in Bekker's tirades against Zachler and the Institute are certainly not coincidental. As we shall see in the discussion of Bekker's relationship to his stepfather, there is a strong analogy between Bekker as he relates to the Institute and the officer as he relates to National Socialism.

[9] Peter Schütze, "Menschenreste mit beschränkter Hoffnung," Deutsche Volkszeitung (November 27, 1980)

[10] Rüdiger Kremer, reviewing Rumor for Radio Bremen on July 20, 1980, pointed out that Strauss has defied the censorship of paragraphs 88a and 130a of the federal penal code, which made "jede auch nur andeutungsweise positive Deutung des politischen Terrorismus" liable to prosecution.

[11] Michael Schneider, "Botho Strauss, das bürgerliche Feuilleton und der Kultus des Zerfalls: Zur Diagnose eines neuen Lebensgefühls," Den Kopf verkehrt aufgesetzt oder Die melancholische Linke: Aspekte des Kulturzerfalls in den siebziger Jahren (Darmstadt/Neuwied: Luchterhand, 1981), p. 253.

[12] A variety of critics allow for some vague social context for Bekker's tale but fail to elaborate on this at all. See for example Peter von Bekker, "'Rumor'," Theater heute, 21 (March 1980), Nr. 3,1; Wolfram Knorr, "Das Vergehen von Hören und Sehen," Weltwoche (April 16, 1980); Peter Laemmle, "Von der Notwendigkeit, böse zu sein," Die Zeit (April 4, 1980); Christoph Munk, "In Botho Strauss rumort es weiter," Kieler Nachrichten (April 18, 1980); Senta Ziegler, "Prinzip Scheitern," Die Furche (September 10, 1980). Christoph Siegrist, in "Bis sich nichts, auch gar nichts mehr bewegt," Badener Tagblatt (December 6, 1980), and Uwe Schutz, in "Das Buch des Monats," Handelsblatt (March 28/29, 1980), see in Rumor a reflection of the political disappointments of the student movement. Rumor's social content, however, is not mere disappointment or resignation but critique extending beyond the student movement per se. Carl Friedrich Geyer, writing "Knirschen in den Fugen," in Christ in der Gegenwart, 44 (1980), notes Rumor's analysis of thirty years of West German society without, however, analyzing the analysis.

[13] This could be an allusion to Chile after the coup against Allende in 1973.

[14] Although the anonymous, technical specialization of Zachler's Institute sounds much like Alexander Mitscherlich's description of fatherlessness of the second degree, neither Bekker's relationship to the Institute nor Grit's relationship to Bekker fits into the scheme of Mitscherlich's analysis. Bekker does not know how to challenge his arch enemy, but he knows who he is and is driven to confrontation. Grit, on the other hand, has clear access to her father but fails to perceive him as a worthy opponent in her struggle for identity--something in which she shows virtually no interest. While Strauss does not concede the fatherlessness of technologically advanced society, he does stress the inability of Grit's generation to feel the need for struggle, let alone execute it. Compare Mitscherlich, Auf dem Weg zur vaterlosen Gesellschaft: Ideen zur Sozialpsychologie (Munich: Piper, 1965), especially page 421.

[15] Michael Schneider, "Botho Strauss," pp. 252 and 254.

[16] It is interesting to note that sexuality as one aspect of corporeality plays a significant role for the first time in Rumor.

[17]Paul Konrad Kurz asks, "Ist Bekker Prophet oder Opfer des Rumor? Ich vermute beides." See Kurz, "Zerfall einer Person--Der neue Roman von Botho Strauss," Die Presse (June 7/8, 1980).

[18]Gustav Bebenmeyer, "Narrenliteratur," Reallexikon der deutschen Literaturgeschichte, ed. Werner Kohnschmidt and Wolfgang Mohr, 2nd ed. (Berlin: Walter de Gruyter, 1968), II, 592-509.

[19]Kindlers Literaturlexikon (Zürich: Kindler, 1965), V, col. 255-258.

[20]Charlotte Ress, "Von Stinkefee und ihren Streichhölzern," Kölnische Rundschau (April 3, 1980).

[21]Robert Musil, Der Mann ohne Eigenschaften: Roman, Gesammelte Werke (Reinbek bei Hamburg: Rowohlt, 1978), I, 1872.

[22]Otto Wimmer, Handbuch der Namen und Heiligen, 3rd ed. (Innsbruck: Tyrolia, 1966), 469-470.

[23]Hans Jansen, "Die begehbare Hölle," Westdeutsche Allgemeine Zeitung (July 1, 1980).

[24]Hilde Rubinstein in fact finds this assumption a credible one in her review, "'Was für ein unnötiges Rätsel'," Frankfurter Hefte, 2 (1981), 69.

[25]One reviewer aptly made the following plea: "Werfen wir diesem Dichter bitte nicht vor, dass er nur Schreiber ist, aber werfen wir seinen Nachbetern vor, dass sie nichts sind als Leser und Zuschauer." Peter Schütze, "Menschenreste mit beschränkter Hoffnung," Deutsche Volkszeitung (November 27, 1980). Schütze thus concurs with Rumor's thrust that the real battle over subjective agency must take place outside literature.

[26]Volker Hage, "Botho Strauss, ein Mann, der sich selbst nie in Szene gesetzt hat, bewegt als Autor wie kein anderer das deutsche Theater," Frankfurter Allgemeine Zeitung (March 21, 1980); also in Botho Strauss Symposium 9.2.1981 - 5.4.1981: Dokumentatieboek (Amsterdam: CREA, University of Amsterdam, 1981), CREA-Dokumentatieboek Nr. 7, p. 12.

[27]Botho Strauss, Paare, Passanten (Munich: Hanser, 1981), p. 26. Further references to this work will appear as PP parenthetically within the text.

[28]"Die vorerst letzte Stätte der subjektiven Produktion wird dann nur noch die Krankheit sein" (PP, p. 195) immediately calls Marlene's sister and Grit to mind.

CHAPTER V

CONCLUSIONS AND BEGINNINGS

I. BOTHO STRAUSS AND MAX FRISCH

Given that the principle of diachronic longing plays such a fundamental role within the corpus of Botho Strauss' prose, it seems only logical that this body of literature would likewise make diachronic reference to other works of literature, particularly those from the past. The wealth of literary allusions in Strauss' work indeed tempts the literary scholar with a variety of possibilities for comparison with earlier periods (Romanticism, for one) or even other cultures (French, for example). Focusing on the different possibilities for prose in post World War II German literature, however, it is of particular interest to note certain similarities between Botho Strauss and an older author who may be considered one of the major representatives of German literature in the latter half of the twentieth century. Max Frisch is certainly not the only writer who could make this claim, nor is he the only member of a post-war generation whose works might fruitfully be compared with those by Botho Strauss. Nonetheless, the diachronic references extending from Strauss' work to texts by Frisch are simply too striking to be overlooked. The scope of the present study forbids a detailed analysis of these intertextual references, but even a brief look at them allows us to see Strauss' prose oeuvre in the broader historical context of post-war German literature, especially as it relates to the status of literary subjectivity and the extratextual challenge to subjective agency.

The similarities between texts by Strauss and Frisch are by no means limited to the most obvious parallel, i.e., that between "Theorie der Drohung" (1975) and <u>Stiller</u> (1953/54).[1] In both instances, the protagonist is proclaimed by others to be a known character, while he himself professes total ignorance of the existence presumed (by others) to be his own. Both "Theorie der Drohung" and <u>Stiller</u> problematize the question of identity and language. <u>Die Widmung</u> (1977) and a more recent work by Frisch, <u>Montauk</u> (1974/75), share a concern for experiential integrity implicit in living a present that is indeed fully present without being devoid of past. Both texts revolve around the love relationship between a man and a woman.[2] <u>Rumor</u> (1980) in turn is strongly reminiscent of <u>Homo faber</u> (1955/57).[3] Walter Faber is a technician by profession and by nature; he believes in rational solutions to mechanical problems but finds that human problems cannot be reduced to mechanics.[4] While <u>Rumor</u>'s central character is not a firm believer in technology, he is trapped by an institute for news and know how, one which annihilates the potential for subjective agency and responsibility, a potential which Faber initially ignores. As fathers of young women they have not seen in many years, the two men have incestuous desire for their daughter. These similarities--between "Theorie der Drohung" and <u>Stiller</u>, <u>Die Widmung</u> and <u>Montauk</u>, and <u>Rumor</u> and <u>Homo faber</u>--are the most conspicuous. There are others, which are neither quite so obvious nor confined to the scheme of textual pairs just listed. The woman who receives Faber's written report of his experiences and the woman to whom Schroubek addresses his journal are both called Hanna(h). Both "Theorie der Drohung" and Montauk devote a great deal of consideration to plagiarism--"Leben im Zitat"[5]--especially with regard to the inability to experience fully one's own present, to speak the authentic voice of "I".[6] Montauk likewise shares with Die Widmung and even with Stiller the fear of repetition as a principle that precludes lived experience.[7] Furthermore, both Stiller and Die Widmung clearly address crises of articulation and identity. "Wir haben die Sprache, um stumm zu werden. Wer schweigt, ist nicht stumm. Wer schweigt, hat nicht einmal eine Ahnung, wer er nicht ist."[8] Strauss uses the word Ausdrucksnot, while Frisch circumscribes it. Stiller asserts: "Das ist die erschreckende Erfahrung dieser Untersuchungshaft: ich habe keine Sprache für meine Wirklichkeit!" Characterized by her silence, Stiller's wife, Julika, dies of tuberculosis, "so ausdruckslos noch im Zustand der schreienden Not."[9] Montauk, Stiller, and Homo faber all address the interplay between past and present, an area which we have seen to be of pivotal concern for Strauss. It is not important here to note the finer points of style and approach separating Strauss from Frisch, nor is it necessary to trace the changes in style from Stiller, written in the fifties, to Montauk, written some twenty years later. What is significant is that both authors, representative of different generations and different post-war experiences, write prose texts in which questions of personal identity and experiential integrity spanning past and present all figure very strongly. The individual constitutes him/herself (or not) through language and in history. For Frisch, particularly as evidenced in Stiller, Homo faber, and Mein Name sei Gantenbein (1960/64),[10] the telling of tales means the production of history and histories as experiential possibilities. An essay from 1960 entitled "Unsere Gier nach Geschichten" elaborates on the notion of narrated memory as an experience whose realm is more that of future possibility than closed past. Yet, any experience needs its past as well as its future. The past can be adapted to allow for a possible future: "Geschichten sind Entwürfe in die Vergangenheit zurück [. . .]."

> Nur die Erfahrung ändert alles, weil sie nicht ein Ergebnis der Geschichte ist, sondern ein Einfall, der die Geschichte ändern muss, um sich auszudrücken. Die Erfahrung dichtet. [. . .] [Die Menschen] entwerfen, sie erfinden, was ihre Erfahrung lesbar macht. Die Erfahrung ist nicht ein Schluss, sondern eine Eröffnung; ihr Bezirk ist die Zukunft. Oder die Zeitlosigkeit. Drum widerstrebt es ihr--so müsste man meinen--, sich als Geschichte zu geben, als Erzählung. Aber wie soll sie sich anders geben?[11]

Botho Strauss' texts abound with characters on the brink of disaster. Marlene's sister suffers from a terminal illness with no termination; Lea disintegrates, while the narrator in "Theorie der Drohung" undergoes a radical transformation; Richard Schroubek suffers from a potentially fatal crisis of articulation; Bekker experiences marasmic changes, and Grit finds no real release from her physical ailments. The struggle for experiential integrity is a matter of utmost importance for subjective survival. It proceeds through and against language. For Frisch's characters, too, the struggle for the articulation of identity is a matter of life and death, "Leben oder Versiechen."[12] Julika, so often characterized as silent, dies unrecognized even by Stiller, who loved her.[13] The daughter/lover in <u>Homo faber</u> dies from a skull fracture unnoticed by hospital personnel preoccupied with her snake bite, while Walter Faber himself cannot be saved from the disease which consumes his body. Beyond the element of survival per se, Frisch's weaving and reweaving of narrated possibilities contain an ethical component as well, which is absent from Strauss' texts. There are numerous narrative possibilities for Frisch's characters to try on for size. The problem is to decide which one is the right story/history for a particular experience. The path not chosen, the unrealized possibility, does not disappear but leaves a negative imprint that poses an ethical question. Faber's encounter with Sabeth opens up the Pandora's box of his past experience --which he had considered closed--with Hanna, whose child he did not want. Hanna knows better than he that their own history cannot be relived with a different outcome. "'[. . .] wir können uns nicht mit unseren Kindern nochmals verheiraten'."[14] <u>Mein Name sei Gantenbein</u> poignantly tells the tale of a man seeking the history to his experience.[15] "Ich probiere Geschichten an wie Kleider!"[16] The protagonist cannot help but recall his encounter with a Nazi in 1942 in terms of what he did not do.

> Ich weiss, es ist lächerlich. Eine Tat nicht vergessen zu können, die man nicht getan hat, ist lächerlich. Ich erzähle auch niemand davon. Und manchmal vergesse ich wieder vollkommen . . . .
> Nur seine Stimme bleibt mir im Ohr.

Regarding the possibilities of flying away from a given situation or not, the conclusion is

> Einerlei:
> Der nämlich bleibt, stellt sich vor, er wäre geflogen, und der nämlich fliegt, stellt sich vor, er wäre geblieben, und was er wirklich erlebt, so oder so, ist der Riss, der durch seine Person geht, der Riss zwischen mir und ihm, wie ich's auch immer mache, so oder so [. . .].[17]

Although the sum constellation of narrated possibilities in any given text by Frisch may not yield an integral subjective voice, each story told is privy to a certain congruity of narration. Each story is a credible, whole possibility. For Strauss, such stories can no longer be told. To be sure, one can find brief anecdotes in his texts, but these cannot be construed as extended histories to a particular experience proper to a subjective agent. Except for Julien, who relates the vampire story in "Marlenes Schwester," Strauss' characters do not tell each other (or themselves) stories as Frisch's characters do. When Lea relates experiences from her past with the narrator in "Theorie der Drohung," she does so from the perspective of what she knows to be true and not from that of how it might have been. Unable to tell such tales, Strauss' characters are thus unable to create their own personal history; neither are they able to produce social history. The self-reflective style of Strauss' texts consistently precludes the possibility for a focused center to his "stories," which after all do not exist as such. This certainly precludes as well the notion of a literary figure (an individual) capable of assuming the responsibility for remembering--maintaining history--for the species.[18]

The points of comparison and contrast between Strauss and Frisch outlined above attest to the advanced stage of fragmentation of the literary subject in the 1970's and the progressive loss of an epistemological framework that would allow either for ethical judgments or experiential integrity. We should not assume from this, however, that the subjective agent of history faced no comparable threats in the 1950's, when Frisch wrote Stiller and Homo faber. Hans Mayer provides a somewhat controversial reading of Stiller when he ascertains that the experiential possibilities narrated in the novel evidence anything but existential freedom in Sartre's vein. Mayer sees Stiller's possibilities as socially defined, that is to say, limited. Modifying Frisch's own words, he writes:

> [. . .] jeder Mensch erfindet sich früher oder später eine Geschichte, die er für sein Leben hält. Er hat aber unter bestimmten realen Lebensbedingungen nur die Auswahl unter einigen vorhandenen Fertigmodellen. Welches auch immer er erwählt, es wird eine Lebensgeschichte daraus, die ebensogut in einer illustrierten Zeitschrift erzählt werden könnte. Umtausch der Modelle im Warenhaus für Lebensgeschichten ist nicht gestattet. Was am Falle Stillers zu beweisen war.

Further: "Der Erzähler dieses Romans wird nicht müde, den Reproduktionscharakter und die völlige Verdinglichung menschlicher Beziehungen in der von ihm dargestellten Welt zu demonstrieren."[19] Mayer clearly understands capitalist pluralism somewhat differently from R. Hinton Thomas and Keith Bullivant, who have written on post-war German literature: "Die Identität der Person wurde nun, deutlicher als je zuvor, als eine Sache gesehen, die man sich auswählen kann."[20] Although Thomas and Bullivant focus on literature of the early 1960's, their uncritical concept of personal pluralism echoes a faint but recognizable adherence to the hypothesis that the end of World War II and the founding of the Federal Republic of Germany gave West German literature and society a clean slate to start anew, unhampered by a cumbersome and controversial past. Others have argued elsewhere that indeed no such "Stunde Null" existed.[21] German literature after 1945 was neither ignorant of nor oblivious to its traditions. By the same token, neither was the world created anew after 1945. To be sure, international politics and national boundaries assumed different demarcations after the war from those they had known previously. The fundamental principles governing the organization of Western European society remained, however, those of advanced capitalism. The point here is that the differences between Frisch and Strauss cannot be attributed to a pseudo-primeval freedom available to Frisch in the fifties but denied Strauss some twenty to thirty years later. There are as many similarities between the two authors as there are differences. The principles of social organization threatened subjective agency and challenged literary subjectivity then as they do now, with the difference that objective possibilities for subjective agency have suffered increasing corrosion. A leading West German sociologist discusses a shift in social behavior resulting from economic concentration, political centralization, and increasing abstraction in social life.[22] The contemporary nature of industrial-capitalist production and its state gives rise, he claims, to a "Rollengesellschaft, die dadurch charakterisiert ist, dass der einzelne nur als 'Merkmalsträger' gefragt ist--im Hinblick auf dieses oder jenes Merkmal, nicht [. . .] auf das, was diese Merkmale zusammenhält, seine Person."[23] All realms of social activity--and what realm is not social?--evidence the progressive erosion of social networks, of possibilities for experiential integrity. "Was gebraucht und geschaffen wird, ist ein Stehaufmännchen ohne Bleigewicht."[24] Narr sees the danger facing the subject in Western society but does not concede the demise of the subjective agent as a <u>fait accompli</u>. Neither does Strauss, although <u>Rumor</u> certainly comes quite close to doing just that.

## II. BOTHO STRAUSS AND THE RECEPTION OF HIS WORKS

Precisely because the advancing fragmentation of the subject and the loss of paradigmatic faith figure so strongly in Strauss' work, it lends itself to a curious denunciation by those who find the consumer-appeal and fashionability of despair distasteful: Botho Strauss is "'Arrièregarde.'"[25] Yet, we have seen that this author's prose project of the 1970's does not wallow self-complacently in the mire of despair. Rather, it weaves an intricately crafted outcry and struggle against the sources of despair, against the threat to subjective agency in contemporary West German society. It is not until <u>Rumor</u> that the tendency to capitulate to that threat is manifested. The failure to note the complexity of Strauss' texts and their aesthetic and epistemological ramifications allows for the glib rejection as <u>arrièregarde</u>. By the very same token, it also allows high praise to be lavished on Strauss' work for its sensitive depiction of universal suffering, humankind in the face of final disaster.[26] To be fair, we must concede that Strauss' characters do lend themselves somewhat to this latter interpretation, primarily since they are not rooted in any fixed, identifiable social context.[27] Yet, this does not reflect the elitist desperation of the privileged few. It may be attributed instead to Strauss' concern for subjective agency. To give his characters real social roots would foster the illusion that integral networks of social experience were not as endangered as they indeed are. This particular manifestation of the concern for subjective agency is, as we have seen in our discussion of Die Widmung, certainly not unproblematic, especially given Strauss' concern for the specificity of experience. These two concerns--the specificity of experience and the threat to subjective agency--render a slick textual resolution impossible. In fact, they structure the dynamic tension in Strauss' prose. The complacent proclamation of Botho Strauss as the aesthetic elite's brilliantly morose prophet of doom would seem to reveal, then, more about his critics than about his actual work.[28]

Let us assume for a moment that there is more to this than the carelessness of readers rushing to meet deadlines with reviews that must be witty, informative, and not overly complicated. What possible explanations can there be for the overriding reception of Botho Strauss' prose as exemplary for the existential-universal suffering of humanity? For purposes of discussion, I should like to tender three possible explanations, none of which I shall attempt to prove. Analyzing the institutional transitions in the writing of literary history following the failure of the 1848 revolution in Germany, Peter Uwe Hohendahl ascertains that this political failure affected changes in literary history after the defeat of liberalism, both with regard to methodology and to content. These changes sought to pave a linear, revisionary path leading to the Second Empire.[29] I would suggest that something roughly analogous may be at play in the critical reception of Strauss' prose in the decade following the demise of the student protest movement. It is not Strauss who is overly eager to mourn the loss of the political hope of that movement but rather the critics themselves who exhibit post-1968 revisionism. In an odd twist, it is not the past they revise but the present; this in turn predetermines the possibilities for the future. Such critics thereby falsely credit Strauss with depicting the universal end of hope and, furthermore, implicitly equate the end of the student movement with the end of any viable social struggle. The question whether this reflects a personal idiosyncrasy--on the part of a conspicuously large number of individual critics--or an institutional pattern merits some consideration.

A second possible explanation for the critics' reception of Strauss indicates the latter. Drawing largely on Alvin Gouldner's analysis of the intellectuals as the new class,[30] David Roberts has written an intriguing essay on the periodization of West German literature since 1960, in which he makes the following point:

> Die neue Klasse bzw. die 'Intellektuellen neuen Typs', die vom Berufsverbot bedroht sind und die ihren verlorenen revolutionären Hoffnungen nachtrauern, registrieren ihre gesellschaftliche Situation in der Form der existentiellen Entfremdung und die sich bildende neue Gesellschaft nicht als die <u>entfremdete</u> Form ihrer eigenen Klasseninteressen.[31]

This has as its consequence, Roberts argues, the regression implicit in <u>Neue Subjektivität</u>, which renews the search for the bourgeois individual.

> Das Verlangen nach Ganzheit bestätigt aber bloss die immer fortschreitende gesellschaftliche Arbeitsteilung und die tatsächliche Zerrissenheit des Subjekts. Die

> Suche nach Authentizität, nach neuen Lebensformen, nach der
> Überwindung von Entfremdung in der Gemeinschaft oder in der
> Natur ist in diesem Sinn der negative Aus- druck des
> Bedürfnisses nach Klassenbewusstsein.[32]

Certainly, Botho Strauss' prose cannot be reduced to the standard attributes commonly ascribed to the so-called new subjectivity.[33] Indeed, one wonders whether the phrase Neue Subjektivität is more appropriate to a wide range of different literary texts or, alternately, to an institutional bandwagon all too eager to ride roughshod over textual specificity in order to homogenize--grasp, control, and label--literary trends. To modify Roberts' conclusion, then, it seems that not the literature of Neue Subjektivität but, rather, its reception manifests a negative expression of the need for class consciousness among intellectuals.

The third possible explanation for the standard reception of Strauss' prose is somewhat less theoretical and historically specific than the other two. It is, simply, the ideological inclination of bourgeois intellectuals to view the world as a mirror reflecting only the eye of the beholder. They see their experience as universal because they fail to perceive any experience other than their own. One surmises this criticism behind Michael Schneider's enraged discussion about "jenes melancholische und depressive Lebensgefühl" in Strauss' work, so savored by the critics.[34]

> Kein Wunder, dass die bundesrepublikanischen Kultur-
> pfleger und Feuilletonisten sich im frostigen Klima
> dieser Kultur-Provinz, die sie ja von Berufs wegen mit-
> verwalten, ausgesprochen heimisch fühlen. Und natür-
> lich stilisieren sie--in altbewährter Weise--das dort
> herrschende desolate Lebensgefühl zum 'einzig wahren'
> Lebensgefühl, zum 'allgemeinen Zeitgeist', ja zur
> 'Grundbefindlichkeit des Menschen' hoch.[35]

## III. BOTHO STRAUSS AND HISTORY: THE CHALLENGE TO LITERATURE IN THE 1980'S

While we have seen that Strauss' prose work of the 1970's does indeed ultimately tend to concede to despair, the critics' response to this capitulation is premature and not based on a careful reading of Strauss' texts. With the exception of Rumor, these texts actively engage in the struggle to address the crisis of articulation, identity, and experience that afflicted the decade. David Roberts characterizes West German literature into the late 1960's as oriented towards political questions of the past, arguing that what followed has focused on existential questions of the present.[36] This schematic dichotomy cannot be upheld for an author like Botho Strauss, whose literary challenge to the crisis of experiential integrity assimilates the need for vibrant present with the call for subjectively appropriated past. The subjective agent is the ground in which past and present fertilize each other; only here can experiential integrity be cultivated. Strauss' work attests to the fact that a living sense of history--personal and social--is crucial for the survival of the individual as well as of the species. History is as pervasive in the texts discussed here, albeit primarily as a menace, dangerous precisely because it itself is threatened with ossification. Die Widmung's plea for open-ended, diachronic extensions into history becomes rigidified into a pattern of petrified disjunctures in Rumor. For all intents and purposes, the subjective agent has been reduced to registering pain or voicing its own demise.

Strauss is certainly not the only contemporary author who acknowledges the crisis inherent in the loss of history. One recognizes a comparable concern, for example, in the prose writings of Alexander Kluge, known primarily for his work in German cinema.

> Kluges ganze literarische Arbeit hat teil an der Anstrengung, die [. . .] irreale Geschichtslosigkeit des Nachkriegsdeutschland zu verändern, die Gegenwart mit der abgekapselten, verdrängten, höchstens in Schlagworten rezipierten Vergangenheit zu verknüpfen, ein Kontinuum wieder herzustellen [. . .].[37]

The continuum cited here does not stem from an uncritical faith in the unbroken integrity of the subject but rather from the critical conviction that history persists in every human act. The relationship between the two is not a harmonious one to be fit neatly into clearly defined conceptual systems. Rather than focus on the threat of history denied, as Strauss does, Kluge concentrates on the potentially fruitful but in any case ever-present, porous aspects of history lived in the present. History becomes in effect a sixth material sense.[38] It is not surprising that this notion of history is given theoretical consideration by Kluge together with Oskar Negt in their 1981 publication on <u>Geschichte und Eigensinn</u>. In a chapter entitled "Verschleierung und Erfahrung," they write:

> Die Erfahrungen, die in Bewegung setzen, müssen nicht nur durch den Kopf hindurch, sondern durch Körper, die Nerven, die Sinne, die Gefühle; sie müssen am Geschichtsverhältnis als einem fasslichen Gegenstand arbeiten können.[39]

Subjectivity, they argue, is by definition historical. While any given individual is privy to the immediate experience of his/her lifetime, any aspect of that experience reflects the mediated experience of the totality of society and the history of the species extending in either direction outside that particular lifetime. At the same time, the human being can manifest and know membership in the species only through specific, unmediated experience in the present.

> Subjektivität ist geschichtlich bestimmt, wenn sie in ihren Partikeln, in allen diesen einander mehrdimensional überlappenden Geschichtsverläufen, untersucht wird, somit eine Gattungsbestimmung erhält--und wenn diese Untersuchung zugleich im individuellen Lebenslauf rezipiert werden kann. Dies ist nämlich die Bedingung dafür, dass Subjektivität als geschichtlich bestimmte, als subjektiv-objektives Verhältnis, wiederangeeignet werden kann.[40]

Negt and Kluge point out further that the common understanding of subjectivity as confined to the private realm of emotions and desires merely sustains a false dichotomy that serves the interests of domination.[41] The same could be said of our failure to ask what is qualitatively new in the "new subjectivity" when we occupy ourselves with labeling texts rather than analyzing them in the historical context of aesthetic epistemology. Strauss' texts make no pretense of resolving the crisis of subjective agency, whose roots are planted in extratextual reality. At the same time, they struggle towards a redefinition of subjectivity and historical experience without actually achieving it. Helmut Kreuzer claimed that the end of the 1970's brought no significant changes in West German literature.[42] Here I would disagree. Botho Strauss' prose responds to the extraliterary loss of paradigmatic faith and the extratextual threats to subjective agency with a literary project that pleads for a qualitatively new understanding of the dynamic between history and experiential specificity, a project evidencing more <u>Subjektskepsis</u> than <u>Sprachskepsis</u>. Considered in terms of Vergangenheitsbewältigung, which by and large has dominated the discussion of West German literature and culture since the Third Reich, the plea for a new epistemological understanding of history and subjectivity indeed has potentially striking significance. It challenges the very notion of the past as a closed entity which must be acknowledged and overcome by positing it instead as a continuous, experiential element of the lived present. In so doing, it simultaneously rescues the issue of Vergangenheitsbewältigung from becoming a mere relic of an archaic past itself. This is perhaps the greatest challenge for the 1980's, to restore the subject to its own personal and social history, and thereby allow for the continued struggle for subjective agency. Such an epistemological understanding of subjectivity calls in turn for a new literary aesthetic. This is then the context in which Botho Strauss' prose assumes ultimate significance.

Notes: Chapter V

[1] Max Frisch, Stiller: Roman, Gesammelte Werke, ed. Hans Mayer (Frankfurt/Main: Suhrkamp, 1976), III, 359-780. Helmut Schödel refers briefly to the similarities between these two works in his essay, "Ästhetik des Verlustes: Zur Literatur des Botho Strauss," Theater heute, 17(1976), Nr. 13, 105. Schödel's piece has been reprinted in Spectaculum 26: Acht moderne Theaterstücke (Frankfurt/Main: Suhrkamp, 1977), pp. 298-303.

[2] Max Frisch, Montauk: Eine Erzählung, Gesammelte Werke, ed. Hans Mayer (Frankfurt/Main: Suhrkamp, 1976), VI, 617-754.

[3] Max Frisch, Homo faber: Ein Bericht, Gesammelte Werke, ed. Hans Mayer (Frankfurt/Main: Suhrkamp, 1976), IV, 5-204.

[4] See Frisch, Homo faber, p. 170.

[5] Frisch, Montauk, p. 685.

[6] Discussing Montauk, Gerhard P. Knapp draws the following conclusions: "Schreiben--und das heisst Erleben 'in dieser dünnen Gegenwart' (103)--ist nicht möglich ohne die Anwesenheit der Vergangenheit. Und wenn Leben sich erinnern bedeutet, dann wird die Erinnerung zum zwangsläufigen Korrelat der Fiktion. 'Leben im Zitat' erweist sich als die einzig noch mögliche Form der Aufrichtigkeit." Knapp oversimplifies the highly complex relationship spanning memory, writing, and experiential integrity of the present and credits Montauk with a resolution which, in my opinion, it does not find. See Knapp, "Noch einmal: Das Spiel mit der Identität, Zu Max Frischs Montauk," Max Frisch: Aspekte des Prosawerks, ed. Gerhard P. Knapp (Bern, Frankfurt/Main, Las Vegas: Peter Lang, 1978), pp. 298-299.

[7] Compare Montauk, p. 628, with Stiller, pp. 420 and 421.

[8] Frisch, Stiller, p. 677.

[9] See Frisch, Stiller, pp. 436 and 747.

[10] Max Frisch, Mein Name sei Gantenbein: Roman, Gesammelte Werke, ed. Hans Mayer (Frankfurt/Main: Suhrkamp, 1976), V, 5-320.

[11] Max Frisch, "Unsere Gier nach Geschichten," Gesammelte Werke, ed. Hans Mayer (Frankfurt/Main: Suhrkamp, 1976), IV, 264.

[12] Frisch, Stiller, p. 752.

[13] Frisch, Stiller, p. 780.

[14] Frisch, Homo faber, p. 139.

[15] See Frisch, Mein Name sei Gantenbein, pp. 8 and 11.

[16] Frisch, Mein Name sei Gantenbein, p. 22.

[17] Frisch, Mein Name sei Gantenbein, pp. 60 and 130.

[18] The issue of the moral capacity of literature is, either implicitly or explicitly, raised in a variety of essays on post-war German prose published in Positionen des Erzählens: Analysen und Theorien zur Literatur der Bundesrepublik, ed. Heinz Ludwig Arnold and Theo Beck (Munich: Beck, 1976). Gisbert Ter-Nedden, for example, makes the following point: "Es geht in diesen Romanen nicht so sehr um konkrete Sozialkritik, sondern um die Restauration ihrer Bedingungen, vor allem um die autonome moralische Persönlichkeit als Gegeninstanz zur Gesellschaft, die Kritik erst möglich macht." Ter-Nedden does not fail to note the problematic nature of this thrust. "Der Rückzug auf die moralische Integrität der Person verfehlt einerseits die Ebene politischer Gesellschaftskritik und bleibt andererseits der traditionell vorgegebenen Selbstdeutungen des Subjekts verhaftet." See Gisbert Ter-Nedden, "Allegorie und Geschichte: Zeit- und Sozialkritik als Formproblem des deutschen Romans der Gegenwart," Positionen des Erzählens, p. 114. Ter-Nedden discusses works by Grass, Böll, Frisch, Johnson, and Lenz.

[19] Hans Mayer, "Max Frischs Romane," Max Frisch: Aspekte des Prosawerks, p. 59.

[20] R. Hinton Thomas and Keith Bullivant, Westdeutsche Literatur der sechziger Jahre, trans. Inge Neske (Cologne: Kiepenheuer & Witsch, 1974), p. 15.

[21] See, for example, the following: Hans Mayer, Zur deutschen Literatur der Zeit: Zusammenhänge--Schriftsteller--Bücher (Reinbek bei Hamburg: Rowohlt, 1967); Hans Dieter Schäfer, "Die nicht faschistische Literatur der 'jungen Generation' im nationalsozialistischen Deutschland," Die deutsche Literatur im Dritten Reich, ed. Horst Denkler and Karl Prümm (Stuttgart: Reclam, 1976), pp. 459-503; Hans Dieter Schäfer, "Zur Periodisierung der deutschen Literatur seit 1930," Literaturmagazin, 7(1977), 95-115; Frank Trommler, "Nachkriegsliteratur--eine neue deutsche Literatur?" Literaturmagazin, 7(1977), 167-186; Frank Trommler, "Der zögernde Nachwuchs: Entwicklungsprobleme der Nachkriegsliteratur in West und Ost," Tendenzen der deutschen Literatur seit 1945, ed. Thomas Koebner (Stuttgart: Kroner, 1971), pp. 1-116; Heinrich Vormweg, "Deutsche Literatur 1945-1960: Keine Stunde Null," Die deutsche Literatur der Gegenwart, ed. Manfred Durzak (Stuttgart: Reclam, 1971), pp. 13-30.

[22] Wolf-Dieter Narr, "Hin zu einer Gesellschaft bedingter Reflexe," Stichworte zur 'Geistigen Situation der Zeit', ed. Jürgen Habermas, 3rd ed. (Frankfurt/Main: Suhrkamp, 1980), II, 489-528.

²³Narr, "Hin zu einer Gesellschaft bedingter Reflexe," p. 494.

²⁴Narr, "Hin zu einer Gesellschaft bedingter Reflexe," p. 498. See also pp. 497 and 503. In many ways, Narr's essay echoes some fundamental tenets in the analysis of contemporary social organization and possibilities for experiential integrity discussed in Oskar Negt and Alexander Kluge, Öffentlichkeit und Erfahrung: Zur Organisationsanalyse von bürgerlicher und proletarisher Öffentlichkeit (Frankfurt/Main: Suhrkamp, 1972).

²⁵Martin Roda Becher borrows a term coined by Christiane Rochefort in the early sixties. See Becher, "Poesie der Unglücksfälle: Über die Schriften von Botho Strauss," Merkur, 32(1978), Nr. 6, 625.

²⁶Strauss' work is not only noted for its sensitivity but for its intelligence as well. Peter Beicken makes this into a category of Neue Subjektivität when he writes: "Botho Strauss bringt in seinen Erzählungen einen Aspekt der neuen Subjektivität zur Geltung, der als Intellektualisierung der Empfindung in der Zeit nach der Politisierung bezeichnet werden kann." See Peter Beicken, "'Neue Subjektivität': Zur Prosa der siebziger Jahre," Deutsche Literatur in der Bundesrepublik seit 1965, ed. Paul Michael Lützeler and Egon Schwarz (Königstein/Ts.: Athenäum, 1980), p. 175.

²⁷Recall Hans Wolfschütz' comments: "Strauss' Figuren bleiben in ihrem gesellschaftlichen Bezug undeutlich definiert, ja sie scheinen, bis auf wenige Ausnahmen, ganz bewusst, aus ihrem normalen sozialen Kontext herausgelöst und in 'künstliche' Handlungsräume gestellt, die als Rückzugsorte und Fluchträume zeichenhaft von einer auf das Private beschränkten Existenz berichten [. . .]." See Wolfschütz' entry on Botho Strauss in the Kritisches Lexikon zur deutschsprachigen Gegenwartsliteratur, ed. Heinz Ludwig Arnold (Munich: edition text + kritik, 1978), II, no pagination.

²⁸While my comments on the reception of Botho Strauss stem from the reviews of his prose work, I suspect that the authors of these reviews are heavily influenced by their reception of Strauss' plays, which seem more emphatically nihilistic than the prose. A careful study of Strauss' work in the dramatic medium would undoubtedly yield fruitful insight into the different possibilities in and challenges to contemporary prose and theater.

²⁹See Peter Uwe Hohendahl, "Post-Revolutionary Literary History: The Case of Wilhelm Dilthey," Literature and History, ed. Leonard Schulze and Walter Wetzels (Lanham/New York/London: University Press of America, 1983), pp. 119-145. Hohendahl writes: "The failure of this Liberalism, its inability to hold its own in the long run against the conservative powers as shown in the revolution of 1848, also brought the Liberal cause into disrepute in those sectors, including the sphere of literary history, where there was no direct contact with political decisions. It is the liberals themselves--men such as the

Neo-Hegelian Robert Prutz or even Theodor Wilhelm Danzel, the Goethe and Lessing scholar--who encourage and carry out the revision of the historical picture. The younger generation, e.g., Dilthey and Scherer, accepts to a great extent this criticism of liberal historiography and turns itself to the task of surmounting the crisis and of formulating a new program" (p. 123).

[30] See Alvin Gouldner, The Future of Intellectuals and the Rise of the New Class (New York: Seabury, 1979).

[31] Although the manuscript has since been published under the title "Tendenzwenden: Die sechziger und siebziger Jahre in literaturhistorischer Perspektive" in Deutsche Vierteljahrsschrift, 56 (June 1982), No. 2, 290-313, I am citing here from the original manuscript, "Zur Periodisierung der westdeutschen Literatur seit 1960: Zwei Modelle," p. 28.

[32] Roberts, "Zur Periodisierung," p. 29.

[33] Interestingly enough, Roberts does cite Die Widmung as one example of Neue Subjektivität. See Roberts, "Tendenzwenden," p. 300, fn. 26.

[34] Michael Schneider, "Botho Strauss, das bürgerliche Feuilleton und der Kultus des Verfalls: Zur Diagnose eines neuen Lebensgefühls," Den Kopf verkehrt aufgesetzt oder Die melancholische Linke: Aspekte des Kulturzerfalls in den siebziger Jahren (Darmstadt/Neuwied: Luchterhand, 1981), p. 236.

[35] Schneider, "Botho Strauss," p. 245.

[36] Roberts, "Tendenzwenden," passim.

[37] Jörg Drews, "Leseprozesse mit paradoxem Ausgang: Neun Mini-Essays über Alexander Kluge," Süddeutsche Zeitung (March 24/25, 1979).

[38] For a taste of Kluge's prose illustrating these points, see Alexander Kluge, Neue Geschichten, Hefte 1-18: 'Unheimlichkeit der Zeit' (Frankfurt/Main: Suhrkamp, 1977), in the preface to which Kluge refers to his stories as "Geschichten ohne Oberbegriff."

[39] Oskar Negt and Alexander Kluge, Geschichte und Eigensinn: Geschichtliche Organisation der Arbeitsvermögen; Deutschland als Produktionsöffentlichkeit; Gewalt des Zusammenhangs (Frankfurt/Main: Zweitausendeins, 1981), p. 777.

[40] Negt and Kluge, Geschichte und Eigensinn, p. 783.

[41] Negt and Kluge, Geschichte und Eigensinn, p. 784.

[42] "Zunächst aber sei festgehalten, dass die ausgehenden siebziger Jahre im literarischen Leben der Bundesrepublik ohne einschneidende Veränderung verstrichen sind." See Helmut Kreuzer, "Neue Subjektivität: Zur Literatur der siebziger Jahre in der Bundesrepublik Deutschland," _Deutsche Gegenswartsliteratur_, ed. Manfred Durzak (Stuttgart: Reclam, 1981), p. 93.

BIBLIOGRAPHY

## A. PRIMARY SOURCES

Bernhard, Thomas. *Der Atem: Eine Entscheidung.* Salzburg and Vienna: Residenz, 1978.

_____. *Der Stimmenimitator.* Frankfurt/Main: Suhrkamp, 1978.

Born, Nicolas. *Die erdabgewandte Seite der Geschichte: Roman.* Third edition. Reinbek bei Hamburg: Rowohlt Taschenbuch Verlag, 1979.

Brinkmann, Rolf Dieter. *Keiner weiss mehr: Roman.* Cologne and Berlin: Kiepenheuer & Witsch, 1968.

Erlenberger, Maria. *Der Hunger nach Wahnsinn: Ein Bericht.* Sixth edition. Reinbek bei Hamburg: Rowohlt Taschenbuch Verlag, 1981.

Frisch, Max. *Gesammelte Werke.* Ed. Hans Mayer. Frankfurt/Main: Suhrkamp, 1976.

Handke, Peter. *Kindergeschichte.* Frankfurt/Main: Suhrkamp, 1981.

_____. *Die linkshändige Frau: Erzählung.* Frankfurt/Main: Suhrkamp, 1976.

Herzog, Marianne. *Nicht den Hunger verlieren.* Berlin: Rotbuch, 1980.

Kirchhoff, Bodo. *Die Einsamkeit der Haut.* Frankfurt/Main: Suhrkamp, 1981.

Kluge, Alexander. *Neue Geschichten, Hefte 1-18: 'Unheimlichkeit der Zeit'.* Second edition. Frankfurt/Main: Suhrkamp, 1978.

Krechel, Ursula. *Zweite Natur: Szenen eines Romans.* Darmstadt und Neuwied: Luchterhand, 1981.

Schimmang, Jochen. *Der schöne Vogel Phönix: Erinnerungen eines Dreissigjährigen.* Third edition. Frankfurt/Main: Suhrkamp, 1980.

Schneider, Michael. *Das Spiegelkabinett: Novelle.* Munich: Autoren-Edition, 1980.

Schneider, Peter. *Lenz: Eine Erzählung.* Berlin: Rotbuch, 1973.

Strauss, Botho. *Marlenes Schwester: Zwei Erzählungen.* Munich: Hanser, 1975.

_____. *Paare, Passanten.* Munich: Hanser, 1981.

_____. *Rumor.* Munich: Hanser, 1980.

Botho Strauss. Schützenehre: Erzählung. Düsseldorf: Eremiten-Presse, 1975.

\_\_\_\_\_. Die Widmung: Eine Erzählung. Munich: Hanser, 1977.

Timm, Uwe. Heisser Sommer: Roman. Munich: Bertelsmann AutorenEdition, 1974.

\_\_\_\_\_. Kerbels Flucht: Roman. Munich: Bertelsmann AutorenEdition, 1980.

Vesper, Bernward. Die Reise: Romanessay. Jossa: MÄRZ, 1977.

Wiener, Oswald. Die Verbesserung von Mitteleuropa: Roman. Reinbek bei Hamburg: Rowohlt, 1969.

Zahl, Peter Paul. Die Glücklichen. Berlin: Rotbuch, 1980.

Zorn, Fritz. Mars. Frankfurt/Main: Fischer Taschenbuch Verlag, 1980.


B. SECONDARY SOURCES

Adorno, Theodor W. Ästhetische Theorie. Ed. Gretel Adorno and Rolf Tiedemann. Second edition. Frankfurt/Main: Suhrkamp, 1974.

\_\_\_\_\_. Minima Moralia: Reflexionen aus dem beschädigten Leben. In: Gesammelte Schriften. Frankfurt/Main: Suhrkamp, 1980. Vol. IV.

\_\_\_\_\_. Noten zur Literatur. Frankfurt/Main: Suhrkamp, 1958.

\_\_\_\_\_. "Was bedeutet: Aufarbeitung der Vergangenheit?" Erziehung zur Mündigkeit: Vorträge und Gespräche mit Hellmut Becker 1959-1969. Ed. Gerd Kadelbach. Fifth edition. Frankfurt/Main: Suhrkamp, 1977. Pp. 10-28.

Arnold, Heinz Ludwig. "Die drei Sprünge der westdeutschen Literatur," Akzente, 20(1973), Nr. 1/2, 70-80.

Arnold, Heinz Ludwig and Theo Buck (eds.). Positionen des Erzählens: Analysen und Theorien zur Literatur der Bundesrepublik. Munich: Beck, 1976.

Arnold, Wilhelm et al (eds.). Lexikon der Psychologie. Freiburg: Herder, 1980.

Baron, Lawrence et al. "Der 'anarchische' Utopismus der westdeutschen Studentenbewegung," Deutsches Utopisches Denken im 20. Jahrhundert. Ed. Reinhold Grimm and Jost Hermand. Stuttgart: Kohlhammer, 1974. Pp. 120-135.

Batt, Kurt. "Die Exekution des Erzählers," Revolte Intern: Betrachtungen zur Literatur in der Bundesrepublik. Leipzig: Reclam, 1974. Pp. 191-273.

Baumgart, Reinhard. Die verdrängte Phantasie: 20 Essays über Kunst und die Gesellschaft. Darmstadt and Neuwied: Luchterhand, 1973.

Bauss, Gerhard. Die Studentenbewegung der sechziger Jahre in der Bundesrepublik und West Berlin: Handbuch. Cologne: Paul-Rugenstein, 1977.

Becher, Martin Roda. "Poesie der Unglücksfälle: Über die Schriften von Botho Strauss," Merkur, 32(1978), Nr. 6, 625-628.

Becker, Peter von. "Die Minima Moralia der achtziger Jahre: Notizen zu Botho Strauss' 'Paare Passanten' und 'Kalldewey, Farce'," Merkur, 36 (1982), Nr. 2, 150-160.

Beckermann, Thomas (ed.). Über Max Frisch. Frankfurt/Main: Suhrkamp, 1971.

Beicken, Peter. "'Neue Subjektivität': Zur Prosa der siebziger Jahre," Deutsche Literatur in der Bundesrepublik seit 1965. Ed. Paul Michael Lützeler and Egon Schwarz. Königstein/Ts.: Athenäum, 1980. Pp. 164-181.

Berg, Jan et al. Sozialgeschichte der deutschen Literatur von 1918 bis zur Gegenwart. Frankfurt/Main: Fischer Taschenbuch Verlag, 1980.

Berman, Russell. "Adorno, Marxism and Art," Telos, 34(Winter 1977-78), 157-166.

Beutin, Wolfgang et al. Deutsche Literaturgeschichte: Von den Anfängen bis zur Gegenwart. Stuttgart: Metzler, 1979.

Biermann, Wolf. "Das gute Wort 'Dableiben'," Der Spiegel, 27(1973), Nr. 50, 142.

Blöcker, Günter. "Innenweltspiele: Botho Strauss als Erzähler," Merkur, 29(1975), Nr. 7, 681-683.

Bolle, Eric. "Subjectiviteit van de mislukking: Over de prozateksten van Botho Strauss," Botho Strauss Symposium 9.2.1981-5.4.1981: Dokumentatieboek. CREA-DOKUMENTATIEBOEK Nr. 7. Amsterdam: CREA, University of Amsterdam, 1981. Pp. 78-81.

Bopp, Jörg. "Der linke Psychodrom," Kursbuch, 55(March 1979), 73-94.

Brückner, Peter. "Über Krisen von Identität und Theorie," Konkursbuch, 1(1978), 39-60.

Buch, Hans Christoph. "Von der möglichen Funktion der Literatur: Eine Art Metakritik," Kursbuch, 20(March 1970), 42-52.

Buck-Morss, Susan. "The Dialectic of T.W. Adorno," Telos, 14(Winter 1972), 137-144.

Bürger, Christa. Tradition und Subjektivität. Frankfurt/Main: Suhrkamp, 1980.

Cobben, Paul. "Foucault's begrip van de waanzin als inspiratiebron voor Botho Strauss," Botho Strauss Symposium 9.2.1981-5.4.1981: Dokumentatieboek. CREA-DOKUMENTATIEBOEK Nr. 7. Amsterdam: CREA, University of Amsterdam, 1981. Pp. 87-103.

Dede, Hans Ewald. "Die Politisierung der Literatur in der Bundesrepublik seit 1968," kontext, 1(1976), 48-67.

Deleuze, Gilles and Félix Guattari. Anti-Ödipus: Kapitalismus und Schizophrenie I. Trans. Bernd Schwibs. Frankfurt/Main: Suhrkamp, 1974.

\_\_\_\_\_. Rhizom. Trans. Dagmar Berger et al. Berlin: Merve, 1977.

Denkler, Horst. "Langer Marsch und kurzer Prozess: Oppositionelle Studentenbewegung und streitbarer Staat im westdeutschen Roman der siebziger Jahre," Der deutsche Roman und seine historischen und politischen Bedingungen. Ed. Wolfgang Paulsen. Bern and Munich: Francke, 1977. Pp. 124-144.

Drews, Jörg. "Antwort auf Jürgen Theobaldy," Akzente, 24(August 1977), Nr. 4, 379-382.

\_\_\_\_\_. "Leseprozesse mit paradoxem Ausgang: Neun Mini-Essays über Alexander Kluge," Süddeutsche Zeitung [Munich], March 24/25, 1979.

\_\_\_\_\_. "Nach der 'neuen Sensibilität': Überlegungen zur jüngsten Lyrik," Protokolle, 1(1981), 3-24.

\_\_\_\_\_. "Selbsterfahrung und Neue Subjektivität in der Lyrik," Akzente, 24(February 1977), Nr. 1, 89-95.

Durzak, Manfred (ed.). Deutsche Gegenwartsliteratur: Ausgangspositionen und aktuelle Entwicklungen. Stuttgart: Reclam, 1981.

\_\_\_\_\_. Die deutsche Literatur der Gegenwart: Aspekte und Tendenzen. Third edition. Stuttgart: Reclam, 1976.

\_\_\_\_\_. Der deutsche Roman der Gegenwart. Stuttgart: Kohlhammer, 1971.

Durzak, Manfred (ed.). Gespräche über den Roman: Formbestimmungen und Analysen. Frankfurt/Main: Suhrkamp, 1976.

Enzensberger, Hans Magnus. "Gemeinplätze, die Neueste Literatur betreffend," Kursbuch, 15(November 1968), 187-197.

Erbslöh, Gisela and Hans Burkhard Schlichtung. "Offener Hermetismus und Theater des Alltäglichen: Über 'Gross und klein' von Botho Strauss," Spectaculum 33: Vier moderne Theaterstücke. Frankfurt/Main: Suhrkamp, 1980. Pp. 312-317.

Faber, Reinhard. "Subversive Ästhetik: Zur Rekonstruktion kritischer Kultur-Theorie," Kursbuch, 49(October 1977), 159-173.

Fischer, Ludwig. "Vom Beweis der Güte des Puddings: Zu Jörg Drews' und Jürgen Theobaldys Ansichten über neuere Lyrik," Akzente, 24(August 1977), Nr. 4, 371-379.

Freud, Sigmund. Gesammelte Werke chronologisch geordnet. London: Imago Publishing, 1946-1949.

Frisch, Max. "Unsere Gier nach Geschichten," Gesammelte Werke. Ed. Hans Mayer. Second edition. Frankfurt/Main: Suhrkamp, 1976. Vol. VII. Pp. 262-264.

_____. "Wir hoffen: Friedenspreis des deutschen Buchhandels, Frankfurt am Main, 19. September 1976," Max Frisch: Aspekte des Prosawerks. Ed. Gerhard P. Knapp. Bern: Peter Lang, 1978. Pp. 15-23.

Glotz, Peter. "Über politische Identität," Merkur, 34(December 1980), Nr. 12, 1177-1187.

Gnüg, Hiltrud. "Was heisst 'Neue Subjektivität'?" Merkur, 32(January 1978), Nr. 1, 60-75.

Gouldner, Alvin. The Future of the Intellectuals and the Rise of the New Class: A Frame of Reference, Theses, Conjectures, Arguments, and an Historical Perspective on the Role of Intellectuals and Intelligentsia in the International Class Contest of the Modern Era. New York: Seabury Press, 1979.

Greiffenhagen, Martin and Sylvia. Ein schwieriges Vaterland: Zur politischen Kultur Deutschlands. Second edition. Munich: List, 1979.

Grimm, Reinhold. "Eiszeit und Untergang: Zu einem Motivkomplex in der deutschen Gegenwartsliteratur," Monatshefte, 73(Summer 1981), Nr. 2, 155-186.

Grossklaus, Götz. "West-östliches Unbehagen: Literarische und Gesellschaftskritik in U. Plenzdorfs 'Die neuen Leiden des jungen W.' und P. Schneiders 'Lenz'," Basis, 5(1975), 80-99.

Habermas, Jürgen. Protestbewegung und Hochschulreform. Frankfurt/Main: Suhrkamp, 1969.

_____. (ed.). Stichworte zur 'Geistigen Situation der Zeit'. Third edition. Frankfurt/Main: Suhrkamp, 1980.

_____. Zur Rekonstruktion des historischen Materialismus. Frankfurt/Main: Suhrkamp, 1976.

Hage, Volker. "Das Ende der Beziehungen: Über den Zustand der Liebe in neueren Romanen und Erzählungen, Eine Bestandsaufnahme," Aufbrüche, Abschiede: Studien zur deutschen Literatur seit 1968. Ed. Michael Zeller. Stuttgart: Ernst Klett, 1979. Pp. 14-25.

Hartung, Klaus. "Die Repression wird zum Milieu: Die Beredsamkeit linker Literatur," Literaturmagazin, 11(1979), 52-79.

_____. "Über die lang andauernde Jugend im linken Getto: Lebensalter und Politik aus der Sicht eines 38jährigen," Kursbuch, 54(December 1978), 174-188.

_____. "Versuch, die Krise der antiautoritären Bewegung wieder zur Sprache zu bringen," Kursbuch, 48(June 1977), 14-43.

Hazel, Hazel E. "Die alte und die neue Sensibilität: Erfahrungen mit dem Subjekt, das zwischen die Kulturen gefallen ist," Literaturmagazin, 4(1975), 129-142.

Hermand, Jost (ed.). Literatur nach 1945. Wiesbaden: Akademische Verlagsgesellschaft, 1979.

Hirsch, Joachim. Der Sicherheitsstaat: Das 'Modell Deutschland', seine Krise und die neuen sozialen Bewegungen. Frankfurt/Main: Europäische Verlagsanstalt, 1980.

Hofe, Gerhard vom and Peter Pfaff. Das Elend des Polyphem: Zum Thema der Subjektivität bei Thomas Bernhard, Peter Handke, Wolfgang Koeppen und Botho Strauss. Königstein/Ts.: Athenäum, 1980.

Hohendahl, Peter Uwe. "Autonomy of Art: Looking back at Adorno's Ästhetische Theorie," German Quarterly, 54(March 1981), Nr. 2, 133-148.

_____. "Post-Revolutionary Literary History: The Case of Wilhelm Dilthey," Literature and History. Ed. Leonard Schulze and Walter Wetzels. Lanham/New York/London: University Press of America, 1983. Pp. 119-145.

Holzer, Horst. "Die realistische Literatur und ihr gesellschaftliches Subjekt," kontext, 1(1976), 133-154.

Horkheimer, Max and Theodor W. Adorno. Dialectic of Enlightenment. Trans. John Cumming. New York: Herder and Herder, 1972.

Hosfeld, Rolf and Helmut Peitsch. "'Weil uns diese Aktionen innerlich verändern, sind sie politisch': Bemerkungen zu vier Romanen über die Studentenbewegung," Basis, 10(1980), 93-126.

Ingold, Felix Philipp. "Das Buch im Buch: Versuch über Edmond Jabès," Akzente, 26(December 1979), Nr. 6, 632-636.

Jameson, Fredric. Marxism and Form: Twentieth-Century Dialectical Theories of Literature. Princeton: Princeton Unversity Press, 1971.

_____. The Political Unconscious: Narrative as a Socially Symbolic Act. Ithaca, New York: Cornell University Press, 1981.

"'Jene Sehnsucht nach den alten Tagen . . .'," Der Spiegel, 27(January 29, 1973), Nr. 5, 86-99.

Jurgensen, Manfred. Erzählformen des fiktionalen Ich: Beiträge zum deutschen Gegenwartsroman. Bern and Munich: Francke, 1980.

Kafitz, Dieter. "Die Problematisierung des individualistischen Menschenbildes im deutschsprachigen Drama der Gegenwart (Franz Xaver Kroetz, Thomas Bernhard, Botho Strauss)," Basis, 10(1980), 93-126.

Kalasz, Claudia. "Vereiste Spuren: Suche nach Erinnerung in Dichtungen von Botho Strauss," Programmheft [Theater der Stadt Heidelberg] (1978/79), Nr. 6, 30-42.

Kallscheuer, Otto. "Das 'System des Marxismus' ist ein Phantom: Argumente für den theoretischen Pluralismus der Linken," Kursbuch, 48 (June 1977), 59-76.

Keulen, Sybrandt van. "Het realisme van Botho Strauss," Botho Strauss Symposium 9.2.1981-5.4.1981: Dokumentatieboek. CREA-DOKUMENTATIEBOEK Nr. 7. Amsterdam: CREA, University of Amsterdam, 1981. Pp. 65-68.

Knapp, Gerhard P. (ed.). Max Frisch: Aspekte des Prosawerks. Bern: Peter Lang, 1978.

Koch, Roland, "Botho Strauss' Die Widmung: Zur Darstellung einer leidenden Persönlichkeit in Krisensituationen." Unpublished paper, University of Siegen, 1980.

Koselleck, Reinhart and Wolf-Dieter Stempel (eds.). Geschichte: Ereignis und Erzählung. Munich: Fink, 1973.

Krahl, Hans-Jürgen. Konstitution und Klassenkampf: Zur historischen Dialektik von bürgerlicher Emanzipation und proletarischer Revolution. Schriften, Reden und Entwürfe aus den Jahren 1966-1970. Frankfurt/Main: Verlag Neue Kritik, 1971.

Krechel, Ursula. "Leben in Anführungszeichen: Das Authentische in der gegenwärtigen Literatur," Literaturmagazin, 11(1979), 80-107.

Kreuzer, Helmut. "Neue Subjektivität: Zur Literatur der siebziger Jahre in der Bundesrepublik Deutschland," Deutsche Gegenwartsliteratur. Ed. Manfred Durzak. Stuttgart: Reclam, 1981. Pp. 77-106.

Kudszus, Winfried (ed.). Literatur und Schizophrenie: Theorie und Interpretation eines Grenzgebiets. Munich: deutscher taschenbuch verlag; Tübingen: Niemeyer, 1977.

―――. "Literaturwissenschaft und Psychiatrie," Die Psychologie des 20. Jahrhunderts. Zürich: Kindler, 1980. Vol. X. Pp. 1121-1130.

Kursbuch, 35(April 1974). Verkehrsformen I/Frauen Männer Linke/Über die Schwierigkeit der Emanzipation.

Kursbuch, 37(October 1974). Verkehrsformen II/Emanzipation in der Gruppe und die 'Kosten' der Solidarität.

Kursbuch, 41(September 1975). Alltag.

Kursbuch, 49(June 1977). Zehn Jahre danach.

Kurz, Paul Konrad. "Protokoll ihrer Abwesenheit," Über moderne Literatur: Zur Literatur der späten siebziger Jahre. Frankfurt/Main: Josef Knecht, 1979. Vol. VI. Pp. 76-78.

Laemmle, Peter (ed.). Realismus--welcher? Sechzehn Autoren auf der Suche nach einem literarischen Begriff. Munich: edition text und kritik, 1976.

Lattmann, Dieter (ed.). Die Literatur der Bundesrepublik Deutschland. Second edition. Zürich: Kindler, 1973.

Literaturmagazin. Reinbek bei Hamburg: Rowohlt Taschenbuch Verlag, 1974-1979.

Lottman, Herbert R. "Fiction is the Forerunner Among Books from Leading Houses Across Germany," Publishers Weekly, December 25, 1978, pp. 32-35.

Lüdke, W. Martin (ed.). Literatur und Studentenbewegung: Eine Zwischenbilanz. Opladen: Westdeutscher Verlag, 1977.

―――. (ed.). Nach dem Protest: Literatur im Umbruch. Frankfurt/Main: Suhrkamp, 1979.

Lützeler, Paul Michael. "Von der Intelligenz zur Arbeiterschaft: Zur Darstellung sozialer Wandlungsversuche in den Romanen und Reportagen der Studentenbewegung," Deutsche Literatur in der Bundesrepublik seit 1965. Ed. Paul Michael Lützeler and Egon Schwarz. Königstein/Ts.: Athenäum, 1980. Pp. 115-134.

Lützeler, Paul Michael and Egon Schwarz (eds.).Deutsche Literatur in der Bundesrepublik seit 1965. Königstein/Ts.: Athenäum, 1980.

Lyotard, Jean-François. La condition postmoderne: Rapport sur le savoir. Paris: Les éditions de minuit, 1979.

Mattenklott, Gert. "Adornos ästhetischer Maßstab," kontext, 1(1976), 32-47.

Mayer, Hans. Deutsche Literatur seit Thomas Mann. Reinbek bei Hamburg: Rowohlt, 1967.

Michel, Willy. "Poetische Transformationen Kierkegaardscher Denkfiguren im neueren deutschen Roman -- Eine wirkungsgeschichtliche Betrachtung zu Max Frisch, 'Stiller' und 'Mein Name sei Gantenbein', Peter Härtling, 'Niembsch oder Der Stillstand', Gabriele Wohmann, 'Ernste Absicht' und Martin Walser, 'Das Einhorn'," Festschrift für Friedrich Kienecker zum 60. Geburtstag. Ed. Gerd Michels. Heidelberg: Groos, 1980. Pp. 153-177.

——. "Poetische und hermeneutische Erinnerung: Ein Gespräch mit Peter Härtling," Die Aktualität des Interpretierens: Hermeneutische Zugänge zu den Werken von Lessing, Lenz, F. Schlegel, Fontane, Kafka, Frisch, Bachmann, Handke, Weiss, Härtling. Heidelberg: Quelle & Meyer, 1978. Pp. 197-204.

Michels, Gerd. "Skeptische Melancholie: Zu Botho Strauss' 'Die Widmung'," Textanalyse und Textverstehen. Heidelberg: Quelle & Meyer, 1981. Pp. 145-168.

Mitscherlich, Alexander. Auf dem Weg zur vaterlosen Gesellschaft: Ideen zur Sozialpsychologie. Tenth edition. Munich: Piper, 1973.

Mosler, Peter. Was wir wollten, was wir wurden: Studentenrevolte -- 10 Jahre danach. Reinbek bei Hamburg: Rowohlt Taschenbuch Verlag, 1977.

Nägele, Rainer. "Die Arbeit des Textes: Notizen zur experimentellen Literatur," Deutsche Literatur in der Bundesrepublik seit 1965. Ed. Paul Michael Lützeler and Egon Schwarz. Königstein/Ts.: Athenäum, 1980. Pp. 30-45.

——. "Geht es noch um den Realismus? Politische Implikationen moderner Erzählformen im Roman," Der deutsche Roman und seine historischen und politischen Bedingungen. Ed. Wolfgang Paulsen. 9. Amherster Kolloquium zur deutschen Literatur. Bern and Munich: Francke, 1977. Pp. 34-53.

Nägele, Rainer. "Geschichten und Geschichte: Reflexionen zur westdeutschen Roman seit 1965," Deutsche Gegenwartsliteratur. Ed. Manfred Durzak. Stuttgart: Reclam, 1981. Pp. 234-251.

Narr, Wolf-Dieter. "Hin zu einer Gesellschaft bedingter Reflexe," Stichworte zur 'Geistigen Situation der Zeit'. Ed. Jürgen Habermas. Third edition. Frankfurt/Main: Suhrkamp, 1970. Vol. II. Pp. 489-528.

Negt, Oskar. "Interesse gegen Partei: Über Identitätsprobleme der deutschen Linken," Kursbuch, 48(June 1977), 175-188.

Negt, Oskar and Alexander Kluge. Geschichte und Eigensinn: Geschichtliche Organisation der Arbeitsvermögen, Deutschland als Produktionsöffentlichkeit, Gewalt des Zusammenhangs. Frankfurt/Main: Zweitausendeins, 1981.

──────. Öffentlichkeit und Erfahrung: Zur Organisationsanalyse von bürgerlicher und proletarischer Öffentlichkeit. Frankfurt/Main: Suhrkamp, 1972.

Piwitt, Hermann Peter. "Rückblick auf heisse Tage: Die Studentenrevolte in der Literatur," Literaturmagazin, 4(1975), 35-46.

Podewils, Clemens Graf (ed.). Tendenzwende?: Zur geistigen Situation der Bundesrepublik. Stuttgart: Ernst Klett, 1975.

Raddatz, Fritz J. "Ich singe aus Angst -- das Unsagbare: Ein ZEIT-Gespräch mit Max Frisch," Die Zeit [Hamburg], April 17, 1981, pp. 37-38.

──────. "Die zeitgenössische Literatur ist Angst-Literatur," Die Zeit [Hamburg], August 7, 1981, p. 17.

Reich-Ranicki, Marcel. "Botho Strauss: Gleicht die Liebe einem Monolog?" Entgegnung: Zur deutschen Literatur der siebziger Jahre. Stuttgart: Deutsche Verlags-Anstalt, 1979. Pp. 17-35.

Reinhold, Ursula. "Interview mit Uwe Timm/Vom Wert eigener Erfahrungen," Weimarer Beiträge, 22(1976), Nr. 8, 45-59; 60-68.

Ritter, Roman. "Die 'neue Innerlichkeit' -- von innen und aussen betrachtet (Karin Struck, Peter Handke, Rolf Dieter Brinkmann)," kontext, 1(1976), 238-257.

Roberts, David. "Zur Periodisierung der westdeutschen Literatur seit 1960: Zwei Modelle." Unpublished manuscript, revised version of which appeared as "Tendenzwenden: Die sechziger und siebziger Jahre in literaturhistorischer Perspektive," Deutsche Vierteljahrsschrift, 56 (June 1982), Nr. 2, 290-313.

Rudolph, Hermann. "Eine neue unbewältigte Vergangenheit?" Merkur, 34 (September 1980), Nr. 9, 870-883.

Rutschky, Michael. Erfahrungshunger: Ein Essay über die siebziger Jahre. Cologne: Kiepenheuer & Witsch, 1980.

Schelsky, Helmut. Die skeptische Generation: Eine Soziologie der deutschen Jugend. Düsseldorf and Cologne: Diedrichs, 1957.

Scherpe, Klaus R. and Hans-Ullrich Treichel. "Vom Überdruss leben: Sensibilität und Intellektualität als Ereignis bei Handke, Born und Strauss," Monatshefte, 73(Summer 1981), Nr. 2, 187-206.

"Schizophrenie," Die Psychologie des 20. Jahrhunderts. Zürich: Kindler, 1980. Vol. X. Pp. 263-433.

Schmidt, Alfred. Die kritische Theorie als Geschichtsphilosophie. Munich: Hanser, 1976.

_____. Zur Idee der kritischen Theorie: Elemente der Philosophie Max Horkheimers. Munich: Hanser, 1974.

Schmitz, Walter (ed.). Über Max Frisch II. Second edition. Frankfurt/Main: Suhrkamp, 1976.

Schneider, Michael. Den Kopf verkehrt aufgesetzt oder Die melancholische Linke: Aspekte des Kulturzerfalls in den siebziger Jahren. Darmstadt and Neuwied: Luchterhand, 1981.

_____. Die lange Wut zum langen Marsch: Aufsätze zur sozialistischen Politik und Literatur. Reinbek bei Hamburg: Rowohlt Taschenbuch Verlag, 1975.

_____. "Von der alten Radikalität zur neuen Sensibilität," Kursbuch, 49(October 1977), 174-187.

Schneider, Peter. "Die Phantasie im Spätkapitalismus und die Kultur-Revolution," Kursbuch, 16(March 1969), 1-37.

_____. "Schreiben in Deutschland," tip, 10(March 3-26, 1981), Nr. 6, 56-58.

_____. "Über den Unterschied von Literatur und Politik (Vortrag)," Literaturmagazin, 5(1976), 188-198.

Schödel, Helmut. "Ästhetik des Verlustes: Zur Literatur des Botho Strauss," Theater heute, 17(1976), Nr. 13, 104-106. Also in Spectaculum 26: Acht moderne Theaterstücke. Frankfurt/Main: Suhrkamp, 1977. Pp. 298-303.

_____. "Kapitalistischer Realismus: Über Botho Strauss' 'Trilogie des Wiedersehens' und die Aufführungen in Basel, Hamburg und Stuttgart," Theater heute, 18(July 1977), Nr. 7, 31-36.

Schülein, Johann August. "Von der Studentenrevolte zur Tendenzwende oder der Rückzug ins Private: Eine sozialpsychologische Analyse," Kursbuch, 48(Jun3 1977), 109-117.

Schütze, Peter. "Die Nuss Kratatuk oder Nostalgie und Sensibilität," kontext, 2(1978), 25-41.

Schweppenhäuser, Hermann. "Tauchen im Schlamm," Programmheft [Theater der Stadt Heidelberg] (1978/79), Nr. 6, 8-17.

Seeba, Hinrich C. "Persönliches Engagement: Zur Autorenpoetik der siebziger Jahre," Monatshefte, 73(Summer 1981), Nr. 2, 140-154.

Siefken, Ursula. "Die Widmung," Neue deutsche Hefte, 25(1978), 361-363.

Spengler, Tilman. "Der Bauch als Avantgarde -- über den aufrechten Niedergang der Theorie," Kursbuch, 65(October 1981), 179-188.

Stephan, Peter. "Das Gedicht in der Marktlücke: Abschliessende Marginalien zur Diskussion über die 'Neue Subjektivität' in der Lyrik," Akzente, 24(December 1977), Nr. 6, 493-504.

Strauss, Botho. "Versuch, ästhetische und politische Ereignisse zusammenzudenken: Neues Theater 1967-70," Theater heute, 11(1970), Nr. 10, 61-68.

_____ and Rolff Mauff et al. Leserbrief und Antwort. Theater heute, 11(1970), Nr. 12, 4.

Theobaldy, Jürgen. "Literaturkritik, astrologisch: Zu Jörg Drews' Aufsatz über Selbsterfahrung und Neue Subjektivität in der Lyrik," Akzente, 24(April 1977), Nr. 2, 188-191.

Thomas, R. Hinton and Keith Bullivant. Westdeutsche Literatur der sechziger Jahre. Trans. Inge Neske. Cologne: Kiepenheuer & Witsch, 1974.

Timm, Uwe. "Peter Handke oder sicher in die 70er Jahre," kürbiskern(1970) Nr. 4, 611-621.

_____. "Realismus und Utopie," kürbiskern(1975), Nr. 1, 91-101.

_____. "Sensibilität für wen?" kürbiskern(1976), Nr. 1, 118-122.

_____. "Über den Dogmatismus in der Literatur," kontext, 1(1976), 22-31.

_____. "Zwischen Unterhaltung und Aufklärung," kürbiskern(1972), Nr. 1, 79-90.

Tohidipur, Mehdi (ed.). Der bürgerliche Rechtsstaat. Frankfurt/Main: Suhrkamp, 1978.

Trommler, Frank. "Der 'Nullpunkt 1945' und seine Verbindlichkeit für die Literaturgeschichte," Basis, 1(1970), 9-25.

Türcke, Christoph. "Auferstehung als schlechte Unendlichkeit: Zum theologischen Leitmotiv des Botho Strauss," Programmheft [Theater der Stadt Heidelberg] (1978/79), Nr. 6, 18-29. Also in Theater heute, 20(1979), Nr. 4, 22-24.

Vassen, Florian. "Geschichte machen und Geschichten schreiben: Gedanken zu Volker Brauns Unvollendeter Geschichte," Monatshefte, 73(Summer 1981), Nr. 2, 207-224.

Vaterland, Muttersprache: Deutsche Schriftsteller und ihr Staat von 1945 bis heute: Ein Nachlesebuch für die Oberstufe. Berlin: Wagenbach, 1979.

Walser, Martin. "Über die neueste Stimmung im Westen," Kursbuch, 20 (March 1970), 19-41.

Wapnewski, Peter. "Der neue Realismus: Glaubwürdigkeit durch Genauigkeit," Theater heute, 16(December 1975), Nr. 12, 26-31.

_____. Zumutungen: Essays zur Literatur des 20. Jahrhunderts. Düsseldorf: Claassen, 1979.

Wilhelm, Edgar. "Das Ende der Verhältnisse: Trennungsproblematik in der gegenwärtigen Literatur," Tageszeitung [Hannover], July 3, 1980.

Wolfschütz, Hans. "Botho Strauss," Kritisches Lexikon zur deutschsprachigen Gegenwartsliteratur. Ed. Heinz Ludwig Arnold. Munich: edition text und kritik, 1978. Vol. II. No pagination.

Zeller, Michael (ed.). Aufbrüche, Abschiede: Studien zur deutschen Literatur seit 1978. Stuttgart: Ernst Klett, 1979.

_____. "Fragen an ein dahingegangenes Jahrzehnt," Merkur, 35(June 1981), Nr. 6, 594-604.

_____. "Poesie und Pogram: Zu Rolf Dieter Brinkmanns nachgelassenem Reisetagebuch 'Rom,Blicke'," Merkur, 34(April 1980), Nr. 4, 388-393.

Zeltner, Gerda. Das Ich ohne Gewähr: Gegenwartsautoren aus der Schweiz. Zürich: Suhrkamp, 1980.

Zimmermann, Hans Dieter. "Die mangelhafte Subjektivität," Akzente, 24 (June 1977), Nr. 4, 280-287.

Zur Lippe, Rudolf. "Gedanken zu 'Bekannte Gesichter, gemischte Gefühle'," Programmheft [Theater der Stadt Heidelberg] (1978/79), Nr. 6, 43-48.

_____. "Innerer, äusserer und öffentlicher Dialog: Zur Aktualität von Individualismus," Merkur, 34(September 1980), Nr. 9, 857-869.

_____. "Objektiver Faktor Subjektivität," Kursbuch, 35(April 1974), 1-35.

## C. INTERVIEWS

Bachmann, Dieter. "Das Ende der Liebe," TagesAnzeiger [Zürich], June 9, 1979.

Bock, Hans Bertram. "Das Leben als Abschied," Nürnberger Nachrichten, May 14/15, 1977.

Hage, Volker. "Botho Strauss: Ein Mann, der sich selbst nie in Szene gesetzt hat, bewegt als Autor wie kein anderer das deutsche Theater," Botho Strauss Symposium 9.2.1981-5.4.1981: Dokumentatieboek. CREA-DOKUMENTATIEBOEK Nr. 7. Amsterdam: CREA, University of Amsterdam, 1981. Pp. 11-12.

Jutting, Ada van Bentheim. "Een schrijver die geen verteller is," Het Parool [Amsterdam], May 2, 1980.

Zacharias, Carna. "Jeder Mann ist auch eine Frau," Münchener Abendzeitung, November 11, 1977.

## D. REVIEWS

### General

Becher, Martin Roda. "Poesie der Unglücksfälle: Über die Schriften von Botho Strauss," Merkur, 32(1978), Nr. 6, 625-628.

Bondy, François. "Der Erzähler und Stückeschreiber Botho Strauss: Erlesene Gefühle," Deutsche Zeitung/Christ und Welt [Düsseldorf], October 20, 1978.

_____. "Undeutliche Menschen, erlesene Gefühle: Zum Erfolg des Erzählers und Stückeschreibers Botho Strauss," Die Weltwoche, October 18, 1978.

"Botho Strauss," Frankfurter Allgemeine Zeitung, August 29, 1980.

Krättli, Anton. "Die Verlassenen oder die Taubheit der anderen," <u>Rargauer Tagblatt</u>, June 18, 1979.

## Marlenes Schwester: Zwei Erzählungen

Amann, Jürg. "Ein Schreibender schreibt unter Vorwänden über das Schreiben," <u>TagesAnzeiger</u> [Zürich], July 21, 1975.

Baier, Lothar. "Lektüre als Blindflug: Zwei Erzählungen von Botho Strauss," <u>Frankfurter Allgemeine Zeitung</u>, May 10, 1975.

Baumgart, Reinhard. "Gefühle als Handlungen," <u>Süddeutsche Zeitung</u>[Munich], May 17, 1975.

Becher, Martin Roda. "Die Bestürzung des Lesers: Tendenzen des Phantastischen in einigen neueren Werken der Literatur," <u>NZ am Wochenende</u> [Basel], October 16, 1976.

_____. "Nekromantische Märchen," <u>NZ Basel</u>, September 13, 1975.

Beck, Gabriele. "Der Tod--ein Traum," <u>Deutsche Zeitung</u> [Düsseldorf], June 13, 1975.

Beckelmann, Jürgen. "Bäumchen, Bäumchen, wechsle dich," <u>Mannheimer Morgen</u>, September 30, 1976.

_____. "Schwirrende Zwei-Personen-Welt: Talentproben des Erzählers Botho Strauss," <u>Stuttgarter Zeitung</u>, July 17, 1976.

Berth, Hans. "Im Taumel der Todesdrogen," <u>Nürnberger Nachrichten</u>, September 6/7, 1975.

"Botho Strauss," <u>Het Vaderland</u> [The Hague], January 24, 1976.

<u>Bücher beim Wort genommen</u>. Bayrisches Fernsehen. Munich, October 5, 1975.

<u>Bücher im Gespräch</u>. Writ. Günter Blöcker. Deutschlandfunk. May 4, 1975.

"Bücher, von denen man spricht," <u>Hessische Allgemeine Zeitung</u> [Kassel], May 31, 1975.

"Doppelkopf," <u>Der Abend</u> [Berlin], April 23, 1975.

Engel, Willem. "Ein Erzähler von Gemütskatastrophen," <u>Südwestpresse</u> [Tübingen], July 2, 1975.

_____. "Komplizierte Gemütskatastrophen," <u>Kieler Nachrichten</u>, June 24, 1975.

"Erzähler von Gemütskatastrophen," <u>Oberhessische Presse</u> [Marburg], June 28, 1975.

Exner, R. "Botho Strauss, Marlenes Schwester: Zwei Erzählungen," World Literature Today, 54(Winter 1977), Nr. 1, 98.

Fellmann, Vreni. "Fiktion mit realen Wirkungen: Botho Strauss," Vaterland [Luzern], June 13, 1975.

Klausenitzer, Hans-Peter. "Der Szene den Rücken gekehrt," Die Welt, Ausgabe B[Berlin-West], May 15, 1975.

Mateen, Gabbo. "Innere Wahnwelt," Kölner Stadt-Anzeiger, June 2, 1975.

Michaelis, Rolf. "Stimmenmeer im Kopf," Die Zeit [Hamburg], March 21, 1975.

Morshäuser, Bodo. "Botho Strauss," Berliner Wochen Magazin, June 7-13, 1975.

Mutius, Dagmar von. "Botho Strauss: Marlenes Schwester," Der evangelische Buchberater [Göttingen] (1976), Nr. 3.

Das neue Buch. Dir. Rolf Haufs and Gabriele Beck. Sender Freies Berlin. Berlin, June 12, 1975.

Völker, Klaus. "Verständigungs- und Gefühlsarbeit," Frankfurter Rundschau, August 23, 1975.


Die Widmung

"Albumblatt 'Für Elise'," Neue Zürcher Zeitung, October 28, 1977.

André, Michael. "Nach Liebensentzug völlig isoliert," Düsseldorfer Nachrichten, July 5, 1978.

Arnold, Heinz Ludwig. "Leid und Trauer -- inszeniert," Deutsches Allgemeines Sonntagsblatt [Hamburg], September 11, 1977.

Becher, Martin Roda. "Botho Straussens Playback der Verstörung," Basler Zeitung, April 1, 1978.

_____. "Trennung," Basler Zeitung, December 17, 1977.

Becker, Peter von. "Die Falle des Trieblesers," Süddeutsche Zeitung [Munich], October 12, 1977.

Bock, Hans Bertram. "Der Rostfrass der Verblendung," Nürnberger Nachrichten, July 31, 1977.

"Bocksprung Frau," Wiener Tagebuch, July/August, 1978.

Botho Strauss: Die Widmung. Writ. Uwe Japp. Hessischer Rundfunk. October 31, 1977.

Botho Strauss: Die Widmung. Writ. Stephan Reinhardt. Westdeutscher Rundfunk. September 1, 1977.

"Botho Strauss: Die Widmung," Abendzeitung [Munich], December 17/18, 1977.

"Botho Strauss: Die Widmung," Bücherschiff, July/August, 1978.

"Botho Strauss' Erzählung 'Die Widmung'," Stuttgarter Nachrichten, October 12, 1977.

"Botho Strauss modern narcisme," Het laatste Nieuws [Brussels], November 30, 1978.

"Buch des Monats," Bücherschiff, January/February, 1978.

"Devotion," Kirkus Reviews, May 15, 1979.

"Devotion," Publishers Weekly, May 28, 1979.

"Devotion," Saturday Review, February 7, 1979.

Duquesnoy, Theodoor., "Een dagboek als liefdespartner," NRC Handelsblad [Rotterdam], February 3, 1978.

"Eine Liebe kommt abhanden," Neue Osnabrücker Zeitung, September 30, 1977.

Eine ungewöhnliche Liebesgeschichte. Writ. Heinz Ludwig Arnold. Deutsche Welle. September 23, 1977.

Fritz, Walter Helmut. "Wagnis grosser Erregungen," Der Tagesspiegel [Berlin], dember 11, 1977.

Für Sie gelesen -- aus neuen Büchern. Writ. Wilhelm Grasshoff. Bayrischer Rundfunk. February 15, 1978.

Gensheimer, Wolfgang. "Vom Verlassensein," Mannheimer Morgen, October 7, 1977.

Grave, Christian. "Botho Strauss: Die Widmung," World Literature Today. 53(Winter 1979), Nr. 1, 106.

Gürtelschmied, Walter. "Protokoll einer Abwesenheit," Salzburger Nachrichten, December 3, 1977.

Hage, Volker, "Das Ende der Beziehungen: Über den Zustand der Liebe in neuren Romanen und Erzählungen," Frankfurter Allgemeine Zeitung, September 9, 1978.

Hartmann, Rainer. "In der Hitze des Sommers ein Abgesang auf die Liebe," Kölner Stadt-Anzeiger, November 19/20, 1977.

———. "Papierne Brücke zur fernen Geliebten," Frankfurter Neue Presse, November 4, 1977.

Henrichs, Benjamin. "Ein Liebesunglück," Die Zeit [Hamburg], September 2, 1977.

Holmes, Jennifer, "Open heart surgery is good for the soul," Detroit Free Press, September 16, 1979.

Hüttenegger, Bernhard. "Die Widmung," Kleine Zeitung Graz, December 21, 1977.

Jansen, Hans. "Schmerz wie Lust geniessen," Westdeutsche Allgemeine Zeitung [Essen], February 4, 1978.

Journal am Morgen. Writ. Gisela Schlientz. Südfunk. October 17, 1978.

Kupfer, Erika. "Spielart des Todes," münchner monat (January 1978), 22-24.

Lenz, Guntram. "Eine poetische Liebesgeschichte," Wetzlarer Neue Zeitung, July 12, 1978.

Lesezeichen: Buchbesprechungen, Informationen, Interviews. Südfunk. July 12, 1978.

"Liebe, Tod und Leidenschaft," Welt der Arbeit [Cologne] (1977), Nr. 51/52.

Limmer, Wolfgang. "Flitterwochen einer Trennung," Der Spiegel, 31(November 28, 1977), Nr. 49, 228-230.

Michaelis, Rolf. "Der Empfindungsforscher," Die Weltwoche, October 26, 1977.

"Neues auf dem Büchermarkt," Südwestpresse [Tübingen], November 4, 1977.

Noble, David. "Devotion: Botho Strauss," Minnesota Daily, October 29, 1979.

Prieser, Uwe. "Reflexionen nach einer Trennung," Kieler Nachrichten, April 19, 1978.

Reich-Ranicki, Marcel. "Deutsche Literatur 1977," Frankfurter Allgemeine Zeitung, October 13, 1977.

———. "Gleicht die Liebe einem Monolog?," Frankfurter Allgemeine Zeitung, September 10, 1977.

Reinhardt, Stephan. "Wünschelrutengang," Frankfurter Rundschau, December 10, 1977.

"Der Roman von Botho Strauss: Qualität bahnt sich immer ihren Weg,"
  Buchreport [Dortmund], November 4, 1977.

Schramm, Godehard. "Traktat über die Trennung," Nürnberger Zeitung,
  November 19, 1977.

Schreibt er den 'Roman seiner Generation'? Der Dramatiker und Erzähler
  Botho Strauss -- Ein Porträt. Writ. Jürgen Sauer. Südfunk. July 12,
  1978.

Schultze, Sabine. "Traktat über die Trennung," Rhein-Neckar Zeitung
  [Heidelberg], September 24/25, 1977.

Schulze-Reimpell, Werner. "Denkzettel: Botho Strauss, Die Widmung," Die
  deutsche Bühne, January, 1978.

_____. "Ein junger Meister," Neue Musikzeitung [Regensburg], June/July,
  1978.

_____. "Seismographische Darstellung sozialer Befindlichkeit," General-
  Anzeiger [Bonn], December 16, 1977.

Siefken, Ursula. "Botho Strauss: Die Widmung," Neue deutsche Hefte, 25
  (1978), Nr. 2, 361-363.

Ulrich, Jörg. "Totunglücklicher Buchhändler," Münchner Merkur,
  November 30, 1977.

"Was Kritiker empfehlen," Westdeutsche Allgemeine Zeitung [Essen],
  February 8, 1978.

"Die Widmung," Der Abend [Berlin], December 7, 1977.

"Die Widmung," akut [Bonn], December 15, 1977.

"Die Widmung," Luzerner Neueste Nachrichten, November 18, 1977.

"Die Widmung," Oberösterreichische Nachrichten [Linz, Austria],
  January 30, 1978.

Die Widmung. Writ. Gabriele Beck. Sender Freies Berlin. October 6, 1977.

Wright, Jay. "Strauss: language, desire intertwined," Houston Chronicle,
  July 22, 1979.

Zacharias, Carna. "Jeder Mann ist auch eine Frau," Münchener Abendzeitung, November 11, 1977.

Zehm, Günter. "Der heisse Sommer eines Missvergnügens," Die Welt [Bonn],
  January 14, 1978.

## Rumor

"Abstieg im Zickzack," Spandauer Volksblatt [Berlin], July 13, 1980.

Auffermann, Verena. "Selbstzerstückelung im Zeitlupentempo," Rhein-Neckar-Zeitung [Heidelberg], April 19/20, 1980.

Ayren, Armin. "Zerfallsprozess in Einzelbildern," Badische Zeitung [Freiburg], May 14/15, 1980.

Bachmann, Dieter. "Der Lärm, in dem man lebt -- und untergeht," Tages-Anzeiger [Zürich], April 16, 1980.

Baumgart, Reinhard. "King Lear, 42, Beruf: Seher," Der Spiegel, 34 February 25, 1980), 211-213.

Becker, Peter von. "Rumor," Theater heute, 21(March 1980), Nr. 3, 1.

Beckmann, Heinz. "Kaugummi fragt Grill," Rheinischer Merkur/Christ und Welt [Koblenz], March 28, 1980.

"Begehbare Hölle," profil, 25(June 16, 1980).

Binder, Hartmut. "Wahrnehmungen eines Gescheiterten," Evangelische Kommentare (January 1981).

Bock, Hans Bertram. "Wehklagen in der Eiszeit," Nürnberger Nachrichten, April 10, 1980.

"Botho Strauss," Pariser Kurier, April 30, 1980.

"Botho Strauss vorn: Die Bestenliste des Südwestfunks," Frankfurter Allgemeine Zeitung, April 10, 1980.

"Dramatiker -- Hoffnung," Kieler Nachrichten, February 13, 1980.

"Entfernung aus der Realität," Augsburger Allgemeine Zeitung, March 15, 1980.

Geyer, Carl Friedrich. "Knirschen in den Fugen," Christ in der Gegenwart, 44(1980).

Glossner, Herbert. "Eine Pathologie der Gegenwart," Deutsches Allgemeines Sonntagsblatt [Hamburg], May 11, 1980.

Grack, Günther. "Ein geheimnisvolles Rumpeln," Der Tagesspiegel [Berlin], August 17, 1980.

Hartmann, Rainer. "Dumpfes Geräusch eines Aufstands," Frankfurter Neue Presse, March 27, 1980.

Herr, Doris. "Messerstich ins Gemüt des hilflosen Lesers," Westfalen-Blatt, April 16, 1980.

Jahnke, Manfred. "Über die Verletzlichkeit eines Lebens," Südwestpresse [Tübingen], May 31, 1980.

Jansen, Hans. "Die begehbare Hölle," Westdeutsche Allgemeine Zeitung [Essen], July 1, 1980.

Kaiser, Joachim. "Gefährliche Chaos-Beschwörung mit privatem Ausgang," Süddeutsche Zeitung [Munich], March 8/9, 1980.

Klee, Gerd. "Bekker, der Stammler," Wiesbadener Kurier, March 27, 1980.

Knorr, Wolfram. "Das Vergehen von Hören und Sehen," Die Weltwoche, April 16, 1980.

Körling, Martha Christine. "Wortreiche Götterdämmerung des Mittelstandes," Berliner Morgenpost, July 31, 1980.

"Kommentar zum Kulturgeschehen," Deutsche Tagespost [Würzburg], June 4, 1980.

Krättli, Anton. "Ein Ziguener am Rand des Universums," Schweitzer Monatshefte (May 1980), 431-436.

_____. "Von Grund auf unversöhnlich," Rargauer Tagblatt, May 24, 1980.

Kurz, Paul Konrad. "Eine Angst geht übers Land," Zeitwende [Karlsruhe], April, 1980.

_____. "Hamlet als Vater richtet die Welt," Bayerische Staatszeitung, June 6, 1980.

_____. "Zerfall einer Person," Die Presse [Stuttgart], June 7/8, 1980.

Laemmle, Peter. "Von der Notwendigkeit, böse zu sein," Die Zeit [Hamburg], April 8, 1980.

"Lehrzeit -- Leerzeit," Neue Zürcher Zeitung, February 29, 1980.

Lüdke, W. Martin. "Schöne Bilder des Schreckens, zerfallen," Frankfurter Rundschau, March 22, 1980.

Meili, Barbara. "Zuviel gewollt, nichts erreicht," Zürcher Oberländer, June 14, 1980.

Meissner, Toni. "Rumor," Vogue (June 1980).

Munk, Christoph. "In Botho Strauss rumort es weiter," Kieler Nachrichten, April 18, 1980.

Neue Bücher -- Neue Platten. Writ. Rüdiger Kremer. Radio Bremen. July 20, 1980.

Orzechowski, Lothar. "Bücher, von denen man spricht," Hessische Allgemeine [Kassel], March 22, 1980.

Ress, Charlotte. "Von Stinkefee und ihren Streichhölzern," Kölnische Rundschau, April 3, 1980.

Rubinstein, Hilde. "'Was für ein unnötiges Rätsel'," Frankfurter Hefte 2(1981), 69-70.

Rumor. Writ. Friedrich Dermanski. Bayerischer Rundfunk. June 24, 1980.

Rumor. Writ. Joachim Jaeger. Rias II. September 17, 1980.

Rumor. Writ. W. Martin Lüdke. Deutschlandfunk. March 2, 1980.

Rumor. Writ. Ernst Wendt. Norddeutscher Rundfunk. April 27, 1980.

"Rumor," Neue Osnabrücker Zeitung, March 24, 1980.

"Rumor um Vater und Tochter," Westermann (June 1980).

Schütze, Peter. "Menschenreste mit beschränkter Hoffnung," Deutsche Volkszeitung [Düsseldorf], November 27, 1980.

Schultheiss, Helga. "Lieber sein als scharren," Nürnberger Zeitung, March 8, 1980.

Schultz, Uwe. "Das Buch des Monats," Handelsblatt [Hamburg], March 28/29, 1980.

Schwartz, Leonore. "Das Panoptikum vom alltäglichen Schrecken," Kölner Stadt-Anzeiger, April 12/13, 1980.

Schweighofer, Martin. "Ohnmacht und Einsamkeit," Wochenpresse Wien, April 4, 1980.

Seeliger, Rolf. "Hier rumort es zwischen den Zeilen," Tageszeitung [Hannover], February 27, 1980.

Siegrist, Christoph. "Bis sich nichts, auch gar nichts mehr bewegt," Badener Tagblatt, December 6, 1980.

Simon, Peter. "Der Mensch: ein Tippfehler der genetischen Übertragung," Schaffhauser Nachrichten, August 25, 1980.

Stadelmeier, Gerhard. "Bekkers Platz wäre die Bühne (Regie: Peter Stein)," Stuttgarter Zeitung, March 15, 1980.

Steinmann, Kurt. "Auf das Inferno folgt kein Aufstieg," Vaterland [Luzern], May 12, 1980.

Tauber, Reinhold. "Literatur-Cocktail: Das Leben, ein Alptraum," Oberösterreichische Nachrichten [Linz, Austria], June 26, 1980.

Tieges, Wouter Donath. "Een positieve verloedering," Vrij Nederland [Amsterdam], March 22, 1980.

"Ullstein setzt auf moderne Literatur und zahlt 100 000 DM für Botho Strauss," Buchreport [Dortmund], March 21, 1980.

Ulrich, Jörg. "Ein Mittvierziger an der Grenze zur Idiotie," Münchner Merkur, March 12, 1980.

Venzlaff, Rolf Dieter. "Problem zwischen Vater und Tochter," Lübecker Nachrichten, April 27, 1980.

Werner, Sigrid. "Die Unruhe bleibt nach," Stader Tageblatt, June 21, 1980.

"'Wir sind Idiot . . .'," ketchup (March 1980).

Wirsing, Sibylle. "Die Gefälligkeit des Missvergnügens," Frankfurter Allgemeine Zeitung, March 1, 1980.

Zacharias, Carna. "Einer, der ausbricht und keine Chance hat," Münchener Abendzeitung, March 4, 1980.

Zehm, Günter. "Wie Bekker auf den Schnuller kommt," Die Welt [Bonn], March 15, 1980.

Ziegler, Senta. "Prinzip Scheitern," Die Furche, September 10, 1980.

## Paare, Passanten

Anz, Thomas. "Die neue Überheblichkeit: Der Dichter als Priester und Prophet -- Anmerkungen zu Botho Strauss und Peter Handke," Frankfurter Allgemeine Zeitung, April 17, 1982.

Barth, Achim. "Ein neuer Mörike zwischen den TV-Kanälen," Münchner Merkur, December 19/20, 1981.

Baumgart, Reinhard. "Verfluchte Passanten-Welt," Die Zeit [Hamburg], September 25, 1981.

Becker, Peter von. "Die Minima Moralia der achtziger Jahre: Notizen zu Botho Strauss' 'Paare Passanten' und 'Kalldewey, Farce'," Merkur, 36 February 1982), Nr. 2, 150-160.

Blöcker, Günter. "Zwei Fussbreit über der Leere," Frankfurter Allgemeine Zeitung, September 26, 1981.

Goetz, Rainald. "Im Dickicht des Lebendigen," Der Spiegel, 43(October 19, 1981), 232 ff.

Kaiser, Joachim. "Botho Strauss geht aufs Ganze: Wie sich der Autor vom dialektischen Denken freimacht," Süddeutsche Zeitung [Munich], October 14, 1981.

Lüdke, W. Martin. "Die Physiognomie dieser Zeit: Botho Strauss' 'Paare, Passanten'," Frankfurter Rundschau, October 17, 1981.

Samsa, Frauke. "Girlanden, Nippes, Tiefsinn und schlechtes Deutsch," konkret (December 1981), 52-53.

Schmid, Thomas. "Der Virtuose am Stammtisch: Botho Strauss' 'Paare, Passanten'," Lesezeichen (Fall 1981), 6.

Amsterdamer Publikationen zur Sprache und Literatur. In Verbindung mit Peter Boerner, Hugo Dyserinck, Friedrich Maurer und Oskar Reichmann hrsg. von Cola Minis und Arend Quak.

1. UTE SCHWAB: Die Sternrune im Wessobrunner Gebet. Beobachtungen zur Lokalisierung des clm 22053, zur Hs, BM Arundel 393 und zu Rune Poem V. 86-89. Amsterdam 1973, 4to. 141 S. Mit 55 Abb. und Tafeln.  95,–
2. DIETER HENSING: Zur Gestaltung der Wiener Genesis. Mit Hinweisen auf Otfrid und die frühe Sequenz. Amsterdam 1972.  65,–
3. ALFRED BERGMANN: Grabbe Bibliographie. Amsterdam 1973. XIX, 512 S.  150,–
4. WALTER A. BERENDSOHN: August Strindberg. Der Mensch und seine Umwelt. Das Werk – Der schöpferische Künstler. Amsterdam 1974. XVIII, 473 S.  70,–
5. TETTE HOFSTRA: Ortsnamen auf -elte in der Niederländischen Provinz Drente. Amsterdam 1973. 132 S. Mit Karten und Abbildungen.  30,–
6. TH. VAN DE VOORT: Het dialekt van de gemeente Meerlo-Wanssum. Amsterdam 1973. 341 p. Leinen.  vergriffen
7. SOLVEIG OLSEN: Christian Heinrich Postels Beitrag zur deutschen Literatur. Versuch einer Darstellung. Amsterdam 1973. IV, 344 S.  70,–
8/9 ROBERT RALPH ANDERSON & JAMES C. THOMAS: Index Verborum zum Ackermann aus Böhmen. Ein alphabetisch angeordnetes Wortregister zu Textgestaltungen des Ackermanns aus Böhmen von Kniescheck bis Jungbluth. Amsterdam 1973-1974. 530, 459 S.  190,–
10. WILLIAM C. McDONALD & ULRICH GOEBEL: German Medieval Literary Patronage from Charlemagne to Maximilian I: A Critical Commentary with Special Emphasis on Imperial Promotion of Literature. Amsterdam 1973. IV, 206 pp.  60,–
11. BRIAN O. MURDOCH: The Recapitulated Fall. A Comparative Study in Mediaeval Literature. Amsterdam 1974. 207 pp.  vergriffen
12. AREND QUAK: Studien zu den altmittel- und altniederfränkischen Psalmen und Glossen. Amsterdam 1973. 196 S.  60,–
13. HANSJÜRGEN BLINN: Die altdeutsche Exodus. Strukturuntersuchungen zur Zahlenkomposition und Zahlensymbolik. Amsterdam 1974. 351 S. 90,–
14. ULRICH MEISSER: Die Sprichwörtersammlung Sebastian Francks von 1541. Amsterdam 1974. 536 S.  100,–
15. PETER N. RICHARDSON: German-Romance Contact: Name-Giving in Walser Settlements. Amsterdam 1974. XI, 372 pp. With 3 maps.  80,–
16. VERONIKA STRAUB: Entstehung und Entwicklung des frühneuhochdeutschen Prosaromans. Studien zur Prosaauflösung "Wilhelm von Oesterreich". Amsterdam 1974. 158 S. Mit 10 Abbildungen.  40,-
17. CORNELIS GEERARD VON LIERE: Georg Hermann. Materialien zur Kenntnis seines Lebens und seines Werkes. Amsterdam 1974. 249 S. Mit Abbildungen.  60,–
18. FRITZ REUTER: Gedenkschrift. Herausgegeben von Heinz. C. Christiansen. Amsterdam 1975. 221 S.  50,–

19. FRANCIS G. GENTRY: Triuwe and Vriunt in the Nibelungenlied. Amsterdam 1975. 94 pp. 30,–
20. SKIÐARIMA. An inquiry into the written and printed texts, references and commentaries. With an edition and an English translation edited by Theo Homan. Amsterdam 1975. 430 pp. 150,–
21. GUNTER SELLING: Die Einakter und Einakterzyklen Arthur Schnitzlers. Amsterdam 1975. 224 S. Mit Abbildungen. 50,–
22. AREND QUAK: Wortkonkordanz zu den altmittel- und altniederfränkischen Psalmen und Glossen. Nach den Handschriften und Erstdrucken zusammengestellt. Amsterdam 1975. 182 S. 42,–
23. ROBERT LECLERCQ: Aufgaben, Methode und Geschichte der wissenschaftlichen Reimlexikographie. Amsterdam 1975. 270 S. 60,–
24. ROBERT LECLERQ: Reimwörterbuch zu 'Sankt Brandan'. Amsterdam 1976. 83 S. 30,–
25. THOMAS I. BACON: Martin Luther and the Drama. Amsterdam 1976. 86 pp. 25,–
26. FRANZ SIMMLER: Synchrone und diachrone Studien zum deutschen Konsonantensystem. Amsterdam 1976. 94 S. 25,–
27. JOHANNES HENDRIKUS WINKELMAN: Die Brückenpächter- und die Turmwächterepisode im 'Trierer Floyris' und in der 'Version Aristocratique' des altfranzösischen Florisromans. Eine vergleichende Untersuchung. Amsterdam 1977. 222 S. 60,–
28. BRIAN O. MURDOCH: Hans Folz and the Adam-Legends. Texts and Studies. Amsterdam 1977. IX, 184 pp. 50,–
29/ CHRISTINE BOOT: Cassiodorus' Historia Ecclesiastica Tripartita in Leo-
30  pold Stainreuter's German Translation. MS ger. fol. 1109. Amsterdam 1977. XXXVIII, 900 pp. 200,–
31. KEES HERMANN RUDI BORGHART: Das Nibelungenlied. Die Spuren mündlichen Ursprungs in schriftlicher Überlieferung. Amsterdam 1977. 174 S. 45,–
32. MANFRED STANGE: Reinmars Lyrik. Forschungskritik und Überlegungen zu einem neuen Verständnis Reinmars des Alten. Amsterdam 1977. 166 S. 40,–
33. CEGIENAS DE GROOT: Zeitgestaltung im Drama Max Frischs. Die Vergegenwärtigungstechnik in 'Santa Cruz', 'Die Chinesische Mauer' und 'Biografie'. Amsterdam 1977. 346 S. 60,–
34. R.A. UBBINK: De receptie van Meister Eckhart in de Nederlanden gedurende de middeleeuwen. Een studie op basis van middelnederlandse handschriften. Amsterdam 1978. 260 p. with ill. 60,–
35. WALTER K. STEWART: Time Structure in Drama: Goethe's 'Sturm und Drang' Plays. Amsterdam 1978. 308 p. 60,–
36. JACOBA HENDRICA KUNE: Die Auferstehung Christi im deutschen religiösen Drama des Mittelalters. Amsterdam 1979. 250 S. Mit Abb. 50,–
37. GERARD JAN HENDRIK KULSDOM: Die Strophenschlüsse im Nibelungenlied. Ein Versuch. Amsterdam 1979. XXVII, 260 S. 60,–

38. GERHARD EIS: Kleine Schriften zur altdeutschen weltlichen Dichtung. Amsterdam 1979. 520 S. 110,–
39. C.E.C.M. VAN DEN WILDENBERG-DE KROON: Das Weltleben und die Bekehrung der Maria Magdalena im deutschen religiösen Drama und in der bildenden Kunst des Mittelalters. Amsterdam 1979. 140 S. + 8 Abb. 30,–
40. P.J.G. SCHELBERG: Woordenboek van het Sittards dialect met folkloristische aantekeningen. Zittesj wie men 't sjprik en sjrif. Amsterdam 1979. 596 p. + map + ill. vergriffen
41. HALLER IN HOLLAND. Het dagboek van Albrecht von Haller van zijn verblijf in Holland (1725-1727). Ingeleid en geannoteerd door G.A. Lindeboom. Delft 1958. 122 p. Nachdruck Amsterdam 1979. 25,–
42. KARL-FRIEDRICH O. KRAFT: Iweins Triuwe. Zu Ethos und Form der Aventiurenfolge in Hartmann's 'Iwein'. Amsterdam 1979. 233 S. 50,–
43. JUNG ÖSTERREICH. Dokumente und Materialien zur liberalen Österreichischen Opposition 1835-1848. Hrsg. von Madeleine Rietra. Amsterdam 1980. 645 S. 140,–
44. SIEGFRIED RICHARD CHRISTOPH: Wolfram von Eschenbach's Couples. Amsterdam 1981. 262 S. 50,–
45. HERMAN CROMPVOETS: Veenderijterminologie in Nederland en Nederlandstalig België. Amsterdam 1981. 474 S. 4to. 130,–
46. COLA MINIS: Zur Vergegenwärtigung verganger philologischer Nächte. Amsterdam 1981. 397 S. 80,–
47. Die altmittel- und altniederfränkischen Psalmen und Glossen. Nach den Handschriften und Erstdrucken neu herausgegeben von Arend Quak. Amsterdam 1981. 231 S. 50,–
48. GERHARD EIS: Medizinische Fachprosa des späten Mittelalters und der frühen Neuzeit. Amsterdam 1982. 361 S. 70,–
49. ADRIANUS KEIJ: Onderzoek naar dialectgrenzen en articulatorische verschillen in het middennederlandse rivierengebied met een verwijzing naar een mogelijke relevantie voor het onderwijs in de moderne vreemde talen. Amsterdam 1982. 720 S. 75,–
50. J.B. BERNS: Namen voor ziekten van het vee. Een dialectografisch onderzoek in het gebied van het Woordenboek van de Brabantse en dat van de Limburgse Dialecten. Amsterdam 1983. 316 S. 45,–